D1712876

Jewish Spain

STANFORD STUDIES IN JEWISH HISTORY AND CULTURE

EDITED BY *Aron Rodrigue and Steven J. Zipperstein*

Jewish Spain
A Mediterranean Memory

Tabea Alexa Linhard

WITHDRAWN

STANFORD UNIVERSITY PRESS

STANFORD, CALIFORNIA

Stanford University Press
Stanford, California

This book was published with support from the Department of Romance Languages
and Literatures and the Program in International and Area Studies at Washington
University in St. Louis.

Printed in the United States of America on acid-free, archival-quality paper

Library of Congress Cataloging-in-Publication Data

Linhard, Tabea Alexa, 1972– author.
 Jewish Spain : a Mediterranean memory / Tabea Alexa Linhard.
 pages cm — (Stanford studies in Jewish history and culture)
 Includes bibliographical references and index.
 ISBN 978-0-8047-8739-0 (cloth : alk. paper)
 1. Jews, Spanish—Historiography. 2. Sephardim—Historiography. 3. Jews—Spain—
History—20th century. 4. Collective memory—Spain—History—20th century.
I. Title. II. Series: Stanford studies in Jewish history and culture.
 DS135.S7L73 2014
 946'.004924—dc23
 2013047791

ISBN 978-0-8047-9188-5 (electronic)

Typeset by Bruce Lundquist in 10.5/14 Galliard

To Adolf Linhard, 1902–1954,
Melanie Linhard, 1905–1979,
and Karin Linhard, 1944–2007
In Memoriam

Contents

Acknowledgments

Like the stories that families tell over and over again, this book came together with the help of many voices; like the stories that families tell, the book has many flaws. I was only able to complete this work thanks to all those who helped me finish it; the responsibility for its shortcomings is mine alone.

My gratitude goes to my colleagues who read earlier and much rougher versions of the different chapters: Nancy Berg, Erin McGlothlin, Rebecca Messbarger, Joseph Schraibman, Michael Sherberg, and Harriet Stone. Daniela Flesler and Adrián Pérez Melgosa have been amazing collaborators and wonderful readers. I am especially grateful for Andrew Bush's generous, intelligent, and thorough reading of the entire manuscript.

At Washington University, I would like acknowledge the support I received from the Department of Romance Languages and Literatures and the Program in International and Area Studies. Tim Parsons provided invaluable advice and support on all things international and interdisciplinary, and beyond.

Generous grants for summer research from Washington University have helped me complete my research. Collaboration with different working groups has greatly enriched and invigorated my work over the years, especially the Mediterranean Studies research group at Duke University and, at Washington University, the reading group on Transnational Approaches to Postmemory and the Research Cluster on Migration and Identity. Beyond my home base in St. Louis, I need to thank Sebastiaan Faber, Dalia Kandiyoti, Jo Labanyi, Jordana Mendelson, and Teresa Vilarós. My students, who provided me with insightful questions and fresh perspectives, have been a great source of inspiration.

In 2010 I had the good fortune of participating in the *Summer Research Workshop on Sephardic Jewry and the Holocaust* at the United States Holocaust Memorial Museum's Center for Advanced Holocaust Studies, which contributed significantly to the development of the research presented in this book. I would like to thank USHMM, especially Leah Wolfson; the seminar leaders, Aron Rodrigue and Daniel Schroeter; and the seminar participants for helping me think about parts of the world I barely knew how to place on a map before our seminar.

I am very grateful to Norris Pope, Stacy Wagner, Friederike Sundaram, Laura Kenney, and Carolyn Brown at Stanford University Press for helping me make this book a reality, and to Aron Rodrigue and Steven Zipperstein for believing in this project and making it part of the Stanford Studies in Jewish History and Culture series.

The years since I first started thinking about this book have been tumultuous, filled with moments of both immense joy and profound sadness that I shared with Silvia Ayuso, Cindy Brantmeier, Amy Sara Carroll, Daniel Chávez, María Devant, Jutta Gsoels-Lorensen, Asimina Karavanta, Anthony Kirk, Stephanie Kirk, María Fernanda Lander, Desirée Martín, Nina Masot, Laura Medem, Margarita Muñoz, Derek Pardue, Mauricio Tenorio, and Selma Vital. Sat Inder Singh Khalsa, Numancia Rojas, and Gigi Werner, my gifted teachers, have helped to keep things in perspective.

I would not have been able to complete even a single sentence without Guillermo Rosas, Emilio Rosas Linhard, and Aitana Rosas Linhard. Aitana told me recently that she did not understand why I was thanking her and her brother in the book's acknowledgments, because, so she claimed, "I did not do anything." I trust that one day she will understand how much she and Emilio do for me every day. Guillermo helped me in more ways that can ever be put into words, and I need to thank him for so much more than his tolerance for my obstinate use of inferior software products. But *la nit es morta i ja és fa clar. . . .* Thank you.

Curiosity about the lives of Melanie and Adolf Linhard inspired this book, and I thank Isabel Linhard de Hoffmann, Mirjam Mahler, and José Linhard for their stories, their relentless support for all my endeavors, and their love. And finally, I thank Karin Linhard, for everything.

Earlier versions of portions of Chapters 2 and 3 appeared in the articles "The Maps of Nostalgia: Juana Salabert's *Velódromo de invierno*," *Revista Hispánica Moderna* 60:1 (June 2007): 72–93, and "Surviving the Holocaust in Sepharad: Trudi Alexy's Story," *History & Memory* 22:2 (Fall–Winter 2010): 97–126. I am grateful to the journals' anonymous readers and editors.

Jewish Spain

Introduction

"Ask the Mediterranean"

One of the most emblematic locations in Barcelona's medieval Jewish quarter, El Call, can be found at the corner of Marlet and Sant Ramon in the heart of the city's Gothic quarter.[1] Three plaques are affixed to the walls of the house located at 1 Carrer de Marlet, a building that was restored in 1820. The first plaque, with a Hebrew inscription, is a copy of a plaque from the early fourteenth century, now kept in Barcelona's history museum, Museu d'Història de Barcelona (MUHBA). The second features an inaccurate translation of the Hebrew inscription. The owner who commissioned the nineteenth-century restoration was probably responsible for encasing the original plaque inside the outer wall of the building and placing the panel that contains the translation.

The replica of the original plaque from the fourteenth century was vandalized: a close look at the plaque with the translation reveals traces of the words "Palestina Libre," written diagonally across the text. Even though the graffito has been removed and the words are now barely visible to the naked eye, their presence can still be detected in Figure 1. The third plaque—affixed during a campaign that MUHBA initiated in the medieval Jewish quarter in 2007 to place explanatory signs on the streets and landmarks of the medieval Jewish quarter—provides a revised translation into Catalan and English of the original Hebrew text and also situates the inscription in the geographical and historical context of Barcelona's medieval Jewish quarter (see Figure 2). The Hebrew text on the plaque from the fourteenth century actually reads: "Pious Foundation by R. Samuel ha-Sardi. His light burns on forever."[2]

*Figure 1.*1 Carrer de Marlet, Barcelona, 2009. Courtesy of Tabea Alexa Linhard.

Figure 2. 1 Carrer de Marlet, Barcelona, 2013. Courtesy of José Linhard.

The three plaques, together with the graffiti damage, speak to the manifold and often contradictory meanings that Jewish presence and Jewish absence attain in public spaces. The attempt to recover and restore remote Jewish history in Barcelona coincides with the conflation of Jewish history in its entirety with the current situation in the Middle East, which in many ways monopolizes discussions of all things Jewish in contemporary Spain.[3] The different forms of writing and rewriting on these plaques—including the actual fourteenth-century inscriptions, the attempts to recover the memory of a population absent in the nineteenth century, the protection of Jewish heritage with the help of historical markers, and even the defacement of symbols of the past in a present-day struggle—conjure up the main themes of this book.

These plaques, along with many other forms of reminiscence to be discussed in the pages that follow, are part of ongoing processes that involve Jewish absence and presence and the fluctuating meanings of the past in the present. The main argument of *Jewish Spain* is that writers and witnesses narrate instances of Jewish life in Spain's turbulent twentieth century by invoking the remote past. Thus, narratives that are only apparently coherent emerge because any story about what was and is Jewish (and was and is perceived to be Jewish) in contemporary Spain is bound to be as contradictory as the expression "Jewish Spain."

This book traces the process through which memory work bundles these contradictions into coherent narratives. A close look at the fissures and inconsistencies in these accounts reveals that any story about Jewish Spain will always be tentative and open-ended. Although the book broadly addresses the multiple relationships that the term "Jewish Spain" entails today, its main argument centers on the uses of the past in texts that depict the memory of the survival of Jews in or because of Spain during World War II. Even after the Francoist dictatorship had ended in 1975, the official version of the events that still circulated held that Francisco Franco was responsible for saving Jews from the Holocaust and that the dictator had pulled the strings all along, even when he was forced to make difficult decisions.

Chaim Avni, Isabelle Rohr, Bernd Rother, and Danielle Rozenberg have studied the complex intersections among political opportunism, personal initiative, and, at times, chance that made deliverance from the Holocaust in Spain possible, either through exile in and transit through the Iberian Peninsula or with the help of Spanish diplomats in occupied Europe. The historians conclude that notwithstanding the narrative the Francoist government spread during the postwar years, saving the Jews from the Holocaust did not result from official government policy, much less from Franco himself.[4]

Jewish Spain centers specifically on the varied ways in which accounts of these events appear in different forms of cultural production. The authors (witnesses, novelists, historians) invoke the past—specifically, the era of *convivencia* (coexistence of Christians, Jews, and Muslims in medieval Iberia), the anti-Jewish violence in the fourteenth century that led to massive conversions, the establishment of the Inquisition, and the 1492 expulsion of Jews from Spain—to provide coherence and meaning to the contradictory circumstances that made surviving in Spain during World War II possible for Jews. Additionally, the book shows that a comprehensive perspective on those circumstances—even on the Spanish Civil War itself—is only possible once they are considered in relation to the Sephardic diaspora and the history of Spanish colonialism in Morocco.

The term "Jewish Spain," however, is a misnomer. Spain was never really Jewish, even though part of the Iberian Peninsula might have been. "Jewish Spain" therefore encompasses a series of historical contradictions that cannot be dissociated from the different representations of cultural memory that are the subject of this book: literary texts, memoirs, oral histories, biographies, films, and heritage tourism material. The book offers close readings of these different texts and discusses the strategies that authors use in their reconstruction of the past. *Jewish Spain* provides a comprehensive analysis of Jewish life in twentieth-century Spain and of the ways in which Jewish communities interact with other communities in key historical moments.

The foundations for modern Spain were set in the late fifteenth century, when Ferdinand and Isabella, *los reyes católicos* (the Catholic monarchs), unified the kingdoms of Aragon and Castile. With the reconquest of al-Andalus and the ensuing conquest of the Americas, Spain became an empire firmly grounded in enslavement, exclusion, and the resulting homogenization of language and religion within the empire's boundaries. But the same monarchs who forged this imperial nation would also sign the expulsion edict, calling into question the very notion of a "Jewish Spain." The term "Jewish Spain," however, involves a nexus of relations centered on the complex history of Spain as it engages with European powers, countries along the Mediterranean, and the New World. Particular historical, geopolitical, cultural, and religious connections that mark contemporary Spain involve critical relations between the Spanish authorities and the Jews, illuminating the ways in which this century inevitably revisits and revises the past—or, in other terms, memories that are distinctively Mediterranean.

The Sephardic diaspora took place across the Mediterranean; the texts to be discussed locate their stories in the Mediterranean cities of Barcelona, Girona, Salonika, Tangier, and Tétouan, and a significant part of this book engages with Spanish colonialism in Morocco in the late nineteenth and early twentieth centuries. The events during World War II that led to deliverance from the Holocaust in Spain also took place in the Mediterranean "theater of war." Location, however, does not explain it all: the texts also involve other non-Mediterranean (at least in the geographical sense) sites, including Paris, Puerto Rico, and Budapest. The final verses of Marta Pessarrodona's poem "Weissensee" illustrate why a Mediterranean framework is useful for understanding how the traumatic memory of exile during World War II traverses both Europe and the Mediterranean world. "Weissensee," which describes the well-known Jewish cemetery outside Berlin, ends with the following lines: "A gravestone is missing / Walter . . . / Ask the Mediterranean . . ." (*Berlin suite*, 57).[5] The missing gravestone would belong to German philosopher Walter Benjamin, who committed suicide in the border town of Portbou in 1940.[6] By bringing up the Mediterranean, Pessarrodona foregrounds the relevance of Benjamin's suicide not simply for German Jews but also for a cultural region that transcends political borders. Today, "Passages," Dani Karavan's memorial to Benjamin in Portbou, reminds us not only of the philosopher's passing but also of the relationship between his turbulent life and times and the ever-changing sea that the monument overlooks. In a later essay, Pessarrodona returns to her own appeal at the end of "Weissensee" and writes of a "bloody sea" ("En defensa de Israel," 229) that connects the violence of World War II with the historical Mediterranean world and the current conflict between Israel and Palestine. This is not to imply that these conflicts are equivalent or even comparable but rather that an emphasis on the sea that "unites and separates" also means that any study of Jewish communities in Spain and in the Mediterranean region will necessarily entail an understanding of historical interactions among Jews, Christians, and Muslims and of the ways in which these interactions appear in different forms of cultural production.

The particular vision of the Mediterranean that materializes in these pages shares the attributes of "old maps," those that according to Pedrag Matvejević "have lost their sharp edges; their colors have faded; they resemble memory" (*Mediterranean: A Cultural Landscape*, 95). The Mediterranean map traced in this book, with its soft edges and worn colors, not only resembles but indeed charts memory or, as Michael Rothberg (and Richard Terdiman) would phrase it, "the past made present" (Rothberg, *Multidirectional Memory*, 4). This understanding of memory implies that memory is "a contemporary phenomenon" and that memory also is "a form of work, working through, labor, or action" (4). The two qualities of memory (memory as of the present; memory as a form of work) are crucial in a book that engages with the ways in which writers and witnesses make meaning of the Jewish past in contemporary Spain. Memory and its depiction are therefore at the center of the conflicts and controversies that inform the contradictory term "Jewish Spain."

The different forms of memory work to be discussed involve a past of loss and a longing for a world that perhaps never was. At times the work of memory resists the drive to resolve the contradictions of the past in a tidy package. The stories that are discussed in the pages that follow have enduring effects in the present; their endings are open and tentative at best, despite ongoing attempts to provide a sense of closure or completeness; and they reveal a longing for a place and a time that never really existed. Thus, different reactions to loss, including trauma, melancholia, and nostalgia, become evident in the narratives that engage with and map the meanings of "Jewish Spain" in the tumultuous twentieth century. Trauma does not refer to a specific event or moment but to the ways in which an event that was not fully assimilated is belatedly experienced in the present. "To be traumatized," writes Cathy Caruth, "is precisely to be possessed by an image or event" (*Trauma: Explorations in Memory*, 4). The actual events include those of distant but also more recent history, ranging from the start of the Inquisition

in 1478 and the 1492 expulsion to the Holocaust, which are often conflated in what Sebastián Miranda, a character in Juana Salabert's novel
Velódromo de invierno (Winter velodrome) calls a "perpetual present"
and a "magma" (73). Challenging simplified connections between the
events that took place in the fifteenth century and those that occurred
in twentieth-century Spain is one of the goals of *Jewish Spain*; underlining the persistent ways in which such connections appear in the different narratives about the past is another.

Melancholia, as formulated by Freud in his seminal essay "Mourning and Melancholia," begins as mourning, as a reaction "to the loss
of a loved person, or to the loss of some abstraction which has taken
the place of one, such as one's country, liberty, an ideal, and so on"
(243). The work of mourning makes it possible to overcome that loss,
allowing, in Freud's terms, the ego to become "free and uninhibited
again" (245). But melancholia ensues if the work of mourning, which
for Paul Ricoeur can also be compared to the work of remembering
(*Memory, History, Forgetting*, 72), cannot be carried out. Much of the
literature on melancholia is devoted to a sense of closure or cure, in
which mourning, not melancholia, is the desirable state following any
kind of loss.[7] Ranjana Khanna, who critiques the relationship between
Freudian psychoanalysis and colonialism in *Dark Continents*, further
emphasizes the differences between mourning and melancholia, arguing that the "success" of the work of mourning will always be tenuous
because "there will always be some remainder of the lost object" (24).[8]
Khanna's understanding of "the inaccessible remainder" as "the ker-
nel of melancholia, unknown, inassimilable, interruptive, and present"
(24) is particularly pertinent: a map of "Jewish Spain" would feature
the remainders that are the part of memory work that resists the drive
to coherence.

"Nostalgia," a term originally coined in the seventeenth century to
name an affliction that, once again, is a consequence of a loss, shares
some of melancholia's traits. Nostalgia is a longing for a home (a place,
a time) that has vanished. Because the 1492 expulsion and Sepharad
itself are such prevalent motifs in texts that engage with twentieth- and
even twenty-first-century Spain, understanding the ways in which nostalgia operates in this context is particularly important. Svetlana Boym
differentiates between "restorative nostalgia," which "manifests itself in

total reconstructions of monuments of the past," and "reflective nostalgia," which "lingers on ruins, the patina of time and history, in the dreams of another place and another time" (*The Future of Nostalgia*, 41). Both forms of nostalgia appear recurrently in the texts that engage with Jewish absence and presence in contemporary Spain. Restorative nostalgia materializes in a specific form in twentieth-century Spanish philo-Sephardism (which also is strongly nationalistic) as well as in colonialist discourse from the same period (which for the present study will be particularly important in relation to Spain's presence in Morocco). The pages that follow, however, will focus primarily on the interaction between the two forms of nostalgia in a range of texts.

As will become apparent in the map that materializes in this book, the work of memory is inexorably linked to geography, to the actual locations on the Iberian Peninsula, the Mediterranean region, and across the space of the Sephardic diaspora. The plaques described at the beginning of this chapter and the four forms of writing that they display are also examples of what Pierra Nora has called *lieux de mémoire*, the places "where memory crystallizes and secretes itself" ("Between Memory and History," 7); they are "moments of history torn away from the movement of history, then returned; no longer quite life, not yet death, like shells on the shore when the sea of living memory has receded" (12). The lieux de mémoire are fragments of a past that in its entirety is as vast and unknowable as the sea. As Michael Rothberg notes, Nora's conceptualization of memory has received substantial and rigorous criticism, despite its evident importance for any approach to the past. It is precisely the flaws of Nora's conceptualization of the past, however, that also make it very suitable for the scope of this book. As Rothberg observes, Nora's work involves a problematic binary opposition between history and memory that is characteristic of a "nostalgia-tinged tale of decline" and a "nostalgic plotting of loss" ("Between Memory and Memory" 4, 6).[9] Because the very concept of a lieu de mémoire is, almost by definition, a nostalgic notion, it is appropriate for a discussion of Jewish Spain and the loss of Sepharad.

This book tells the story not only of the earlier-mentioned plaques but of many "moments of history torn away from the movement of history," ambiguously located in the in-between, "no longer quite life, not yet death," including the ruins of Jewish quarters across the Iberian Peninsula that have been restored to showcase a heritage attraction for national and international tourists; the now vanished Vélodrome d'hiver (winter velodrome) where the Paris Jews were rounded up in 1942; the train tracks that once crisscrossed Europe, all leading to death and suffering; the plaques in Budapest, Israel, Zaragoza, and Rome that today commemorate the actions of two men (a Spanish diplomat and an Italian heroic impostor) to protect the Jews of Budapest; and the signposted route across the Pyrenees that Walter Benjamin took fleeing the Nazis and Vichy France in 1940. These more tangible places also conjure up other realms of memory of a more distant past: of Jewish life before 1492 (and, possibly, before 1391)—with the highly mythologized keys to their homes that Iberian Jews supposedly took with them on their long diaspora—and even Sepharad itself, or at least what Sepharad was and is imagined to be. These are the places of a Mediterranean memory.

The location of *Jewish Spain* within the field of Mediterranean studies—a field that Sharon Kinoshita has discussed as "less a way of defining or delimiting a geographic space (as in the famous formulation of the Mediterranean as the region of the olive and the vine) than a heuristic device for remapping traditional disciplinary divides" ("Medieval Mediterranean Literature," 602)—makes it possible to tackle questions that are pertinent within a national and a transnational framework. Both contexts (and the relations between them) need to be addressed simultaneously in a book that is grounded in Spanish cultural studies and Jewish studies. The Mediterranean framing does not imply an easy evasion of the issues that arise when considering "the national" as a category of analysis. Rather, a close understanding of Jewish Spain within a Mediterranean context makes evident some of the unresolved questions and conflicts that lie at the heart of the Spanish nation today: the historical identification with a specific race, religion, and ethnicity; the consequent exclusion of all others; and the relationship between past and present.

Current conflicts in the Middle East polarize perceptions of Jews in such a way that, as seen with the plaques in Barcelona, remainders of a Jewish medieval past in Iberia have become part of a contemporary struggle over the meaning of Jewish absence and presence. *Jewish*

Spain will chart the relationships among these remainders, relationships that reveal what Michael Rothberg has called "multidirectional memory." Rothberg's *Multidirectional Memory: Remembering the Holocaust in the Age of Globalization* provides a productive way to understand how different histories of violence relate to one another. To move beyond a model of "competitive memory"—in which, for example, Holocaust memory and "historical memory" of the Spanish Civil War (1936–1939) would compete in "a zero-sum struggle for scarce resources"—Rothberg delineates a multidirectional form of memory, "subject to ongoing negotiations, cross-referencing, and borrowing; as productive and not privative" (*Multidirectional Memory*, 3). This suggests that rather than uncritically reassigning concepts developed in the context of traumatic memories of the Holocaust (such as Marianne Hirsch's notion of "postmemory" in *Family Frames*), multidirectional memory makes it possible to understand instances in which memories of different moments come together, sometimes forcefully. According to Rothberg, "recognizing the multidirectionality of memory encourages us to pay close attention to the circulation of historical memories in encounters whose meanings are complex and overdetermined, instead of proceeding from the assumption that the presence of one history in collective memory entails the erasure or dilution of all others" (*Multidirectional Memory*, 179). Rothberg demonstrates that there is far more room for "the past made present" in national memories than we might initially think, but this does not mean that competition over memory is not a reality—it certainly is, as even the three historical plaques in the medieval Jewish quarter of Barcelona show. The ways in which the memories of different histories of violence relate to and even invigorate rather than silence one another (for the purposes of this book, memories of the Holocaust and the Spanish Civil War) constitute a crucial component of what "Jewish Spain" means today.

The debate on memory in Spain may have reached its zenith with the passing of the Law of Historical Memory in 2007. Although this debate takes place along clearly defined ideological lines, Spain's extremely contradictory relationship with Jews in the 1930s and 1940s blurs these lines. Because projections of "what Jews are" constantly changed in this period, philo-Sephardic and anti-Semitic attitudes cannot be clearly aligned with either Republican or Nationalist Spain.

Thus, before discussing how the "historical memory" of the period operates, we need to understand the ways in which depictions of Jews were produced in reactionary and progressive discourse at the time and how these representations intersect with colonial discourse. In addition to revealing the importance of including Spain's colonial relationship with Morocco in the history of the Civil War and the dictatorship, *Jewish Spain* will consider texts produced in Spain, the colonial metropolis, about the Spanish Protectorate of Morocco (1912–1956) that show the ways in which the identifications and roles of Jews constantly shifted, adjusting according to historical circumstances.

A historically informed scrutiny of these interactions will prevent an all-too-easy fusion of the medieval convivencia (a term that philologist Américo Castro uses to name the coexistence of the three cultures in medieval Iberia) and contemporary encounters, crises, and clashes among Christians, Jews, and Muslims in the Mediterranean world. Castro, described by David Nirenberg as "the most influential advocate for the study of Jewish and Islamic influence on Spanish culture" ("Figures of Thought and Figures of Flesh," 40), began paying attention to Jewish culture early in his career in the 1920s, when he was conducting a linguistic study of the language that the Jews of Morocco spoke.[10] With his book *España en su historia* (Spain and its history, 1948), written from his exile in the United States, Castro was the first Spanish intellectual to argue that, before the 711 invasion, "Spain" did not exist.[11]

> I think that the adjective "Spanish" (*español*) cannot be strictly applied to those who lived in the Iberian Peninsula prior to the Moorish invasion. If we call the Visgoths, the Romans, the Iberians, etc. Spanish, then we must find another name for the people in whose lives is articulated everything that has been created (or destroyed) in that Peninsula from the tenth century till today. (*The Structure of Spanish History*, 46)

Castro's argument lies at the heart of one of the main claims I make in this book, that understanding Spain today necessarily involves an engagement with the Muslim and Jewish past; Spain did not become "Spain" in spite of its Jewish and Muslim past (in many ways the position put forth by Castro's opponent, Claudio Sánchez Albornoz) but because of it. Castro's own work—which he also continuously challenged and revised in his lifetime—cannot today be taken at face value either. His vision of Jews in medieval Iberia is undoubtedly problematic, and although he made it possible, in 1948, to consider Spanish reality as one of religious, cultural, and ethnic pluralism rather than singularity, Castro's work contributed to a "mythification," as Ana Menny terms it, of Judeo-Spanish history ("Entre reconocimiento y rechazo," 143); or, in Paul Julian Smith's succinct account, "having rejected the shibboleths of racial purity and exclusivity, Castro goes on to set up a role for Jews and *conversos* that is dangerously ahistorical" (*Representing the Other*, 47).

Nevertheless, Castro's work shows that a Jewish element is always and unvaryingly present in Spain in the form of its remainders, traces, projections, fears, and desires. A similar argument may be made for Muslim presence, as María Rosa Menocal, David Wacks, Patricia Grieve, and Barbara Fuchs have shown in the context of medieval and early modern Spain, and as Luce López-Baralt has traced in the fourteen centuries her work spans.[12] Writing about twentieth-century Spain, Susan Martin-Márquez and Daniela Flesler show the intrinsic ways in which the past also informs the present in relation to Muslim Spain, and, more specifically, in Spain's relationship with Morocco. Martin-Márquez's *Disorientations* centers specifically on colonial discourse and Spanish colonialism in Africa, while Flesler's *The Return of the Moor* focuses on the depiction of contemporary immigration of Africans to Spain in relation to Spain's historical (and literary) relationship with the figure of the "Moor." Both books are significant contributions that make it possible to further understand and articulate the international and trans-Mediterranean implications of the Spanish Civil War and the Francoist dictatorship and to include the history of Spanish colonialism in Morocco—mostly ignored or marginal at best—within contemporary international perspectives on coloniality and postcoloniality. Historians Sebastian Balfour and Isabelle Rohr discuss in great detail the contradictory policies and opportunistic rhetoric that shaped the Spanish presence in Morocco in the early twentieth century. In Martin-Márquez's and Flesler's books it becomes clear how these contradictions played out in everyday life, in low and high forms of cultural production, and how these contradictions persist in contemporary representations of North African immigration in Spain. Both books are stellar examples of cultural analysis, revealing how important it is to understand Spain's colonial past in relation to the nation's increasingly multicultural society because, without taking into account both "Muslim Spain" and "Jewish Spain," it is not possible to understand and articulate what Spain was, is, and will be.

Since the three cultures that once shared the Iberian Peninsula are still involved in wide-ranging conflicts in the Mediterranean world, it is easy to turn convivencia into an object of nostalgia. We must understand this historically unique cohabitation through a consideration of the antagonistic relationships among the different cultures and the ways in which exchanges, ranging from trade to cultural translations, were possible. Demystifying medieval convivencia is beyond the purpose of this book because the events under discussion take place in the twentieth century, not in medieval Iberia. However, the era of convivencia, the establishment of the Inquisition, the expulsion, and the emergence of crypto-Judaism are recurrent themes in narratives of deliverance from the Holocaust in Spain.

In narratives of deliverance, different and often contradictory understandings of what convivencia entails always play a key role, revealing a fusion of past and present that effaces a 500-year history. David Nirenberg explains why such a fusion is so problematic in *Communities of Violence: Persecution of Minorities in the Middle Ages*:

> This focus on the *longue durée* means that events are read less within their local contexts than according to a teleology leading, more or less explicitly, to the Holocaust. Similarly, instead of emphasizing local or even individual opinions about minorities, they focus on collective images, representations and stereotypes of the "other." The actions of groups or individuals are ignored in favor of structures of thought that are believed to govern these actions. Historians therefore act as geologists, tracing the ancient processes by which collective anxieties accreted into a persecutory landscape that has changed little over the past millennium. (5)

Following Nirenberg's model, *Jewish Spain* will focus on "difference and contingency" rather than on "homogeneity and teleology," but it will also show that in different works the authors clearly and perhaps consciously recreate the kind of "persecutory landscape" that Nirenberg discusses. Thus, this book will not reveal what convivencia was or was not; rather, it will examine the shifting meanings that convivencia attains in specific moments in history that include the Spanish Second Republic (1931–1936), the Spanish Civil War (1936–1939), World War II, the different commemorative events that took place in 1992, and, finally, the first decade of the twenty-first century, as new migratory flows, mainly from North Africa and Latin America, are radically redefining Spain's complex history of inclusions and exclusions.

The events and texts discussed in this book are by no means the only ones that are relevant for Jewish Spain; the essays collected in "Revisiting Jewish Spain," a 2011 special issue of the *Journal of Spanish Cultural Studies*, reveal the wide variety of forms in which "Spanish/Jewish junctures" (Flesler, Linhard, and Pérez Melgosa, "Introduction," 1) intersect with Spanish modernity.[13] *Jewish Spain* is therefore not an exhaustive account but instead offers a series of multidirectional inquiries, ultimately aiming to show that constant processes of identification and disidentification with a Jewish other and with "Jewish Spain" intersect with cultural debates in different moments in the late nineteenth and twentieth centuries, as well as in the past decade.

Hazel Gold points out that "in the later eighteenth and nineteenth century the figure of 'the Jew' inhabits the principal discourses of Spanish society—theology, philosophy, philology, politics, art, literature, journalism—even though Jews are nowhere to be found within the borders of the nation" ("Illustrated Histories," 90). Twentieth- and early twenty-first-century Spain saw many instances in which Jews and Jewish culture (for the most part perceived as absent from the Iberian Peninsula) resurfaced in cultural life and political discourse. These instances include the philo-Sephardic movement in the early twentieth century, which was inextricably linked with Spain's colonial ambitions and failures, the highly mythologized protection of Jews (Ashkenazim and Sephardim) during World War II, and the reconstruction of Jewish heritage for tourism purposes. The revalorization of Jewish cultural elements (which, like Muslim elements, form part of the cultural fabric of the Spanish past, present, and future) was marked by political opportunism throughout the twentieth century.[14]

Since 1992, when King Juan Carlos welcomed the descendants of the once expelled Jews back to Spain in a landmark speech at a synagogue in Madrid, a return to Sepharad has become a common motif in diverse cultural fields. Because the Jewish population in Spain remains significantly small (approximately 40,000 individuals), this return is both symbolic and uneven, standing out against the absence, or at least near absence, of Jews. In the introduction to "Revisiting Jewish Spain," the authors note that "this absence is overdetermined with meanings connected to questions of Spanish identity in relation to its silenced histories; to the current reaffirmation of local, regional, and intra-national identities within Spain; and to the remapping of these historical, local, regional, and intra-national identities within Europe" (1).

Contemporary representations of the historical relationship between Spain and the Jews—in popular fiction and mass media, as well as in Jewish cultural heritage tour materials—follow the kind of "conventional narrative structure" that Dominick LaCapra describes, with "a beginning, a middle, and an end, whereby the end recapitulates the beginning after the trials of the middle and gives you (at least on the level of insight) some realization of what it was all about" (*Writing History, Writing Trauma*, 156). Within this narrative structure "Jewish Spain" begins in medieval Iberia and the era of coexistence; the trials of the middle include persecution in the fourteenth century, the establishment of the Inquisition, and the expulsion. Throughout this narrative, struggles over "purity of blood" defined inclusions and violent exclusions in Spain. Jews remained absent from the Iberian Peninsula until commemorations of the expulsion initiated a complicated restoration of "Jewish Spain." The narrative would then come full circle with a mythical return to Sepharad.

In 1990 the Sephardic Communities received the Prince of Asturias Award for Concord, an award that in 2007 was given to Yad Vashem, the Holocaust Museum in Jerusalem. Today, the most visible manifestations of Jewish heritage in Spain are the restored synagogues, Jewish quarters (calls, juderías, or aljamas) of many cities and towns, the Jewish-themed museums (in Toledo, Girona, and Cordova), and the increasing opportunities to visit, either literally or virtually, the remnants of "Jewish Spain." Tourism, despite its more leisurely connotation, therefore forms one of the ways in which the relationship between present and past is depicted in contemporary Spain. Tourism also needs to be taken seriously as one of the major factors that contributed to the country's modernization process.[15] Daniela Flesler and Adrián Pérez Melgosa, who have studied Jewish heritage tourism in Spain, show that although efforts to recover, reconstruct, and package Spain's Jewish quarters certainly provide new visibility for Jewish heritage on the Iberian peninsula, past prejudices and antagonisms toward Jews persist within the institutions (or are voiced by individuals who work for these institutions) that are staging the ruins of Sepharad. The Spanish publishing market has also benefited from a renewed interest in all things Sepharad: stories about convivencia, the Inquisition, the expulsion, and the return to the lost homeland have become popular subjects for bestselling novels.[16]

The narrative that culminates with the symbolic return to Sepharad after a 500-year absence is partial, even misguided, but it nevertheless continues to appear in diverse forms of expression. Rather than rectifying the deficient yet popular version of the history of "Jewish Spain," this book centers on the meanings that a perceived absence and a complicated presence of Jews entailed in the twentieth century. Thus, understanding "Jewish Spain" today requires zeroing in on those moments when Jewish history, literature, and identities intersect with Spanish history, literature, and identities, revealing the ways in which Jewishness is written in and out of Spanish national narratives. Although parts of *Jewish Spain* address Sephardic culture and history, this book is not about the Sephardim or about "Sephardism," a concept that Yael Halevi-Wise calls a "politicized literary phenomenon" (*Sephardism*, 5). Halevi-Wise recognizes a "Sephardic paradigm"(26), in a variety of literary texts that arise from diverse national and cultural contexts. She argues that "two political systems" inform the Sephardic paradigm: "on the one hand, the ethnic and religious pluralism known as *convivencia*, associated with certain periods of Islamic rule and the multicultural court of Alfonso X, and on the other hand, expulsion and inquisition associated with Catholic homogeneity in Iberia and its colonies" (26). The literature analyzed by the contributors to Halevi-Wise's collection shares common themes with the texts discussed in the pages that follow, particularly with regard to the ways in which the conflict between pluralism and homogeneity appears consistently in the texts that feature intersections between Jewish and Spanish life.[17]

Spain's historical relationship with the Jews partially explains why a number of individuals were able to save their lives in and through Spain during the World War II. In the early twentieth century the physician and senator Ángel Pulido established contact with Sephardic communities in Greece and in the Balkans. He then initiated a state-sponsored program that would facilitate communication and trade with Sephardic communities across the Mediterranean. Yet even Pulido's initiatives functioned within the context of patriotism and pan-Hispanic—even neoimperial—ambitions, which was particularly desirable in the aftermath of the 1898 "disaster," when the Spanish Crown lost the remaining three colonies (Cuba, Puerto Rico, and the Philippines) of its former empire. Philo-Sephardism was not so much about establishing affective affinities with the "Jews of the Spanish homeland,"[18] even though it was often perceived as such, as it was about securing Spanish influence in the Mediterranean that would, as Rozenberg writes, make up for the loss of colonial empire.[19] Rother explains that patriotism, not philo-Semitism, motivated Pulido's campaign to search for new economic opportunities across the Mediterranean; with the pro-Sephardic movement, Pulido fought for the restoration of Spain's greatness, not for religious freedom ("España y los judíos," 156). As Joshua Goode has argued, Pulido's initiative needs to be viewed in relation to his understanding of race in the immediate historic context of the early twentieth century:

> The repatriation of Jews for Pulido was always defined as a political
> act: to rejuvenate Spain by reintroducing an element of the Spanish
> racial fusion inherent in its makeup, the removal of which, with the
> expulsion of Jews from Spain in 1492, had caused the decay of the
> Spanish nation. However, Pulido's mission to repatriate Sephar-
> dic Jews must be viewed through the lens of the racial ideas that
> underlay them. Encouraging fusion and counteracting racial decay
> were Pulido's two primary motives for repatriating Jews. For Pulido,
> this act would in turn foster a healthy and thus prosperous Spain.
> (*Impurity of Blood*, 184)

It is in this climate that, in 1924, the Spanish dictator Primo de Rivera issued a royal decree granting Spanish citizenship to Spanish "protégés" (*protegidos*) in the former Ottoman empire. Although the decree could be interpreted as an attempt to restore a Jewish presence on Spanish soil, the Spanish authorities had no intention of actually facilitating a Jewish "return" to what once was known as Sepharad. Rather, because the new nations that emerged after the breakdown of the Ottoman Empire no longer recognized the former protégés of other nations, Spain chose to emulate the French policy promising all its protégés full citizenship. Therefore, Rother argues, one can see that international diplomacy, not Pulido's pan-Hispanic and pro-Sephardic initiative, motivated the government to establish the royal decree ("España y los judíos," 164–165). In other words, the passage of this royal decree did not mean that the government was interested in giving all Sephardic Jews Spanish citizenship, much less in welcoming back the descendants of the once expelled Jews to Spain. In the end, about 5,000 Sephardic Jews, mainly from Salonika, were eligible to become Spanish nationals in this period. The 1924 decree by no means guaranteed that Spain would guard its so-called protégés once Nazi violence became a threatening reality across the Mediterranean, even if this interpretation may fit at least some individual cases.

Spanish philo-Sephardism in the early twentieth century did not, however, preclude anti-Semitism. Only Jews who were descendants of those who once shared the Iberian Peninsula with Christians and Arabs were acceptable: the rhetoric of the period shows that a prolonged stay in Spain "purified" Sephardim and differentiated them from the Ashkenazim.[20] If we are aware of the genealogy of this rhetoric (born in the fourteenth century and undoubtedly evolving over time and according to different circumstances), the constructed and historical nature of the alleged "superiority" of the Sephardim should be apparent. This "superiority" is often invoked in the 1940s and corresponds to the notion of *hispanidad*, an "eternal Catholic-Spanish essence," as Rohr describes it in *The Spanish Right and the Jews* (4) that was a keystone of Francoist rhetoric and—this is where the contradictions lie—ironically helped to save lives.

Recurrent myths about deliverance from the Holocaust in Spain include the speculation that a supposed crypto-Jewish ancestry explained Franco's benevolent policy toward Jews and the story that, to protect the Jews, the Spanish dictator assured Hitler during their famous meeting in Hendaye in 1940 that the Catholic monarchs had

already taken care of the "Jewish problem" in 1492.[21] Although the
reasons that ultimately explain why these lives were saved are multiple
and often appear to contradict each other, they are not a direct consequence of any feelings, positive or negative, Franco may have had
toward the fate of Jewish people in occupied Europe. In other words,
Franco's policies did not programmatically undertake the protection
of the Jews, even though it often may appear that way, especially when
suppositions about Franco's alleged crypto-Jewish ancestry are mentioned to justify his benevolence toward Jews during World War II.
Needless to say, a personal connection between the dictator and the
individuals who needed his protection makes for a good and coherent
story because, in this version of history, Franco becomes the dictator who rescues the Jews and thereby rescues his own international
reputation in the post–World War II world. Rozenberg challenges this
assertion, pointing out that although Franco is a common surname in
the Sephardi diaspora, not all Francos have Jewish ancestry (*La España
contemporánea y la cuestión judía*, 255).

Lives of Jews were saved in or through Spain because Spain had
no clear policy regarding Jewish refugees and because the nation declared itself nonbelligerent during World War II. As Rohr points out,
even these positions shifted in relation to the developments of the
war, mainly for opportunistic reasons (*The Spanish Right and the Jews*,
149). According to Rother, roughly 20,000–35,000 Jews were able to
find exile in or transit through Spain; in spite of the alliance between
Franco and Hitler, these exiles were not turned away at the French
border. Rother also writes that around 5,000 Jews survived thanks to
the efforts of individual Spanish diplomats in occupied Europe (*Franco
y el Holocausto* 158, 408–409).

Separating these isolated events from mythologized versions that
aim to explain why deliverance from the Holocaust in Spain was possible in the first place is no easy task. Rother debunks earlier myths that
held that humanitarian motivations—even Christian charity—explain
the government's policies toward exiled Jews and that Spain exhausted
all its resources and saved all the lives it possibly could. Rohr goes one
step further in her analysis of both historical contingencies and discursive struggles over what was often perceived to be a Jewish presence
in Spain. From philo-Sephardism in the early twentieth century to the

appearance of a "Jewish-Masonic conspiracy" in the government's rhetoric in the 1940s, Rohr shows that political opportunism was what in the end made saving Jews in Franco's Spain possible. Constant invocations of the past, specifically of the 1492 expulsion signed by the Catholic monarchs, played a crucial role in the anti-Semitic rhetoric prevalent among the conservative sectors in Spain even in the years that preceded the Civil War (*The Spanish Right and the Jews*, 157).

The specific political and historical circumstances that allowed for Jewish transit through and exile in Spain during World War II are immensely complex and contradictory. The Iberian Peninsula was a point of transit for European Jews on their way to Palestine or the Americas. Under the Franco regime, although Jewish refugees in Spain were not exactly protected, they were generally not returned to Nazi-occupied Europe. In other words, if refugees could make it across the Pyrenees and into Spain, whether as illegal or legal aliens, they were treated as refugees. This meant that although some of the refugees had to spend time in prison or at the labor camp in Miranda del Ebro, they were usually not deported back to Nazi-occupied Europe. Walter Benjamin's case, to be addressed in Chapter 5, is a well-known exception. At the same time, attaining asylum in Spain was not easy, particularly because the government had no intention of allowing large groups of Jews to settle in Spain. A number of diplomats, among them Ángel Sanz Briz, the chargé d'affaires of the Spanish legation in Hungary, procured protection letters (*cartas de protección*) that stated that specific Budapest Jews (not all of them Sephardic or with direct connections to Spain) were under Spanish consular protection.

Sanz Briz and other diplomats who found themselves in similar circumstances did not follow strict orders from the Franco regime, nor did they exactly adhere to the conditions expressed in the 1924 royal decree (the decree had been long-expired by the 1940s). Rather, these individuals managed to bring into play the connections that had been established decades earlier between Spain and the Sephardim who were residing in Eastern Europe and the Mediterranean region. In this way they managed to save a number of Jews from deportation, both Ashkenazim and Sephardim.

Unlike this multifaceted reality, the story that the Francoist government would popularize and disseminate was one of a heroic rescue, motivated by Christian charity. A 1949 document from the Office of Diplomatic Information states that Christian charity and love ultimately motivated Spain's attempt to rescue all Jews.

> Spain, imbued with its universal Christian spirit of love for all the races on earth, contributed to the rescue of Jews, and acted more for spiritual than for merely legal or political reasons. Our government's aid was extended not only to Spanish Jews dispersed throughout the Continent, but also, whenever the opportunity presented itself, to all Jews irrespective of their nationality or place of residence.[22]

The official version of the events that the government disseminated in the postwar years and that remained unchallenged throughout the Francoist dictatorship is not the only narrative that suppresses the historical complexity of what Jewish exile and transit in Spain during World War II entailed. Witnesses, survivors, journalists, and novelists also reduce and sometimes efface the complexity of the contradictory historical events that led to deliverance from the Holocaust in Spain by articulating coherent narratives, usually centered on an invocation of the past. My focus on such narratives in the chapters that follow intersects with the debate on the "recovery of historical memory" that has marked public discourse, cultural production, and academic inquiries since the late 1990s in Spain.

The developments that led to the Spanish Civil War cannot be separated from Spain's colonial presence in Morocco, revealing again how important it is to consider memory's multidirectionality. Recovering the memory of the Spanish Civil War and its aftermath also involves recovering the memory of Spain's presence in North Africa and its repercussions north and south of the Mediterranean. Franco forged his early military career in the Spanish Protectorate of Morocco; the conspiracy that led to the 1936 coup d'état took place on African soil; and Moroccan mercenaries fought for the Nationalists in the war. Spanish colonialism in Morocco would also result in a constantly changing relationship between the ruling powers in Spain and the Jewish communities in Morocco.[23]

Spain's complex postcolonial relationship with Morocco represents a crucial aspect of the paradoxes contained in the term "Jewish Spain," thus provoking questions about how representations of Moroccan

Jews are related to representations of Jews in Spain in key moments that include the 1859–1860 Guerra de África (African war), the Spanish rule over the Protectorate starting in 1912, the Spanish Civil War, and World War II. Such questions can lead to an understanding of the intricate relationships among identity, race, ethnicity, and religion in a postcolonial Mediterranean world in general and in Spanish-Moroccan and Spanish-Jewish relations in particular.

In the late nineteenth and early twentieth centuries, Spanish writers and politicians depict Moroccan Jews as victims of Muslim rule, nostalgic for Queen Isabella herself, and in need of protection by a benevolent colonial power; however, during the Spanish Civil War and in the ensuing years, Moroccan Jews became the infidels who justify the need for a twentieth-century crusade.[24] Although Christians, Jews, and Muslims coexisted in the Protectorate, this coexistence took place in a colonial context. Thus, what at first glance might appear to be tolerance for Islam in Spanish Morocco was actually, as Abel Albet-Mas explains, the shrewd political opportunism of a colonizing power: "Morocco had little opportunity to influence the perception and the image of the 'Muslim Other' held by the colonizing power in Spain and after some decades of direct contact in Morocco, the new regime assumed that 'another' religion could be accepted not because of tolerance, but as a military reward for the participation of Moroccans on Franco's side in the Spanish Civil War" ("Three Gods, Two Shores, One Space," 581).[25] Tolerance for Judaism in the Protectorate was just as illusory.

That the Civil War became a crusade in the Nationalists' rhetoric is a widely known commonplace, but unlike the medieval Crusades, the external enemies were not Muslims but rather the infidel and atheist Republicans, Bolshevists, Freemasons, and Jews. As a matter of fact, by the 1930s Moroccans and Spaniards had become "brothers" in Spanish colonialist discourse—in the press, in literature, and in historiography—that aimed to redefine Spain's position in the international arena. Although the invention of a Spanish-Moroccan brotherhood dates back to the nineteenth century (the Africanist writer Joaquín Costa articulated this notion repeatedly), it gained new momentum in the twentieth century in the wake of the 1898 "disaster" (Martin-Márquez, *Disorientations*, 49). This idealized but uneven brotherhood resolves some of the contradictions that mark Spanish colonialism in Morocco. Spanish

Christians and Moroccans are represented as unified in an invented, trans-Mediterranean fraternity committed to fighting the infidels (Jews, Communists, Freemasons, etc.) on the Iberian Peninsula and beyond.

Although Spain gained control of the cities of Melilla and Ceuta—enclaves that remain under Spanish control today—in 1497 and 1668, respectively, it was not until the nineteenth century, when Spain was already in competition with other European colonial powers, that Spanish troops again forcefully intervened in Africa.[26] In 1859 the Spanish government faced a number of internal problems. Repeated attacks in Ceuta from native troops made it possible for Spain's prime minister, Leopoldo O'Donnell, to proclaim the need for an invasion in Morocco, possibly because, as C. R. Pennell suggests, it was "the only enemy that the Spanish army could conceivably beat" (*Morocco*, 65). War was declared in October 1859, and by the end of March 1860 Spanish troops had taken Tétouan and were ready to march toward Tangier. Yet the victory was short-lived. Under British mediation the peace treaty of Wad-Ras was signed in April 26, 1860. Although the Spanish government waged war as a distraction from internal problems, it nevertheless set a precedent and opened up the possibility of further invasions in Morocco.

Martin-Márquez argues that the war fulfilled its purpose because it "had been immensely successful in boosting national spirits among Spaniards, who felt confident that their country had regained a position of respect alongside other European powers" (*Disorientations*, 54). In official rhetoric the war aimed to pursue "the restoration of national honor and not conquest," but, in fact, colonial ambitions—"the colonization of some portion of Morocco beyond the enclaves" (54–55)—were behind the war effort. The 1859–1860 war also left ambitions for a Moroccan conquest, pending since Queen Isabella's reign, firmly entrenched within the most reactionary sectors of the Spanish public.[27] These same ambitions, however, would eventually lead to such events as the Setmana Tràgica (tragic week) in Barcelona in 1910; the Rif War from 1911 to 1926, which included the devastating defeat in Annual in 1921; the use of chemical weapons against the Moroccan population; the participation of Moroccan mercenary troops to violently repress the striking mineworkers in Asturias in 1934; and, last but not least, the development of Franco's rapidly rising military career and the conspiracy in Morocco preceding the 1936 coup that initiated the Spanish Civil War.[28]

The colonization of what would become the Protectorate takes place in the context of the "scramble for Africa" and in the wake of Spain's loss of its last overseas colonies in 1898. The war-mongering rhetoric from the period reveals a weakened metropolis attempting to flex its colonial muscle, or what was left of it, in the face of the advance of other European nations in the "Dark Continent." In *Deadly Embrace: Morocco and the Road to the Spanish Civil War*, Sebastian Balfour explains that "after the loss of the old empire in the Americas, expansion in Morocco came to epitomize 'an advantageous compensation for past disasters' in keeping with Spain's 'historic and geographic destinies'" (11). Colonial rule over the Protectorate from 1912 to 1956 results directly from Spain's rivalry with other European powers (France, Great Britain, Italy, and Germany) and not from a timeless, fraternal connection between the two nations.[29]

Spanish colonial rule would also have serious consequences for Jewish communities in Morocco. From the nineteenth century onward, and for the duration of the Civil War and World War II, Spanish attitudes toward Jews in Morocco oscillated between a paternalistic philo-Sephardism and virulent anti-Semitism, mirroring similar trends on the peninsula. The government of Marshal O'Donnell represented the 1859–1860 war as a "crusade against infidel Moors," and, as Rohr point outs, the roughly 6,000 Jews living in Tétouan at the time actually benefited (even economically) from the invader's presence (*The Spanish Right and the Jews*, 11–12). Sixty years later, however, a different crusade—the Spanish Civil War—was taking place. The Nationalists' dominance in the Protectorate in many ways made the situation for Jews far more severe than on the peninsula. Moroccan Jews, who in the philo-Sephardist discourse of the past functioned as agents of Spanish colonialism, now became the target of Nationalist violence because they were believed to support the Republic (*The Spanish Right and the Jews*, 85).

Not a single one of the chapters in *Jewish Spain* tells a complete story, nor is this book an exhaustive history of Jewish life in Spain or an account of the Sephardic diaspora. Instead, the chapters speak to and relate to each another, drawing on the blurred old maps that Matvejević describes.

The structure of the book is multidirectional, aiming to address a "productive, intercultural dynamic" (Rothberg, *Multidirectional Memory*, 3) of the ways in which the different memories literally "work" and are put to work. Chapter 1 focuses on the ways in which Jewish exile and transit in Spain appear in the Spanish literary world. An analysis of Muñoz Molina's *Sepharad* and Salabert's *Velódromo de invierno* reveals how nostalgia for Sepharad plays a crucial role in both novels. Although the idea of Sepharad never represents a blueprint for the solution of present conflicts, *Velódromo de invierno* and *Sepharad* enact but also question the myth of returning to a lost home in the Iberian Peninsula, to a place that in both novels becomes ghostly, unreachable, and yet undeniably present. These are stories that fall somewhere between Spain's "memory boom" and the articulation of the trauma of the Holocaust. The first chapter further reveals what nostalgia means today in relation to the current debate on "historical memory" in Spain as well as to the representation of Holocaust survival in literary texts.

The contradictory appeal of a return to a mythical home also informs Chapter 2. This chapter examines the symbolic uses of the past in narratives of Jewish exile in Spain during World War II, such as Trudi Alexy's memoir of surviving the Holocaust in Spain, *The Mezuzah in the Madonna's Foot*. The author went into exile in Spain in 1942, when she was a young child, and converted to Catholicism with her family. In her memoir she draws a spiritual connection between her exile in Spain in the 1940s and the struggles of crypto-Jews in earlier centuries. This link provides a desired coherence as her narrative confronts the contradictory circumstances that led to deliverance from the Holocaust in Francoist Spain. Contrasting Alexy's narrative with an oral history of the Jewish community in Barcelona, *Memorias judías*, I argue that Alexy's invocation of the past to make sense of her complex present is a common strategy in representations of Jewish exile in Spain.

Chapter 3 centers on historical accounts of Spanish diplomats who were instrumental in protecting Jews in Eastern Europe and the Balkans and who have been designated as "Righteous among the Nations" at Yad Vashem, the Holocaust Museum in Israel. I examine biographical texts produced in Spain and Italy about Sanz Briz, the Spanish chargé d'affaires in Budapest credited with saving more than 5,000 lives, and Italian-born Giorgio Perlasca. A veteran of the Civil

War and staunch Franco supporter, Perlasca found himself stateless and trapped in Budapest in 1944. He offered to help the Spanish legation protect Jews. After Sanz Briz left Budapest, Perlasca remained in the Hungarian capital and continued assisting Jews until the end of the war. Although Sanz Briz's work was officially recognized in Francoist Spain after World War II, when the government spread the word that Spain had exhausted all resources in saving Jews, Perlasca's story was ignored and remains little known in Spain, even though Perlasca was honored in the early 1990s in the United States and Israel. By contrasting Diego Carcedo's *Un español frente al Holocausto: Así salvó Ángel Sanz Briz a 5.000 Judíos* (A Spaniard facing the Holocaust: How Ángel Sanz Briz saved 5,000 Jews) with Enrico Deaglio's *The Banality of Goodness: The Story of Giorgio Perlasca*, as well as other historiographies and oral histories, this chapter develops a transnational perspective on the events in Budapest, focusing specifically on the ways in which the diplomats' efforts were interpreted in different national contexts and different historical moments.

Chapter 4 focuses on literary representations of Jewish women in the Spanish Protectorate in Morocco. Contrasting "Itinerario lírico de Sultana Cohén" (a text that nationalist writer Luis Antonio de Vega published in 1938 in the Falangist magazine *Vértice*) with Ángel Vázquez's 1976 novel *La vida perra de Juanita Narboni* (Juanita Narboni's wretched life) and Farida Benlyazid's 2005 film version of Vázquez's work, I establish a dialogue among literary, visual, and historical representations of Jewish women in the Protectorate to critique a colonialist narrative that, as Benlyazid's film shows, persists in contemporary Spain. The analysis reveals the ways in which the construction of both a Muslim and Jewish "other" constantly shifts according to historical contingencies, specifically, during the Spanish Civil War, when the discourse of a Spanish-Moroccan "brotherhood" was prominent in nationalist propaganda; during World War II, when Spanish officials voiced anti-Semitic rhetoric in both the Iberian Peninsula and the Protectorate; during the decolonization of Africa; and also today. I show that the gendered dynamics of Spanish colonial rule, with separate and inferior status accorded to women, persist in contemporary relationships between Spain and Morocco, as well as in published depictions of identity, race, and religion involving relations between these countries. I argue, however, that these dynamics were also in constant flux and changed in response to specific historical circumstances.

Finally, Chapter 5 focuses on "memory tourism"—that is, the reconstruction and signposting for touristic purposes of specific locations where Spanish history and Jewish history intersect. The first four chapters of the book center on events in the 1940s; the last chapter takes a close look at Spain today, focusing specifically on the reconstruction of a Jewish cultural heritage. In a number of Spanish cities, the reconstruction of the juderías is a thriving and also economically profitable enterprise. Daniela Flesler and Adrián Pérez Melgosa have discussed the different strategies that have turned Jewish heritage in Spain into a visible and easily accessible destination, recognizing "the underlying ambivalence to the enterprise of marketing the Spanish Jewish tradition for the purposes of tourism" ("Marketing Convivencia," 69). The production of a Jewish heritage in Spain reflects in part a trend that has been common in other parts of Europe for the past two decades. Ruth Ellen Gruber's *Virtually Jewish* establishes the ways in which Jewish heritage tourism in Europe today is mainly "without Jews." In Spain, all things "virtually Jewish" need to be examined bearing in mind the mass conversions (which took place in 1391, following attacks on Jewish quarters across the country), the expulsion, the complex forms of identification, and the history of the conversos. Thus, in medieval, early modern, and contemporary Spain, absence and presence can never be absolutes. The challenge lies in recognizing shades of absence in presence and shades of presence in absence in the palimpsestic Jewish quarters of such cities as Barcelona, Girona, Seville, and Toledo.

Many of the same contradictions can also be found in the various travel guides and guided tours that have been published in the past decade. These are texts that ultimately tell stories that offer a comforting solution to the problems of past and present, providing a message of both historical reconciliation and historical erasure. The reconstruction and national and international promotion of Jewish cultural heritage therefore represents a crucial component of the ways in which Jewish culture and history become increasingly visible in today's Spain. I analyze how newly restored medieval Jewish quarters and signposted escape routes across the Pyrenees contribute to our understanding of the historic relationship between Spain and Jews and of the ways in which the question of memory informs debates on public spaces in Spain today. The debate over the "recovery of historical memory" in Spain takes place most persistently in the legal, cultural, and academic arenas. Yet the relationship between the tourism industry, responsible for the influx of capital and modernization since the 1960s, and the representation of other expressions evident in legal texts, artistic works, and academic discussions merits further discussion. The first section of the chapter focuses on reconstructed Jewish quarters in Barcelona and Girona, and the second section centers on the historically designated routes and memorials of Jewish exile in transit at the Spanish-French border during World War II. In the first part of the chapter I focus specifically on *Les set portes del Call* (2004), the script for a tour of the Call, the medieval Jewish quarter in the city of Girona, to discuss the problematic representations of Jewish history and Jewish memory in relation to the virtual absence of Jews in Girona, a situation that does not differ greatly from that in other cities that now include restored or partially restored Jewish quarters among their sites. The second part of the chapter tackles the debate on the recovery of historical memory in Spain from an unexplored angle. The geographical and physical remainders from the Spanish Civil War and the ensuing political repression in the 1940s—ranging from unearthed mass graves and execution sites to symbols of the Francoist regime in public spaces in Spain—have been at the center of many of the debates on memory. In this context, the Spanish-French border, once a site of legal and illegal crossings of exiles and refugees between 1939 and 1945, has received renewed attention. Signposted escape routes, memorials (such as Dani Karavan's "Passages" in the city of Portbou), exhibits, and museums in Portbou and La Jonquera make it possible to revisit the paths of exile and transit.

Tourists and armchair travelers who catch a glimpse of the past in Spain's recovered quarters may not understand that this easily accessible past belongs to an intricate web of relations between Spanish history and Jewish history, between Spanish culture and Jewish culture, that once covered the "Mediterranean map" charted in *Jewish Spain*. The chapters that follow will look at—or rather "ask," as Pessarrodona would have it—the Mediterranean to learn more about the ways in which the past informs the present, about visible absences and indiscernible presences, about actual and imagined journeys away from, across, and into the Iberian Peninsula, and about the multiple and contradictory meanings that the term "Jewish Spain" encompasses.

One Mapping Nostalgia

Velódromo de invierno and *Sepharad*

In the Andalusian city of Seville, as in any widely visited city today, tourists often choose to get acquainted with the most important sites on double-decker buses that provide headsets so that visitors can listen to prerecorded historical and cultural information in a variety of languages. As they pass near the Barrio de Santa Cruz, the old Jewish quarter, visitors will hear about a "wonderful time of coexistence and tolerance" and about the "melodic Spanish" that only Seville's Jews used to speak. According to the tour script, in those times, before 1492, these same Jews already expressed their "yearning for Sepharad" in that melodious Spanish.

Needless to say, one can hardly expect a detailed description of the complexity of Jewish life in Seville before 1492 in sound bites that accompany affordable bus tours designed for tourists. And yet, beyond the idealization of convivencia in this characterization, it is worth noting its irony: the "Spanish" that only Jews spoke attained its melodic quality only after Sephardic Jews had been exiled and the language that endured in different Ladino-speaking communities became marked by its difference.[1] The notion that Andalusian Jews longed for Sepharad before the 1492 diaspora sounds absurd: how could they express nostalgia for a homeland from which they had not (yet) been expelled? Nevertheless, within the context of the tour the reference to the yearning Sephardim adds to the Barrio de Santa Cruz's appeal.

Like a siren's song, nostalgia is both seductive and treacherous. The idealized and inaccurate picture of the Sephardic experience that comes across on the bus tour is not an isolated incident in contemporary Spain. Indeed, a homogenizing and anachronistic vision of Sephardic Jews remains widespread (see Díaz-Mas, *Sephardim*, 168).

31

This mythicized version of the past also shapes narratives of Jewish exile in Spain during World War II that appear, even if fleetingly, in the Spanish literary world.

In memoirs (as will be shown in Chapter 2) and in literary texts the representation of complex historical circumstances that allowed for deliverance from the Holocaust in Spain is interwoven with invocations of the remote past. This does not mean, however, that what happened in 1391 or 1492 directly explains what happened in 1942, as tempting as it might be to link these dates.[2] My exploration of Juana Salabert's *Velódromo de invierno* and Antonio Muñoz Molina's *Sepharad* aims to show that the two novels in many ways take place in what David Nirenberg has called a "persecutory landscape" (*Communities of Violence*, 5). The nostalgic invocation of Sepharad that appears in both novels further reveals that the texts engage with the historical contradictions and ambiguities that made deliverance from the Holocaust in Spain possible. At the same time, and notwithstanding the complexity of the novels, they do reflect the same kind of teleological fallacy that Nirenberg addresses in his book, as noted in the Introduction.

This does not, however, mean (as Erich Hackl argues in a somewhat cursory critique of Muñoz Molina's novel) that the Sephardim who appear in *Sepharad* as well as in Salabert's *Velódromo de invierno* are necessarily noble characters—or noble victims.[3] The novels share more than their publication date (2001), more than their representation of deliverance from the Holocaust in Spain, and far more than the portrayal of their Sephardic central characters, Sebastián Miranda and Isaac Salama. The novels also reflect on what a nostalgic invocation of Sepharad means in relation to both the current debate on "historical memory" in Spain and literary representations of Holocaust survival. Nostalgia is a blessing and a curse in both novels, which reenact a mythical (and failed) return to Sepharad, the ancestral homeland that serves as a means to bridge the past and the present. The characters, however, end up lost, found, and then lost again in their nostalgia for what may be the ultimate lieu de mémoire, Sepharad, trapped within the grasp of history and the impossibility of a return to a home that no longer exists.

Although, strictly speaking, these texts are not historical novels, they certainly engage with history: Salabert's novel centers on the Vélodrome d'hiver round-up in Paris in July 1942, which was the first step in the deportation of more than 13,000 Jews, initially to a concentration camp in Drancy and later to Auschwitz-Birkenau. Salabert's novel also includes a small number of footnotes that provide historical information, as well as a photograph of the location. In Muñoz Molina's novel biographical sketches of historical figures intersect with the author's own biography. In addition, in both novels the characters themselves are seduced by nostalgia for Sepharad, despite but also because of the ambiguous relationship of nostalgia with history and memory.

In Salabert's novel, young Ilse Landermann is able to escape the Vel d'hiv, where both her mother and young brother, along with more than 13,000 other Parisian Jews, have been confined. Although Ilse's mother and brother perish in the Holocaust, Ilse survives and eventually makes her way to Puerto Rico. An organization named Sefarad, coordinated by Sebastián Miranda, makes Ilse's deliverance possible. My analysis of Muñoz Molina's *Sepharad* will center on one of the tales, "Oh You, Who Knew So Well," but will also consider the larger "frametale"—or "novel of novels," as its subtitle calls it.[4] In "Oh You, Who Knew So Well," Isaac Salama, a young Hungarian Jew, is able to escape deportation to a concentration camp thanks to the efforts of a Spanish diplomat in Budapest.[5] Together with his father, Salama finds exile in Tangier, Morocco, while his mother and sister, like Ilse's family members, die in Nazi concentration camps in Eastern Europe. When Salama is ready to begin his studies in Madrid, he finally feels free of his burdensome inheritance of loss, which in many ways is embodied by his perpetually mourning father. But the mythical return to Sepharad becomes a failure for young Salama: he suffers a traffic accident that leaves him disabled. Isaac returns to Tangier, where he will spend the rest of his days working as a forgotten cultural ambassador in the derelict Spanish Athenaeum.

Salabert's and Muñoz Molina's novels situate twentieth-century Spanish history in relation to the trauma of World War II, thereby sharing the understanding of witnessing and trauma that Shoshana Felman and Dori Laub develop in *Testimony: Crises of Witnessing in Literature, Psychoanalysis, and History*. The authors base their analysis on a notion of a history that is "essentially *not over*, a history whose repercussions are not simply omnipresent (whether consciously or not) in all our cultural activities, but whose traumatic consequences are still actively *evolving* . . . in today's political, historical, cultural and artistic scene" (xiv). Both novels engage with broader debates on literary representations of the Holocaust and, more specifically, with the historical contingencies in Spain: the Civil War, its repressive aftermath, and, more important, the debates on the "historical memory" of these events.

Both novels represent the experience of traumatic loss, although in different manners. Trauma studies tend to converge in three observations: first, the effects of trauma occur in an expanded time frame, and its symptoms are potentially somatic, "disguised or symbolic in their manifestations" (Douglass and Vogler, *Witness and Memory*, 10). Second, the effects and symptoms of trauma reach beyond the person who actually experienced it, passing on to family members and younger generations. Third, the connections between an actual event and trauma are often indirect and blurred: no single event has the same traumatic effect on all subjects; sometimes, as Douglass and Vogler point out, trauma appears to be completely disconnected from an actual event (11). Its effects invariably alter the processes of the mind and, as a result, the language in which devastating events are narrated. In the particular context of the Holocaust, history needs to be examined in conjunction with the ways in which the events themselves structured the possibilities (or the impossibility) of representation. Post-Holocaust history, explains Michael Rothberg, "has a traumatic structure—it is repetitive, discontinuous, and characterized by obsessive returns to the past and the troubling of simple chronology" (*Traumatic Realism*, 19). Rothberg's notion of "traumatic structure" also poignantly describes the composition of both Salabert's and Muñoz Molina's novels. These are complex and circular texts that illuminate the ways in which trauma structures memory and language as well as the cultural and discursive relationships among very different moments in the past, echoing what Rothberg has called the multidirectionality of memory.

Rothberg's *Multidirectional Memory* addresses the intersections of decolonization and Holocaust memory, centering on public discourse and cultural production in France in the early 1960s, when the Eichmann trial coincided with public debate on the Algerian War.

The book also is relevant to a discussion of the theoretical relation between the memory of the Spanish Civil War and the trauma of the Holocaust. Rothberg argues that "far from blocking other historical memories from view in a competitive struggle for recognition, the emergence of Holocaust memory on a global scale has contributed to the articulation of other histories—some of them predating the Nazi genocide, such as slavery, and others taking place later, such as the Algerian War of Independence (1954–62) or the genocide in Bosnia during the 1990s" (6).

Discourse about Holocaust remembrance has also influenced the memory of the Spanish Civil War; its most deliberate but also its most polemic manifestations are possibly the title and subtitle of Paul Preston's *The Spanish Holocaust: Inquisition and Extermination in Twentieth-Century Spain* (2012). Rather than attempting to compare or equate these two events, I will focus, following Rothberg, on the ways in which the discourses on memory and trauma of the Spanish Civil War and the Holocaust (depicted in both novels) pose new questions in relation to the debate on the "recovery of historical memory" that has been central to the cultural, academic, and even the legal realm in Spain since the mid-1990s.

Along with countless novels, successful films, such as Fernando Trueba's *Soldiers of Salamis* (2002), Guillermo del Toro's *The Devil's Backbone* (2001), and Emilio Martínez-Lázaro's *13 Roses* (2007), and historiographies and works of cultural analysis have contributed to the still expanding bibliography on the Spanish Civil War and its violent aftermath.[6] A key player in the public debate on historical memory is the "Asociación para la recuperación de la memoria histórica" (Association for the Recovery of Historical Memory), which was founded in 2000 with the explicit aim of unearthing mass graves in which the remains of Republican victims had been thrown. The ARMH has grown into an umbrella organization that has also lobbied for the Ley de Memoria Histórica (Law of Historical Memory), which the Spanish Congress approved in 2007. The law dictates that the victims of the war and the repression should be recognized as such; it provides funds for further investigation of mass graves and enforces the removal of Francoist and Falangist symbols in public venues. Undoubtedly, the Spanish Civil War and its aftermath still affect Spanish political life in a way that the Holocaust and its consequences do not. Nevertheless, Salabert's and Muñoz Molina's novels reveal that the memory debate may not have reached its point of exhaustion quite yet.

"Does the remembrance of one history erase others from view?" asks Rothberg in the opening pages of *Multidirectional Memory*. His model of multidirectional memory suggests the opposite—that is, that "pursuing memory's multidirectionality encourages us to think of the public sphere as a malleable discursive space in which groups do not simply articulate established positions but actually come into being through their dialogical interactions with others; both the subjects and spaces of the public are open to continual reconstruction" (5). The "multidirectional" model (as opposed to a competitive model) allows for an understanding of the relations between the historical memory of the Spanish Civil War and the memory of the Holocaust without bracketing them together and eliding the radical differences between the two. In a critique of the debate that has accompanied the "memory boom"—the phenomenally large number of publications centering on memory in Spain—Jo Labanyi considers these differences. The "boom," she argues, "has not been translated into an increased interest in the workings of memory but into an assumption that the past can be unproblematically recovered" ("Memory and Modernity in Democratic Spain," 106). Labanyi adds that "what is tending to become lost with the current memory boom is a sense of the difficulty of articulating the traumatic impact of past violence" (106). This traumatic past has often been narrated in the form of ghost stories, such as del Toro's film *The Devil's Backbone*, which Labanyi discusses.

Trauma theory, as it has been articulated in relation to the Holocaust, would then provide a path not so much to exorcise the ghosts of the past as to learn to live with them. Paying attention to the spectral presences and their meaning in contemporary Spanish culture is crucial for Labanyi. She argues that "it is only by capturing the resistances to narrativization that representations of the past can convey something of the emotional charge which the past continues to hold today for those for whom it remains unfinished business" (107). Such "resistances to narrativization" are also part of narratives and testimonies of Holocaust survivors, although in the context of Francoist Spain these resistances have a different cause. Noting that "in the case of the

Francoist repression, the resistances to narrativization have clear political causes," Labanyi continues:

> The testimonies of repression that have appeared in Spain in recent years do not suggest a biological inability to register the event at the time but habits of silence induced by decades of repression and a lack of willing interlocutors, which become hard to break. For this reason also, an aesthetics of haunting, which listens to the voices from the past that have not previously been allowed a hearing, seems more appropriate in the Spanish case than an aesthetics of rupture, which is predicated on the classic notion of trauma as the blocking of recall. (109)

These aesthetics coalesce in Salabert's and Muñoz Molina's novels, both of which span the early history of Francoism, including the political repression that took place in Spain in the 1940s, and the history of the Holocaust. The two novels represent singular instances of overcoming the resistance to narrativization that Labanyi locates as a side effect of Francoist repression. In a later essay, Labanyi reads the term "historical memory" in relation to "those forms of memory work that take place in transitional justice contexts," citing Stephanie Golob, for whom the transition to democracy in Spain was a "transition without transitional justice" ("The Politics of Memory in Contemporary Spain," 122). A concern for justice is undoubtedly a crucial component of the debates that center on the memory of the Holocaust. As Rothberg argues, public awareness of the Eichmann trial in the 1960s in many ways shaped discourse on Holocaust memory. I would suggest that *Velódromo de invierno* and *Sepharad* also emphasize matters that are relevant to but also go beyond a concern for justice—surviving a massive extermination, the burden of memory for future generations, exile and displacement—thereby revealing the multiple layers of posttransitional justice in Spain.

The characters in these novels survive the Holocaust partly because specific circumstances in Francoist Spain made this possible. Ilse Landermann and Isaac Salama survive both because and in spite of the consequences of the Spanish Civil War; thus, their stories fall somewhere between Spain's "memory boom" and the articulation of the trauma of the Holocaust. Nevertheless, neither the "the aesthetics of haunting" nor the "aesthetics of rupture" suffices to locate fully their significance.

Indeed, an ambivalent nostalgia for Sepharad ultimately lies at the heart of both novels.

More than ghostly voices that address the unresolved past, places become ghostly in both texts; this is also why nostalgia is so crucial for these two novels. Although the nostalgically invoked home may have an actual location or even a geographic reference, the return to that home is usually more intricate than a line that can be traced on a map. *Velódromo de invierno* and *Sepharad* enact but also question the mythical return to Sepharad: a remainder, a place that in the novels becomes spectral, unreachable, and yet undeniably present. Thus, although both novels evoke the nostalgia of an impossible return, they are also about irrecoverable losses and constant attempts (always doomed to fail) to recover what is gone: Ilse abandons her mother and her little brother at the Winter Velodrome in Paris; Isaac leaves behind his mother and his sisters in occupied Budapest. In both cases the protagonists obsessively return to the brief moment in the past that would change their lives forever, tragically aware that neither recovery nor return is possible.

The irreversible losses in both novels also suggest that these texts are not just about nostalgia but about the melancholia, as Muñoz Molina writes in the last sentence of *Sepharad*, "of an endless exile." Melancholia and nostalgia are by no means equivalent, and yet both afflictions share a number of traits. Both are, after all, the consequence of a loss that cannot be overcome. Although melancholia is by definition open-ended, a "reflective" nostalgia dwells instead in the realm of what could have been and what was believed to have been.

Drawing from Robert Burton's understanding of melancholia in the seventeenth century, Boym notes that, "unlike melancholia, which was regarded as an ailment of monks and philosophers, nostalgia was a more 'democratic' disease that threatened to affect soldiers and sailors displaced far from home as well as many country people who began to move to the cities" (*The Future of Nostalgia*, 5). While melancholia, according to Boym, "confines itself to the planes of individual consciousness," nostalgia is "about the relationships between individual biography and the biography of groups or nations, between personal and collective memory" (xvi). The novels engage with the respective characters' individual consciousness and the ways in which they come into being in the form of a collective memory that has the loss of Sepharad at its very core. The importance of a lost home (in this case, Sepharad) and the sensuous appeal of nostalgia influence and even shape the melancholia that the main characters endure. Ilse Landermann, her son, Herschel, and Sebastián Miranda in *Velódromo de invierno* and Isaac Salama in *Sepharad* cannot overcome their respective losses (even though they attempt, at least initially, to do so), so that they ultimately dwell in an endless longing that corresponds thematically to the longing for a return home, to Sepharad, that will never happen.

Nostalgia for Sepharad

The term "nostalgia," Svetlana Boym explains, was coined from the "nostalgically Greek" *nostos* (homecoming) and *algia* (pain) (Boym, *The Future of Nostalgia*, 3). Nostalgia is a longing for a home that no longer exists or never existed, and for this reason the concept of nostalgia is so prevalent in the discourse on the loss of Sepharad in the fifteenth century. Even though the term "nostalgia" is the creation of a seventeenth-century medical student, artistic rather than medical discourse explains the seductive appeal of nostalgia in the modern world: "Modern nostalgia is a mourning for the impossibility of a mythical return, for the loss of an enchanted world with clear borders and values; it could be a secular expression of spiritual longing, the edenic unity of time and space before entry into history" (8).

The difficult question that arises is whether nostalgia is essentially "history without guilt" (Kammen, *Mystic Chords of Memory*, cited in Boym, *The Future of Nostalgia*, xiv), which would render this analysis of nostalgia questionable. If nostalgia is nothing but "an abdication of personal responsibility, a guilt-free homecoming, an ethical and aesthetic failure" (*The Future of Nostalgia*, xiv), then Sebastián Miranda and Isaac Salama would be merely idealized characters. But none of the characters in *Velódromo de invierno* or *Sepharad* suggests that the "possibility of a guilt-free homecoming" is likely. Rather, in both novels a return to a safe home (before the Holocaust, before the 1492 expulsion) is futile. The constant yearning for such a return remains both present and—as the script of the bus tour discussed at the beginning of this chapter shows—appealing.

Nostalgia, Boym explains, is more than a longing for a place that might or might not exist; it is a "yearning for a different time—the time of our childhood, the slower rhythms of our dreams. In a broader sense, nostalgia is a rebellion against the modern idea of time, the time of history and progress" (*The Future of Nostalgia*, xv). Boym proposes a constant interplay between restorative and reflective impulses. Restorative nostalgia "puts emphasis on *nostos* and proposes to rebuild the lost home and patch up the memory gaps"; indeed, nostalgics of this type "do not think of themselves as nostalgic; they believe that their project is about truth." Reflective nostalgia, however, "dwells in *algia*, in longing and loss, the imperfect process of remembrance." Further, "restorative nostalgia manifests itself in total reconstructions of monuments of the past, while reflective nostalgia lingers on ruins, the patina of time and history, in the dreams of another place and another time" (41).

Reflective nostalgia therefore comes into being as a constant play between past and present, disavowing any yearning for the fixity of a teleological plot or for a stable home that will never again fall apart. Both forms of nostalgia, however, "are not absolute types, but rather tendencies, ways of giving shape and meaning to longing" (41). Even though reflective nostalgia may be more engaging because it relies on doubt as opposed to a fixed or essential truth, restorative nostalgia should not be simply dismissed as a constitutive element in the articulation of nationalist, patriarchal, or even fascist ideology.

The interplay between these two tendencies informs the ways in which characters such as Herschel in *Velódromo de invierno* and Isaac Salama in *Sepharad* experience their respective processes of identification with Spain, with Jewishness, and also as a survivor, in Salama's case, and the son of a survivor, in Herschel's case. A focus on these dynamic, open-ended, and enduring processes (rather than on identity, which may connote certainty and closure) is a productive way to engage with characters inexorably marked by such events as the Spanish Civil War, World War II, and the Holocaust. Restorative and reflective nostalgia shape the ways in which these processes take place. Both novels also show that a restorative nostalgia always lies at the heart of a fixed and static notion of identity.

The interplay between restorative and reflective nostalgia is also visible in the ways in which time and space collapse in the maps of nostalgia that emerge in the novels. Boym emphasizes the intricate relationship between time and space and both forms of nostalgia: "If restorative nostalgia ends up reconstructing emblems and rituals of home and homeland in an attempt to conquer and spatialize time, reflective nostalgia cherishes shattered fragments of memory and temporalizes space" (*The Future of Nostalgia*, 49). This notion of "home" captured in nostalgia cannot, however, be dissociated from a particular time, the time before this home, whether real or imagined, was irrevocably lost. More concretely, reflective nostalgia does not pretend to rebuild a mythical place called home. Thus, Salabert's and Muñoz Molina's novels can be read as topographies of both forms of nostalgia. In these literary representations of Jewish exile during World War II we find not only that restorative and reflective nostalgia are in constant tension but also that if nostalgia is a blessing, it is also a curse. The unfolding meanings of Sepharad in relation to Spanish history and the history of the Holocaust become apparent in both novels. In the end, however, they remain trapped within the same nostalgic discourse that they challenge.

Velódromo de invierno

The consequences of the Spanish Civil War and World War II have marked Juana Salabert's writing. Her parents left Spain during the Francoist dictatorship and Salabert grew up in France. *Velódromo de invierno*, for which she received the prestigious Biblioteca Breve award, is her third novel, and her first novel to deal directly with the Spanish Civil War, World War II, and the Holocaust. In *La noche ciega* (The blind night, 2004) Salabert reimagines her own family's experience during the Civil War, and in *El bulevar del miedo* (The boulevard of fear, 2007), which takes place in Madrid and Paris, she turns to stories surrounding illegal traffic of artworks before and during World War II.

Three moments in history merge in *Velódromo de invierno*: the expulsion of the Jews from Spain in 1492, the confinement of Jews in France and their eventual deportation to concentration camps in 1942, and, finally, an impossible reconciliation and return to the lost homeland of Sepharad in 1992. Different temporalities intersect seamlessly in the text: the novel takes place between 1942, when Ilse is able to escape from the Vél' d'Hiv and certain death in a concentration camp, and 1992, when her son, Herschel, confronts his mother's traumatic past. A third character, Sebastián Miranda, a Sephardi from Salonika, connects the past and the present, so that twentieth-century diaspora becomes a consequence of 1492. Similarly, the characters' nostalgic invocation of Sepharad provides meaning and coherence to the dramatic events narrated in the text. The exchanges between Herschel and Sebastián also mark an encounter between the first and second generations, memory and postmemory, nostalgia for a pre–World War II Mediterranean childhood where everything seemed to be certain, even comforting, and a post-Holocaust Atlantic childhood profoundly marked by doubt and ambiguity.[7]

The novel ultimately shows that the relationship between the two forms of nostalgia, reflective and restorative, lies at the root of any identification process. Such a process is structured through the open-endedness and ambiguity of the questions posed by Herschel and the novel's other characters: his mother, Ilse, Sebastián Miranda, and also Faustino Lagranja, a staunch defender of the nationalist cause during the Spanish Civil War who yearns to save Sephardim.[8]

At the end of the novel young Herschel recovers a lost object, an engraving of a mermaid that at first glance might provide a sense of closure and circularity to the text. As in Muñoz Molina's novel, the main character desperately tries to make up for irrecoverable losses, attempts that ultimately prove to be futile. More than giving a sense of closure to the novel, this recovered object allows the protagonist to sketch a map of his past, present, and future: a topography of nostalgia. In a text filled with journeys that can never reach their destination, the engraving signals the traumatic history of the twentieth century, in which diaspora, displacement, and a futile return to a lost homeland come together.

The engraving reappears in a secondhand bookstore in Paris. It is a German work from the eighteenth century that once belonged to Herschel's grandmother Annelies Landermann. She was forced to sell it before being deported from France to the Nazi death camps. We think that we are witnessing a moment of closure: Herschel has just found the same engraving that Annelies Landermann hurriedly sold in Paris in 1942, when the German-controlled government had closed the French borders and would soon after round up Jews, regardless of their citizenship, at the Vélodrome d'hiver for deportation to concentration camps, where most Jews, including Annelies, her husband, and her son, would be put to death. Only Ilse, Herschel's mother, survives; she escapes from the Vél' d'Hiv, leaving the others behind.

Velódromo de invierno takes place in a perpetually painful, dissociated, and traumatic present. Such an understanding of time (and place, as will shortly become evident) gives the novel its structure; it may also be the most productive way to understand and narrate the ways in which trauma arranges the memory of such events as the Holocaust, the Spanish Civil War, and its repressive aftermath—notwithstanding the radical differences among these events and the divergent ways in which they have been memorialized. A brief look at the thoughts of one of the novel's narrators, Sebastián Miranda, highlights the ways in which a perpetually reexperienced present is a consequence, or even a symptom, of a traumatic past. Sebastián blames this amalgam of past, present, and future on his old age. However, the traumatic events he experienced certainly reveal that not just his memories but also the entire novel is, to use Rothberg's terms, structured by trauma. In an aside, during one of the many conversations with Herschel, the old man reflects on this situation: "Because at my age one consciously rejects the coherence of grammar and the flow of logic, choosing to place oneself in a *perpetual present*, where everything, yesterday with its steaming, years-old turmoil, and getting up a few hours ago, and the appointment with the rheumatologist for tomorrow, get mixed up in a magma made out of fools' drool" (Salabert, *Velódromo de invierno*, 73; my emphasis). Even though Sebastián believes otherwise, old age alone does not explain the complex ways in which memories of the past constantly intersect with the more than symbolic present of 1992. Salabert depicts the associations and disassociations between a broken self and a search for an at least partially hidden narrative that materializes in the maps of nostalgia.

An attempt to read these maps begins with the lost object, the engraving. Annelies Landermann has regarded the mermaid engraving as a charm that would protect her family "from an ancestral memory of pogroms, persecutions and twists of fate" (17). Even though she promised her mother that she would take care of this precious heirloom, she knows in 1942 that the mermaid will only help by leaving the family (18). Annelies therefore sells the engraving to raise the funds she will need to pay Sebastián Miranda, who may be able to save her children from being deported to a concentration camp. Miranda leads Sefarad, an organization dedicated to helping Sephardic children escape across the Pyrenees, away from the Nazis in France, and into Spain.[9] Even though the date has been set for Miranda to take Ilse Landermann and her younger brother, Herschel, to safety away from occupied France, the sold mermaid already seems to have lost all its protective power: along with the other Jewish families in Paris, the Landermanns are brought to the Vél' d'Hiv to await deportation and an almost certain death.

The novel does not end here, however; this is only the beginning of the story: Ilse manages to escape from the Vél' d'Hiv. She finds Sebastián, who will lead her to freedom (first in Portugal, eventually in Puerto Rico) and to Javier Dalmases, the man who in Spain collaborates with Miranda's organization. Dalmases falls in love with Ilse—who, although still very young, has been forced to grow up quickly—and later marries her in absentia (she is already living with her relatives in Puerto Rico, while Dalmases chooses to remain in Spain). Shortly after the wedding, Ilse gives birth to a son she names Herschel, in memory of her little brother, who along with her mother and father perished in the Holocaust.

Velódromo de invierno begins when Herschel, now an adult, travels to Spain after his mother and Javier Dalmases have died. The purpose of his trip is to determine the details of the bequest he is to receive from the man who married his mother; however, his inquiries into Dalmases's material inheritance only partly explain his journey. Among the many questions that Herschel carries with him across the Atlantic, the most pressing is the identity of his unknown father. At the end of the novel, Herschel still wonders whether Javier Dalmases or Sebastián Miranda is his father. In *Velódromo de invierno* this and many other questions remain unanswered, although Herschel indeed recovers the mermaid engraving, happening upon it in the secondhand bookstore in Paris. Jokingly, Herschel asks the Jewish storeowner whether the artist's having been German might allow for a discount. Instead of answering, the storeowner inquires whether Herschel is Sephardic.

Herschel replies: "Maybe. I am Spanish and I come from Puerto Rico. But my grandmother was German. A German Jew" (259). This moment represents Herschel's first hesitant answer; up to this point, his identification process has mainly consisted of question upon question about his family's fate.

If the recovery of the engraving at the end of the novel conveys the idea of restoration, the desire Herschel expresses to pass on the engraving of the mermaid to his own young child might also suggest that good fortune will return, confirming the family mythology that the mermaid stands for their survival. Gazing at the engraving, Herschel remembers Hans Christian Andersen's original fairytale, "The Little Mermaid," as "atrociously sad," radically different from "Walt Disney's horrible little mermaid, who was nothing but an impostor, a happy lie invented by cowards looking for a happy ending on the screens, so that they never have to face the endings of the real world" (259).[10] The distance between the two versions of the fairytale reflects the distance between the family's mythology and its history. Salabert's novel reproduces neither such a clean and happy ending nor "a guilt-free homecoming" (Boym, *The Future of Nostalgia*, xiv). The recovery of a trope, the engraving, cannot cure Herschel's trauma, much less provide an answer to all his questions. Rather, the engraving and its recovery represent a symptom of loss and displacement.

Velódromo de invierno takes place in the fictional city of Finis, a name that evokes Spain's still repressed colonial past and the topography of a former empire.[11] The rhetoric of the Francoist government grounded part of its legitimacy in a sense of *hispanidad*, an imperial and undoubtedly restorative nostalgia. In Finis, then, Herschel Landermann and Sebastián Miranda circulate on "the long avenue of the Reyes Católicos" (*Velódromo*, 108); they stay at the Hotel Colón (109); a Cuban taxi driver takes them around town (178) and back to the "the luxurious hotel that once was the headquarters of the Inquisition and later, during the last civil war, the headquarters of anarchists who filled the roof's volutes with slogans and turned the kitchen into a perpetual feast of scarcity" (121).

The use of such a location is of course not new; it recalls Gabriel García Márquez's Macondo, Juan Rulfo's Comala, Elena Garro's Ixtepec, Juan Benet's Región, and even Faulkner's Yoknapatawpha, or any other literary place that condenses a nation's history and a nation's nightmares. This compression of past and present becomes particularly clear in a description of a mysterious café in Finis, a haunted place that houses at least some of the ghosts of Spain's colonial past. Boym writes that seeing ghosts is an early symptom of nostalgia, and ghosts are what Herschel encounters in the café. He happens upon the café during one of his wanderings in the city and later shares the experience with Sebastián. Referring to the café, he explains that it seemed not to exist,

> or to exist solely in the closed down and dead space of another time and place. As a matter of fact, the waiters dressed in frock coats and very white gloves, who were looking at him in silence, without approaching him, without showing any intention of leading him to a table and offering him the cocktail menu or a list of strange teas or of "something, whatever it was," had the rigid bearing of specters or of zombies from Haiti. (*Velódromo*, 179)

The presence of the Haitian zombies recalls Herschel's Caribbean childhood, just as the specters evoke the silenced issue of postcoloniality in contemporary Spain. Although Herschel makes the comment laughingly, dismissing it as the childish play of his imagination, his laughter is of a nervous sort that also represents a premonition. As the parallel between the waiters' refusal to acknowledge Herschel's presence and his failure to get answers suggests, he will gain neither a clear answer to his questions about his father's identity nor any certainty about his roots from this overly symbolic return to the lost homeland of Sepharad in 1992. Later in this chapter, I will discuss how Isaac Salama's attempt to return to the lost homeland in Muñoz Molina's *Sepharad* will prove even more traumatic: beyond being fruitless, Salama's journey to Spain results in a literal and metaphorical paralysis.

Instead of gaining clear answers, Herschel experiences a seamless fusion of past and present and, with it, a new topography of nostalgia. At the outset of the novel, he complains about his rootless past, calling himself "another child of mystery" and "rootless, out of nowhere" (48). Sebastián's response resounds with clichés: "Roots are dangerous. . . . The worst crimes are almost always committed in the name of damned roots" (48). Sebastián's comment associates roots with the hazards of nostalgia. According to Boym, restorative nostalgia "tends to confuse the actual home and the imaginary one. In extreme cases it can create a phantom homeland, for the sake of which one is ready to kill or die. Unreflected nostalgia breeds monsters" (*The Future of Nostalgia*, xiv). The problem is not only that the worst felonies are committed in the name of imagined roots or an imagined homeland but also, as the novel reveals, that nostalgia is tremendously appealing for someone who, like Herschel, has been searching for concrete answers his entire life. At this point, however, Sebastián's caveat comes almost too easily: he simply dismisses restorative nostalgia. Later in the novel, Sebastián will need to come to terms with his own identification process in relation to the implications of a mythical (and failed) return to Sepharad. Thus, the conflict between restorative and reflective nostalgia comes across through the dialogues between the two characters.

In a different café in Finis, Herschel briefly tells Sebastián Miranda the anecdote about the seemingly haunted place. During the same conversation, Sebastián explains how Ilse, safe in Portugal with Javier Dalmases after the end of World War II, found out about the death of the other members of her family. As Sebastián reminisces, the memories of his own dead, the members of his family, invade his narrative. He remembers that after finding out about the Landermanns' deaths, he informed Dalmases but was unable to explain to Ilse that her father, her mother, and her brother had been put to death. Such reminiscences constantly appear in the text, revealing the ways in which both Sebastián's and Herschel's stories are fatally intertwined in the topography of nostalgia:

> Because my head was filled with all the names that *wurden vergast* [were gassed], Josué Miranda, *wurden vergast*, Antonina Miranda, *wurden vergast*, Esther Miranda, *wurden vergast*, Ramona Miranda, *wurden vergast*, their children, my nephews and nieces that I never met, and their fiancées and husbands that played with me when I was a child . . . all of them, they *wurden vergast*. And many of my friends and companions, that refrain after their names, those two obsessive words, *wurden vergast, wurden vergast*. (*Velódromo*, 205)[12]

Both Sebastián and Ilse did survive, and with their lives they also carried away from burning Europe the burden of survival. Ilse, as noted earlier, moves to Puerto Rico, where she later gives birth to Herschel; Sebastián stays in Europe. In the remaining years of her life (she dies years before Herschel's journey to Spain in 1992), Ilse is unable to live in a home with gas heating, even to stand the smell of cooked meat. Throughout the text, Herschel, who has grown up with the sometimes invisible burdens his mother carried on her shoulders every day of her life, reflects on his own survival and the trauma that will remain with him, situating him undoubtedly in the realm of postmemory, a condition that Marianne Hirsch distinguishes "from memory by generational distance and from history by deep personal connection" (*Family Frames*, 22). Postmemory, according to Hirsch, "characterizes the experience of those who grow up dominated by narratives that preceded their birth, whose only belated stories are evacuated by the stories of the previous generation shaped by traumatic events that can neither be understood nor recreated" (22). Herschel inherits his mother's sorrowful memory, and, even though he is generationally and geographically removed from her traumatic childhood, her story burdens him in such a way that silence and rejection of the past have always accompanied him.

Ilse refuses to speak German, to speak about the past, to ever return to Europe, to acknowledge their Jewish heritage, and to tell her son who his father is. She leaves behind a fragmented history, which does not begin to make sense until after she is gone. Only after her death does Herschel receive her life story, which she had written for him. Yet even this very intimate writing does not satisfy her son's inquiries. Because his mother's silences have engendered the ghosts Herschel finds when he returns to Spain in 1992, his coming across the haunted café in Finis is hardly surprising. It is also no coincidence that, once she moves across the Atlantic, Ilse dedicates her life to an obsessive collection of antiques, holding on to a past that was not hers and possibly finding a partial consolation or palliative cure for her nostalgia in lost and reclaimed objects.

The ghosts in the café also perform an additional role in the novel: they are premonitions of conversations Herschel will hold with Sebastián in the other café in Finis. As mentioned earlier, Sebastián's memories of his own past, his family, and their fate in the death camps constantly invade the unfolding of his narrative in 1992. Sitting across from Herschel in the café, Sebastián tells the young man about his mother, but his narrative is constantly punctured by memories of his own family and their fate in the Nazi death camps, a fate the Mirandas shared with the majority of the Sephardic community in Salonika.[13] Visions of this now vanished community constantly appear within Sebastián's recollection of the past, mixing with what he sees in the present:

> the woman in the corner, for example, with her shoes with buckles and her purse sitting on her skirt, the man who was reading the paper in the back, the girl burning her lips with a fried calamari ring . . . and the waiter who was approaching me, yelling: "I'm coming, just a minute!" Control myself, I had been controlling myself for years, I knew how to manage those brutal panic attacks . . . expelling the image of the corpses piled up next to the barracks, corpses that us, myself, God, yes myself and all of us, in the morning hurled on the carts, pushing then to the doors of the gigantic furnaces. . . . The furnaces . . . (*Velódromo*, 206)

At this point, a voice interrupts Sebastián's thoughts, saying: "One thousand five hundred and thirty seven" (206). Sebastián's thoughts are still focused on the deaths he saw at the concentration camp, but this number is just the amount of the bill that a waiter requests from Sebastián and Herschel. Past, present, and future come together in the "magma" to which Sebastián himself referred earlier. The kind of nostalgia that breaks into the flow of the narrative is often sensual and seductive: it consists of smells, sounds, textures, and flavors from Sebastián's childhood. Sebastián's memories mirror what Boym calls reflective nostalgia. Boym also reminds us, however, that nostalgia is rarely only reflective and that both forms of longing are tendencies rather than absolutes.

Even Sebastián's first encounter with Ilse leads him back to Salonika and, in a sense, to the lost homeland of Sepharad. The shivering child who just fled, leaving her mother and brother and friends and neighbors behind at the Vél' d'Hiv, has arrived in Miranda's home, bringing back Sebastián's memories of the community he left behind in Greece: "For an instant I longed for the world in Salonika, for our age-old traditions that required that women comforted one another and only among women when in mourning" (52). The possibility of mourning—so difficult, if not impossible for Ilse throughout her life—lies at the center of Sebastián's memories of his vanished community. It may be mourning in a more traditional and gendered fashion, when women and men mourned separately and in different ways, but it still represents an opportunity that neither Ilse nor Sebastián ever had. Both Ilse and Sebastián lost their families, their communities, their childhoods; these multiple losses also connect the diaspora that started in the fifteenth century with the twentieth-century events narrated in the novel.

The connections among the ordeals both characters endure throughout the text become particularly evident in Sebastián's thoughts when he first meets the terrified Ilse, who has just escaped the velodrome. The sensuality of the images represents a fundamental aspect of Sebastián's longing for a community that no longer exists:

> I looked at her again, with a terrified insistence, because she was thirteen years old and was the daughter of the temperate and good-hearted Landermann, and had just escaped from the Winter Velodrome, and in that instant was more daunted by having run away from there than all the Nazi menaces together. I saw myself at her age, hanging around a harbor that smelled of fried calamari, frequented late at night by women and off-duty sailors. I remembered myself jumping over ditches in far away orchards, biting warm watermelons, their hearts taken out with knives, that we all had stolen, laughingly, I almost felt the juice on my chin, the chin of a boy who secretly dreamt of starting to shave soon. (53)

The recollection of a moment and a place to which Sebastián can no longer return reveals the allure of nostalgia. Years before he would end up living in Spain, Sebastián dreams of the mythical, always nostalgic return to Sepharad. Still at a young age, he decides to join the international brigades during the Spanish Civil War. He fights his own "good fight" because Sebastián himself as well as the members of his family consider this first return to the Iberian Peninsula an opportunity to find the family's old village in Castile. This desire supports the myth that all Sephardic Jews remained in isolation and that their lives focused solely on the impossible return to the lost homeland, precisely as though time had simply stopped in 1492.

The mythical return to Sepharad, which also erases the enormous diversity among different Sephardic communities and the different historical, cultural, and linguistic contingencies that marked their experiences, takes place at least in part in the realm of restorative nostalgia. Restorative nostalgia relies on an absolute truth: it "manifests itself in total reconstructions of monuments of the past" (Boym, *The Future of Nostalgia*, 41). Thus, Sebastián's dreams of a return to the homeland take him back to a particular place, a particular street, a particular home. It is not only a journey across space, from Greece to Spain, but also a journey across time—possible only in the imaginary—as Sebastián yearns to find his old home exactly as his elders told him it had been left, including a few expressions in Judeo-Spanish at the end of the paragraph:

> I saw myself entering silos, looking down dry wells, looking at the bottom from the concave opening of walls that had not filtered any water for centuries. I saw myself walking next to the corner of a patio with a jungle of weeds that nobody had dared to care for after their owners had left, right next to the corner of the Callejón de la Sangre, the small street where butchers worked, three steps away from the synagogue that had risen out of its own ashes, next to a wine cooperative or a convenience store, where peddlers that might share a range of genes with me once worked. My own memory and my family's memory, we have remembered the location with a mapmaker's accuracy. . . . In the autumn of '36 I often imagined myself telling my father at the end of a won war that I wandered around the stone *kamaretas*, that I pulled the *brocal* and I drank the water from the *mozuelas* of yesteryear. Yet the Callejón de la Sangre no longer exists, or it must have a different name, as also without a doubt the *casa del recodo*. (*Velódromo*, 94–95)[14]

It is important once again to consider the different levels of narrative in the novel: in 1992, on their way to Finis, Sebastián remembers—nostalgically—the restorative nostalgia that accompanied him as he left Salonika, moving first to Berlin and later to Spain in search of a lost homeland. The yearned-for victory of the Republic has the potential to be restorative in the sense that it "stresses nostos and attempts a transhistorical reconstruction of the lost home" (Boym, *The Future of Nostalgia*, xviii).

This is what Sebastián may have felt in 1936, or even in the years that preceded the war and his first trip to Spain. In 1992, however, he knows well that such a transhistorical possibility of reconstruction, fixed on a notion of an absolute truth, is simply not available.

Salabert's choice not only to include Sebastián Miranda's story but also to have him narrate most of the novel shows how important it is to consider the role that nostalgia plays in potential representations of deliverance from the Holocaust in Spain. Sebastián's nostalgia is neither just reflective nor simply restorative; it always oscillates between the two extremes. Sebastián is seduced by nostalgia for Sepharad; however, because he emulates some of the misconceptions of the Sephardim prevalent in Spain, he also obfuscates the meanings of Sepharad. He mentions "the intact Spanish of our ancestors" (*Velódromo*, 56), revealing the common misconception that, as Paloma Díaz-Mas notes, a language and a community "could avoid evolution over five hundred years" (198). This misconception appears again when Sebastián mentions his mother's memories of how conversos treated Sephardic Jews at the moment of the expulsion. Referring to Faustino Lagranja, Sebastián wonders whether he was, as a matter of fact, a converso: "Even though he behaved the way my mother told me *they* did, in April, and in May and July of 1492" (75).[15] Sebastián's mother was probably born in the late nineteenth century in Greece: she never witnessed the actual behavior of the conversos in Spain in the fifteenth century. Rather, she witnessed how memories were transmitted among communities already in an endless exile. The "they" that Sebastián's mother uses is a thorny pronoun: it refers immediately to conversos or *cristianos nuevos* but also suggests potential conflicts over personal and group identities that may even end in treason and death. Such conflicts lie at the heart of the novel, and, as the text itself suggests, at the crux of Spanish history, culture, and identity.

The complex histories of Ilse, Sebastián, and Herschel not only reveal that nostalgia plays a crucial role in their identifications with nations (Germany, Spain, Greece, Puerto Rico), with Jewishness, and as survivors, they also show that such a fixed notion of identity always has an additional corollary: the production of exteriority or otherness. If restorative nostalgia is founded on a fixed and essential truth and "manifests itself in total reconstructions of monuments of the past"

(Boym, *The Future of Nostalgia*, 41), it can only come into being once an external enemy exists. Underneath the reconstruction of these monuments of the past lies the threat of radical otherness. Such monuments, ultimately, are fortresses, built for protection against past and future invasions.

Returning to Faustino Lagranja, who appears early in the novel, will clarify this point. Lagranja is a character who in many ways embodies some of the early twentieth-century notions of Sephardim based fundamentally (yet not exclusively) on a restorative nostalgia that is characteristic of Spanish nationalism in the wake of the 1898 "disaster."[16] He is a dubious character, a defender of the Francoist government in Spain, who in Salabert's text initially seems to support the creation of the organization Sefarad. His attitude reflects the commonly held notion within Spanish philo-Sephardism that Sephardic Jews were more Spanish than Jewish and therefore superior to Ashkenazim. He vociferously argues that Sephardim are not "'racially Jewish,' but the victims of a historical error, the product of an absurd religious obstinacy, that comes from the tragic political refusal to accept the son of the true god that the hawkish leaders of the era in an unfortunate moment planted in the heads of our naïve ancestors" (*Velódromo*, 69). Sebastián quickly recognizes Lagranja's anti-Semitism as he listens to him emphasize once and again that Sephardic Jews had nothing whatsoever to do with the "other" Jews who were, according to Lagranja, "that spiteful horde of 'European' Jews, who had come from God knows where, and who in the past two centuries had been busy invading universities and factories, and parliamentary chambers and administrative boards of banks left and right, and we just did not realize it, but come on man, it is enough to look for a second at the sharp noses of the moneylenders, and at the licentious nature of the pornographic declaimers of the 'Song of Songs'" (70).

Salabert's novel shows that contradictions such as those Lagranja expresses are part of any articulation of nostalgia. This becomes clearer in an interaction between Sebastián and Arvid Landermann (Ilse's father and Herschel's grandfather). Landermann attempts to convince Sebastián that the history of Spanish literature can only be understood in relation to the lies that are entangled with a nostalgia for a homeland that no longer exists. Identification with Spain *and* Jewishness becomes particularly thorny for those who converted, and for those who left:

> You have not quite been able to understand because you belong to those who left, Bas. But underneath every lie remains a powerful nostalgia. In the case of those who stayed behind, it is about having been unable to become what they could have been and needing to face the reality of continuing to be what they were never going to be. . . . It is the nostalgia of an infinite journey, Bas, you don't understand . . . because the journey of expulsion was taken centuries ago, a journey that others took, who are already dead. All of us, and especially you, the Sephardim, we are their lost legacy, Bastián, their mirrors without a reflection. Their Ithaca. (213)

Arvid Landermann is explaining to Sebastián how Spanish culture and identity can be understood in relation to an uncertainly about one's own identity and a yearning for a stable home that never existed. In Landermann's vision of history, the massive conversions of Jews after the massacres of 1391, the establishment of the Inquisition in 1478, and the 1492 expulsion led to an open-ended conflict between those who left (Sephardim, like Miranda) and those who stayed behind (the conversos). The reference to Ithaca suggests that, for both groups (those who left, those who remained in Spain), a desired return to a lost homeland is a powerful but also impossible drive. While Lagranja believes in a fixed and static "Spanish" identity, radically different from a "Jewish" identity, Landermann understands that such an identity is only a fiction, oftentimes a dangerous one.

In the end, the novel shows that the return to a mythical home, be it Sepharad, Ithaca, or even Finis, is a burden that traps those longing to return to the home they have remembered and idealized. Those who long to return are always caught in the trauma of the present, always cursed to know what separates them from their desire. Indeed, surviving devastating events such as those narrated in the novel may be as much a blessing as a curse.

As noted earlier, when Herschel finds the old engraving of the mermaid, he reflects on Hans Christian Andersen's fairytale, in which the main character also yearns to live because what attracts her more than the earthly love for a handsome prince is the possibility of attaining a soul and, with it, eternal life. Ultimately, the mermaid's story is also one of survival. The young mermaid longs for an eternal life, although she knows that this desire will only be satisfied if others perish for her. She thus shares the solitude that Ilse, Sebastián, and Herschel also endure. In the fairytale the little mermaid is given the choice to either commit a murder or dissolve forever into sea foam. Unable to commit the crime, she plunges back into the sea, expecting simply to disappear among the waves.

This devastating moment is not where the fairytale ends. Instead, the author chose to add a possibly uplifting, although prescriptive, ending that in many ways spoils the sadness and with it the sincerity of the tale. The little mermaid does not dissolve into sea foam; instead, she becomes a "daughter of the air." She still has no immortal soul, but she can procure one for herself after three hundred years of hard work. Even her new fate seems to have a twist, however; she has been put, so to speak, on probation and in the meantime needs to earn her soul. She has a chance to enter the gates of heaven even earlier, for it is prescribed that every day she witnesses a child's good behavior her probation period will be shortened by one year. A misbehaving child, however, will make her cry, and, for every tear she sheds, one day is added to her time of trial.

The mermaid's yearning models the conflict between the positive force of desire and the negative force of the "curse" that thwarts her desire. Her fate, which lies where desire and curse intersect, may bring Herschel much closer to his mother and her fate than the answers that Herschel has been expecting all along. Ilse simply could not provide Herschel with coherent answers or a consistent life story; all she could do was survive, and for him her survival was both a desire and a curse. If the recovered object does not provide a sense of closure to a text that can only remain open-ended, it still shows the ways in which stories of survival and, with them, the memories of traumatic events, such as those that Salabert narrates in this novel and Muñoz Molina reveals in *Sepharad*, are always traced onto the maps of nostalgia. Although both texts reflect on the shifting meaning of Sepharad in relation to deliverance from the Holocaust in Spain, neither suggests that returning to what Sepharad once was is remotely possible. Antonio Muñoz Molina's titling his novel *Sepharad* expresses precisely this idea.

Sepharad

Antonio Muñoz Molina's *Sepharad* followed other successful novels that include *Beatus Ille* (A manuscript of ashes, 1986), *El invierno en Lisboa* (*Winter in Lisbon*, 1987), *Beltenebros* (Prince of shadows, 1989), *El jinete polaco* (The Polish rider, 1991), and *Plenilunio* (Full moon, 1997). The prolific fiction writer, frequent contributor to *El País*, member of the Spanish Royal Academy since 1995, and former director of the Cervantes Institute in New York City also published a novel about the Civil War, *La noche de los tiempos* (The depths of time, 2009) and, most recently, the book-length essay, *Todo lo que era sólido* (Everything that was solid, 2013). *Sepharad*, however, stands out among his novels. This "frametale" evokes such texts as the *Thousand and One Nights*, the *Decameron*, and much more recent texts, such as Bernardo Atxaga's *Obabakoak*. The tradition of the framed narrative is tightly intertwined with the Mediterranean world. The stories that are now part of the *Thousand and One Nights*, for instance, reached Spain in medieval times, much earlier than Antoine Galland's French translation brought the tales to rest of Europe (Cinca i Pinós, *Las mil y una noches*, 5). Both Américo Castro and later María Rosa Menocal have pointed out the ways in which these tales belong to a Mediterranean heritage.[17] In Muñoz Molina's novel, however, the narrative frame remains partially concealed: unlike *One Thousand and One Nights* and the *Decameron*, no group of storytellers gathers to delay death or just to have a good time, although storytelling remains "at the heart of the novela de novelas" (Herzberger, "Representing the Holocaust," 85).

Like *Velódromo de invierno*, Muñoz Molina's novel also has a traumatic structure; Alexis Grohmann views *Sepharad* as an example of "errant writing," which is "both wandering and travelling and straying or deviating from the (supposed) right course or accepted standards" ("Errant Text," 233). *Sepharad* thereby becomes "a deviant narrative: it is an arabesque that weaves together biographical, autobiographical, and travel writing, memoir and fiction, stories and fragments of lives and journeys into an ultimately interconnected tapestry" (233). A close look at the different narratives that form this "interconnected tapestry" leads to a number of themes that connect them: exile, displacement, solitude, and war. Yet the words that end the novel, "the melancholy of a long exile" (*Sepharad*, 231), ultimately turn the different parts of the text into a whole that is more than the sum of its parts.[18]

Herzberger observes that in *Sepharad* "much of the storytelling centers on Jewish identity with a specific historical foundation rooted in fifteenth-century Spain and twentieth-century Nazi Germany" ("Representing the Holocaust," 85). The unfolding meanings of Sepharad in relation to the expulsion and to World War II further tie these stories together. In the final tale in the collection, "Sepharad," the author suggests a rationale for writing a frametale rather than a more conventional novel. The narrator reflects on a list of Sephardim who were deported from the Greek island of Rhodes to Auschwitz, acknowledging that each of the stories hidden behind the listed names needs to be told; each story is worthy of its own novel.

> You would have to read them one by one, aloud, as if reciting a strict and impossible prayer, to understand that not one of these names can be reduced to a number in an atrocious statistic. Each had a life unlike any other, just as each face, each voice was unique, and the horror of each death was unrepeatable even though it happened amid so many millions of similar deaths. How, when there are so many lives that deserve to be told, can one attempt to invent a novel for each, in a vast network of interlinking novels and lives? (*Sepharad*, 365)

Although the narrator readily acknowledges that there is a "true" story attached to each name (and each death) on the list, he also recognizes that, as an author, he has the possibility of inventing, of somehow fictionalizing, these lives and deaths. In a sense, he justifies his very creation: interconnected narratives of death, survival, and exile that, although based in reality (the Holocaust, the Spanish Civil War, the Republican exile), are in the end his fiction.

It is no accident that Muñoz Molina writes a novel emulating the "frametale" that flourished in medieval Iberia. As one story flows into the next, as autobiography, biography, and history merge, the stories connect in an endless chain, suggesting that a novel that ultimately narrates "the melancholy of a long exile" (*Sepharad*, 381) needs to remain open-ended. Rather than the melancholy of a long exile, however, *Sepharad* displays the nostalgia of a long exile. As in *Velódromo de invierno,* Muñoz Molina's characters (specifically, Isaac Salama) articulate a nostalgia for Sepharad that is filled with contradictions, displaying both the most alluring and the most perilous aspects of nostalgia. As in Salabert's novel, the return to the lost homeland functions as both a blessing and a curse.

In this novel Muñoz Molina muses on the life stories of a number of historical characters, including Franz Kafka and Milena Jesenská, Victor Klemperer, Willi Münzenberg, Jean Améry, Evgenia Ginzburg, and Margarete Buber-Neumann. The novel also includes the stories of unknown characters, possibly an amalgam of historical characters, chance, the author's own biography, and, of course, fiction, including Isaac Salama's story.[19]

Isaac Salama comes from a Sephardic family who had lived in Budapest. Thanks to the efforts of Ángel Sanz Briz, the Spanish chargé d'affaires in Budapest, Salama and his father are able to leave Hungary in 1944 and find exile in Tangier. Isaac's mother and sisters, however, perish in the Holocaust. The story of the fictional Isaac Salama reflects the reality of Eastern European Jewish exiles in the North African city. (The diverse population of Tangier and of the Spanish Protectorate in Morocco will be discussed further in Chapter 4.)

In the 1960s Salama finally returns to Spain to pursue a law degree. As noted earlier, he is involved in a devastating car accident that leaves him disabled, or, as he calls it, "crippled": "None of this 'impaired' or 'disabled' drivel, which is what those imbeciles say now, as if changing the word could erase the stigma and give me back the use of my legs" (*Sepharad*, 114). Even though the accident and the return to Spain do not share a historical causality, Salama still always reads his own fate in relation to what comes and goes, like the tides, between the North African shore and the Iberian Peninsula: everything Salama does, everything that happens to him ends up invariably tied to nostalgia for what Sepharad entails. Salama's story is relevant for a study of "Jewish Spain" not simply because of the actual historical facts that Muñoz Molina narrates but also because the story's profound engagement with nostalgia (epitomized in Baudelaire's poem "À une passante," which the character obsessively quotes) reveals how crucial it is to consider the role of nostalgia in any discussion of the representation of Jewish exile in Spain during World War II.

Salama's father succumbs to endless grief and regret that drive him to a renewed sense of religiosity, which his son does not share. Instead, the father's perpetual mourning shames the young Salama. He feels smothered by the burden of the past, "the terrifying weight of responsibility" (105). His father mourns "not just for his mother and sisters but for all his relatives, for his neighbors and his father's colleagues and the children he'd played with in the public parks of Budapest—for all the Jews annihilated by Hitler" (103). The rift between father and son continues to grow as the surviving members of the Salama family settle in Tangier, as other refugees from Eastern Europe did during the period. In spite of relative economic stability, however, the Salamas remain marginalized from both the Jewish community in Tangier and, naturally, the mythical Sepharad. Their isolation also only intensifies the father's religiosity.

Even after the father's death, the mourning does not end. The young Isaac Salama inherits his father's guilt and shame, and part of this burdening inheritance foisted on him as a young man is his journey to Poland out of respect for his father's last wishes: "When I die, you will say the Kaddish for me for eleven months and one day, like a good firstborn son, and you will travel to the northeast corner of Poland to visit the camp where your mother and two sisters died" (105). Although the visit to the concentration camp initiates his narrative, Salama, years before the father's death, expects his crossing of the Mediterranean, the mythical return to Sepharad, to somehow help him exorcise the ghosts of the past and the residues of memory. His expectations for the visit across the Mediterranean are stronger than those he will have later when he goes to Poland to fulfill his father's wishes. When the young Salama is about to embark on his journey to Spain and to what he anticipates to be a freer, lighter future, his response to his father's presence at the harbor already conveys that Isaac Salama's proverbial return to Sepharad might not be as liberating as he expects.

> I would have done anything to keep him from going to the port with me, but didn't even hint at it for fear he would be offended, and when he came with me and I saw him among the people who'd come to see the other passengers off, I was mortified, wild for the boat to get under way so I wouldn't keep looking at my father, who was the caricature of an old Jew. In recent years, as he grew more religious, he'd

also grown old and stooped, and in his gestures and way of dressing
he was beginning to look like the poor Orthodox Jews of Budapest,
the eastern Jews whom our Sephardic relatives looked down on and
whom my father, when he was young, had regarded with pity and
some contempt as backward, incapable of adapting to modern life, impaired by religion and bad hygiene. (107)

As in Salabert's novel, the perceived difference between Sephardim and
Ashkenazim underscores the tension between Spanish philo-Sephardism
and Spanish anti-Semitism, and once again the problem remains unresolved. For Isaac Salama, a return to Sepharad will be not a liberation
but rather a confrontation with the ghosts of nostalgia. Unlike Herschel, who is tormented by ghosts in a café and even a recovered engraving, Isaac Salama is haunted by Sepharad itself.

Years before the war, when the family was still living in peace in Budapest, the old Señor Salama talked about the lost homeland, Sepharad,
running through many of the commonplaces typical of nostalgia for
Sepharad, including the keys to the homes that were left behind.[20] Like
Sebastián Miranda's mother, he speaks as though he personally experienced the expulsion and the five centuries that followed: "My father
told me that for generations our family kept the key of the house that
had been ours in Toledo, and he detailed every journey they'd made
since they left Spain, as if he were telling me about a single life that
had lasted nearly five hundred years" (110). For the father, different
moments in time collapse into the same unbearable present: 1492 and
1944, even Tangier during the decolonization process in the 1950s,
are one and the same. He mutters: "I only hope that they throw us
out with better manners than the Hungarians, or the Spanish in 1492"
(117). For the melancholic Señor Salama all diasporas are one, or, to use
Rothberg's term, the different "histories of violence" become just one
repetitive present. For this character, traumatic loss dissolves time and
space: there is nothing left but endless sorrow.

Young and arrogant, Isaac Salama wants very much to escape his
father's stifling grief; his journey to Spain, which signals the mythical
return to Sepharad, seems to provide the kind of escape from reality that he so desperately needs. When Salama makes it to Spain, his
speeding on a winding road leads to the accident that leaves him disabled. Salama cannot but see causality: he did not suffer an accident

but rather "a consequence and punishment of his own pride, for the self-indulgence that had pushed him to be ashamed of his father and to reject him in his deepest heart" (112). The accident's happening in Spain and Salama's blaming himself for it—as his father blamed himself for his wife's and daughters' deaths—serve to reinforce the pattern, locking him within history's grip. Salama followed up on his desire: for him Sepharad represented a yearned-for freedom (from himself and his family's history); ironically, however, he returns to Tangier cursed and trapped within the confines of his own body.

As Salama himself recognizes years after his accident and years after his father's death, Sepharad remains unattainable, no matter how many 500-year-old keys one might have: "Spain is so remote that it is nearly nonexistent, an inaccessible, unknown, thankless country they called Sepharad, longing for it with a melancholy without a basis or excuse" (111). Speaking from Tangier, Salama echoes the first lines of Juan Goytisolo's *Don Julián*, although he certainly does not advocate the sort of apocalyptic re-reconquest that Goytisolo imagines at the end of his novel. Instead, Salama's story ends with a Mediterranean mélange, a pastiche in which memory, nostalgia, poetry, and Muslim and Jewish religiosity come together: "Oh you, whom I would have loved, he recited that evening in his office in the Ateneo Español, moved as deeply as if he were chanting the Kaddish in his father's memory, the sound of a ship's horn and the music of a muezzin's call came through the open window. Oh you, who knew so well" (159). Salama speaks to Sepharad from a distance: the last words of Salama's story are those that end Baudelaire's poem "À une passante" and that give the narrative its title.

The many myths and preconceptions about Sephardic culture that other characters voice in "Oh You, Who Knew So Well" reveal Isaac Salama's exotic but ultimately inconsequential presence in their memories of Tangier. For the few intellectuals visiting the now decayed Spanish cultural center in the Moroccan city, he has become a sort of tabula rasa on which stereotypes about Sephardic culture, and Jews in general, can be displayed. One writer who once visited Tangier remembers him in the following terms: "It seems he came from a moneyed family, from Czechoslovakia or somewhere like that, and they had to pay an enormous sum to the Nazis to get out. I can't remember the details, it was a thousand years ago. . . . Tedious as he was, he was very pleasant on the phone, lots of flowery talk, right?" (117–118). Yet Salama's own story reveals, to an extent, what lies behind these myths: Sepharad is just a memory. Later, it becomes a broken dream when his car accident forces him to return to North Africa, where his father, forever trapped in the traumas of the past, still lives in perpetual mourning.

At the beginning of the story, an aging Isaac Salama describes a visit to the concentration camp where his mother and sisters perished, so that it is clear already in the first few paragraphs that his story is a tragic narrative that emerges out of two moments of regret (the death of Isaac Salama's mother and sisters and the accident), which the character experiences enduringly as "an entire life shattered forever in one fraction of a moment, an eternity of remorse and shame" (*Sepharad*, 113). Nothing but a sign bearing the name of a train station that no longer exists and "rusted rails and rotted ties" (84) are left of this unnamed camp. The image of these ruins evokes the tracks that once crossed Europe, transporting prisoners to death camps. It is a recurrent image throughout *Sepharad*; the train, as Grohman points out, "becomes one of the vehicles crisscrossing the narrative, just as it is said to crisscross Europe's dark age of the twentieth century" ("Errant Text," 283). In this text filled with fatal moments, the main character articulates his own multiple losses with Baudelaire's words from "À une passante," in which, as Boym notes, "the chance of happiness is revealed in a flash and the rest of the poem is a nostalgia for what could have been; it is not a nostalgia for the ideal past, but for the present perfect and its lost potential" (*The Future of Nostalgia*, 21). The image of the train tracks therefore connects the "fraction of a moment" that led to Isaac Salama's family's demise and to his own brief excursion into the realm of what could have been.

Trains reappear at the end of the story, when, on a trip to Casablanca, Salama has an encounter with a woman who will ultimately lead him to dwell obsessively on Baudelaire's "À une passante." The crippled Salama finds himself sharing the train compartment with a beautiful and charming young fellow traveler. Salama is immediately and permanently smitten, but he is unable to establish a relationship with the woman he so desires, unable to tell her about his disability. His shame on account of his disability wins out: he keeps his crutches hidden, along with his paralyzed legs. When he reaches his destination, rather than get up, which would mean revealing his disability to his interlocutor, he remains seated. As the woman departs, Salama gives her incorrect contact information. This brief encounter haunts Salama: he cannot forget her; he speaks of her incessantly, telling this story to whoever does or does not want to hear it. This lost opportunity also connects to other great losses in Salama's life, the loss of his sisters and mother, his father's perpetual and burdensome mourning, and his loss of mobility.

Like the engraving in Salabert's novel, the woman in Baudelaire's poem is, as Boym describes her, "lost and found and then lost again and then found again in the poem" (*The Future of Nostalgia*, 21). Although the engraving and Baudelaire's *passante* (female passerby) are "found again," the losses in both novels remain irrecoverable. Similarly, Sepharad attains a spectral quality in the novels, linking the narrative of Holocaust survival in Spain with the debate on the recovery of historical memory in Spain, a debate in which the specter is a central figure.

Lost and Found

In the final chapter of Muñoz Molina's "novel of novels," the author exhibits some of the same stereotypes that shape perceptions in Spain of Sephardic Jews and Sephardic history. He begins his reflections with an itinerary of his hometown's Jewish quarter, remembering a Jewish home there (*Sepharad*, 343). The narrator, speaking in a semi-autobiographical or even autobiographical voice, details the description further, noting, as Salama's father does in "Oh You, Who Knew So Well," the house key that future generations would inherit. Not unlike the elder Señor Salama, the narrator cannot avoid fusing the consequences of the 1492 expulsion with the Holocaust. He describes the Jewish home, speculates about the carefully guarded key that would one day make a return to Sepharad possible, and then finally remembers the "poems and children's songs that Jews of Salonica and Rhodes would carry with them on the long, hellish journey to Auschwitz" (350). Muñoz Molina continues to dwell on the connections between the 1492 expulsion and the Holocaust. Rather than a historical link, however, the novel suggests a literary and cultural connection. Just like the engraving or Baudelaire's "passante," the poems and children's songs, the Sephardic ballads about "women who disguised themselves as men in order to do battle in wars against the Moors, ballads about enchanted queens" (350) that he remembers point to an absence that can never again be filled.

In "Sepharad," the last tale in the novel, the author reveals the concealed narrative frame of his text. Muñoz Molina joins different stories, and forms of exile, and forms of loss and absence, so that ultimately the "melancholy of a long exile" is all that remains. Although the author does not state this directly, it is not the sadness of melancholy but rather the promise of nostalgia that ends up unifying the different texts that in one way or another narrate an impossible return to a home that no longer exists and the grief that results from this impossibility.

In the end *Sepharad* does and does not show that all stories of homecoming are one and the same. In a brief reference to the *Odyssey*, Boym points out that "even the most classical Western tale of homecoming is far from circular; it is riddled with contradictions and zigzags, false homecomings, misrecognitions" (*The Future of Nostalgia*, 8). The novel, and in particular "Oh You, Who Knew So Well" and "Sepharad," are not exactly circular tales. Instead, Muñoz Molina, like Salabert, shows that a desired return to a lost and consequently mythical homeland necessarily leads to fragmented and open-ended narratives. Both novels also show that in the specific historical context—that of Jews who survived the Holocaust in Francoist Spain—the idea of a return to a lost home is not only meandering and often misleading, it is never to be realized. Despite the permanent rupture of history, however, the fantasy of a return haunts the characters in both novels. In a way, the script for the bus tour of Seville does not suggest otherwise: the yearning of Sepharad still seems to echo in Spanish cities and towns. Reading *Velódromo de invierno* and *Sepharad*, we now see where this yearning comes from and what it means in contemporary Spain.

Two

Exile in Sepharad
The Mezuzah in the Madonna's Foot
and *Memorias judías*

Sophía, whose life story appears in Martine Berthelot's oral history of the Jewish community of Barcelona, *Memorias judías: Barcelona 1914–1954*, was born to a Jewish family in Dresden, Germany, in 1907. In 1933, fleeing the Nazi menace, Sophía and her family find their way to Montcada, a small village outside Barcelona, where the family starts a small brewery. Eventually, Sophía and the members of her family become Spanish citizens. The unrest caused by the Civil War forces the family to leave once again, this time to Locarno, Switzerland. After Franco's victory, Sophía is on her way back from Switzerland to Spain, traveling through Italy. While resting in a pension in Italy, she is confronted by an Italian Jewish woman who is shocked to find out that Sophía and her young daughter are returning to the nation that had once expelled its Jewish population. "How is it possible that you are going to Spain? Don't you know that Spain is damned and that Jews cannot go to Spain? Because of 1492, Spain, the Jewish people have condemned Spain. But, how is it possible that you are on your way to Spain? You cannot go to Spain" (Berthelot, *Memorias judías*, 439). The woman's words reflect the contradictions that mark the life story of Sophía and of many of the other individuals whose testimony Martine Berthelot collects in her oral history, and also of Trudi Alexy, who writes about her own exile in Spain and her conversion from Judaism to Catholicism in *The Mezuzah in the Madonna's Foot*, the memoir that will be the main focus of this chapter.

The Italian woman's words did not, of course, stop Sophía from returning to what was now Francoist Spain; the comment is still worth noting, however, because it reflects the ways in which references to the remote past, most notably the establishment of the Inquisition and the 1492 expulsion, are interwoven with the memories of Jewish exile in Spain before and during World War II. Even though 20,000–35,000 individuals found both exile and transit in Spain (see Rother, "España y los judíos," 409), Jews in Spain did face a hostile environment—not because of the events that had taken place in Spain more than five centuries ago but because of Franco's alliance with Hitler. Unlike other European nations, Spain never enacted racist laws, and for the most part the Jews who suffered the government's repressive policies did so because they were associated with either republicanism, anti-Franco-ism, or freemasonry or because they had entered the country illegally, but not because they were Jewish.

Nevertheless, Francisco Franco himself and especially his second-in-command during the war, Ramón Serrano Suñer, gave numerous anti-Semitic speeches that echoed Nazi rhetoric. Mobs repeatedly harassed individuals and damaged Jewish property, and recent research has revealed that the Francoist government ordered local governors to create a census of all Jews living in Spain. The government provided Himmler with the list but later attempted to make all traces of its involvement with Nazi Germany disappear.[1]

Making sense of this complex situation—in which one might save one's life with the help of a government that signaled a very real threat to all Jews—is maybe best illustrated in Alexy's memoir and in Berthelot's oral history. In both cases invoking the past becomes a way to provide coherence to the contradictory circumstances that made surviving the Holocaust in Spain possible.

Trudi Alexy was eleven years old when her family precipitously left Normandy for Spain. The year was 1939, and the Alexys, who had moved from Prague a few years earlier, not only relocated from one country to another, the four of them were also baptized as Catholics. "Until that moment," writes Alexy, "I never knew we were Jews. Only later did I discover how dangerous it was in those times to be Jew-ish" (*The Mezuzah in the Madonna's Foot*, 11). Alexy and her family remained in Spain in relative safety for two years. In 1941, the family left for the United States, where Alexy continued to practice Catholicism. As she came of age, her family's complicated history of exile and conversion continued to unsettle her. In the late 1960s a melancholy Alexy returned to Spain, where she would discover her "spiritual heritage," as the second subtitle of *The Mezuzah in the Madonna's Foot* states. Yet the subtitle, "Marranos and Other Secret Jews," might reveal even more than the other titles about the ways in which Alexy articulates her memory of exile in Spain during the early years of World War II.[2]

Alexy's own narrative of exile, conversion, and eventual return to Judaism serves as a frame for the narratives of exile and survival of others that she collected in Spain and recounts in the remainder of the text.[3] *The Mezuzah in the Madonna's Foot* commences with a preface and a foreword; the final chapter is followed by a postscript and an epilogue. In these framing chapters the author establishes a spiritual and emotional link between Marranos (Alexy's term of choice) and her own experience in Spain during World War II. Alexy justifies her terminology in the following manner: "'Marrano' is a pejorative name meaning 'swine,' given to secret Jews by suspicious Christians during the Spanish Inquisition. I have used it in the book reluctantly—only because it is a historical term with which most people are familiar and because it symbolizes the demeaned status and fear suffered by Jews who were forced to convert during that terrible time" (*Mezuzah*, 9).

The author makes sense of the broader political events of the 1940s in relation to her own personal history by invoking the past, specifically, the history of crypto-Judaism, which in the book resonates with Alexy's own experience in Spain. Alexy's narrative is endowed with meaning and coherence because, long before her own conversion and exile, others had also undergone conversion to Catholicism on Spanish soil while continuing to practice Judaism in secret. *The Mezuzah in the Madonna's Foot* is not only a reflection on the meanings of exile and conversion to Catholicism in the context of Spain's historical relationship with the Jews, it is also a record of the author's attempt to come to terms with her own history and is thus more invested with the meanings given to historical events than with actual facts. This does not mean that the facts Alexy does include are irrelevant; rather, the correlation between the experience of crypto-Jews in Spain five centuries earlier and Jews during World War II ultimately provides a context for the author's own story: "Just as my family sought to escape Nazi persecution by pretending to be Catholic, so centuries before, the Marranos had hoped to escape the Inquisition's savagery by submitting to baptism. For them, being found out meant torture on the rack and death by fire. For us and others like us, getting caught meant the horrors of concentration camps and death in gas chambers" (*Mezuzah*, 14). Evoking the past (specifically, the age of *convivencia*, the establishment of the Inquisition, and the expulsion) is a common tendency in depictions of Jewish exile in Spain during the Holocaust.

In the introduction to *Memorias judías* Berthelot emphasizes repeatedly that, rather than being *the* story of the Jewish community in Barcelona, the book is *a* story of that community. The forty individuals whose stories appear in the oral history were born in the early twentieth century and arrived in Barcelona between 1914 and 1954, the first date signaling the arrival of the first narrator, the second coinciding with the inauguration of Casa Sefardita Jewish Community Center, the first Jewish cultural and social center to be built in Spain since the expulsion decree in 1492 (see *Memorias judías*, 17–18). The forty life stories are divided into thematic units, ranging from "Origins" to "New Perspectives." This chapter will center on those narratives that refer specifically to the early Francoist years and World War II. Following Berthelot's own definition of her book as *a* history of the Jewish community in Barcelona, it is important to emphasize that, although not all exiled Jews invoke the past when discussing their memories of World War II, it is remarkable that, when specifically addressing Spain's contradictory policy (or, rather, lack of policy) toward Jews, the references to the past become ubiquitous. Ultimately, these references provide coherence to the different life stories.

Although it might be simply taken as a historical inaccuracy at worst and wishful thinking at best, coherence is an important and necessary aspect of the way in which these traumatic events are remembered and narrated by those who have direct or mediated connections to them. According to linguist Charlotte Linde's definition, "coherence is a property of texts; it derives from the relations that the parts of a text bear to one another and to the whole text, as well as from the relation that the text bears to other texts of its type" (*Life Stories*, 12). Linde later adds that the process of creating coherence "is in fact a social obligation that must be fulfilled in order for the participants to appear as competent members of their culture. In the case of narratives that form part of a life story, this demand amounts to an obligation to provide coherence—usually in the form of a chain of causality that is neither too thick nor too thin" (16). A memoir and an oral history require different reading strategies that take into account the respective conditions of their production. However, the cases are comparable because of the way the individuals who experienced the same historical circumstances mitigate the contradictions of the present by making references to a seemingly more coherent past. As Alessandro Portelli observes, oral history "tells us less about events than about their meaning" (*The Death of Luigi Trastulli*, 50). This quality also means that there is no such thing as "wrong" oral history; rather, "the diversity of oral history consists in the fact that 'wrong' statements are still psychologically 'true,' and that this truth may be equally as important as factually reliable accounts" (51). This does not imply that Alexy or the individuals whose narratives appear in Berthelot's book are falsifying history with their respective invocations of the past. Instead, the oral histories provide us with a window into what surviving the Holocaust in Spain might mean.

Although my analysis shows that the invocation of the past is a constitutive part of different representations of exile in Spain, it also challenges easy fusions of past and present, in which events that took place in medieval and early modern Spain account for the complex circumstances of Jewish life in Spain during World War II. Alexy's representation of the past, specifically of the history of Spain's secret Jews, reflects what David Nirenberg has called a "genealogical form of collective memory" ("Mass Conversions and Genealogical Mentalities," 7). In the context of the mass conversions that took place in 1391, Nirenberg discusses the "genealogical mentalities" that in many ways continue to mark the discourse on Jewish presence and absence in Spain. In the late fourteenth century, lineage became the means for restoring a sense of identity that the mass conversions and suspicions about the converted subjects had created.[4] Alexy's evocation of a "meaningful kinship link" (*Mezuzah*, 12) with Spain's secret Jews echoes the ways in which the fusion of genealogy and history still informs discourse on Jewish life in Spain and, more specifically, narratives of deliverance from the Holocaust.

The substance of the analysis that follows lies in the relation among the terms "survival," "Holocaust," and "Sepharad." All three have complicated and widely studied meanings and implications; in relation to each other, new meanings, contradictions, and open-ended narratives take shape. Spain's long and conflictive relationship with the Jews, its fragile neutrality during World War II, and the politics and poetics of memory therefore come together. The Holocaust is the central element in this analysis. Although, according to Andreas Huyssen, the Holocaust has become "the ultimate cipher of traumatic unspeakability or unrepresentability" (*Present Pasts*, 12), this by no means implies that the death and suffering of millions could be taken out of its immediate and violent context. Susan Rubin Suleiman argues that the Holocaust "has become a template for collective memory in areas of the world that had nothing to do with those events but that have known other collective traumas" (*Crises of Memory and the Second World War*, 2). Thus, a cross-disciplinary and cross-geographical dialogue is invaluable for further understanding the deep impact of the Holocaust in different parts of the world and on all paths its victims crossed, either by force or by choice.

When Spain becomes such a path, as it does in Alexy's story, the crypto-Jews become part of an exemplary narrative: "The Marranos' stubborn but contained commitment to their spiritual heritage stands as a shining example of fortitude under fire" (*Mezuzah*, 10). But the book, despite its subtitle, is not a history of secret Jews. Instead, it allows us to understand the ways in which the author comes to terms with her own story by creating a myth of the past. In *Zakhor: Jewish History and Jewish Memory*, Yosef Yerushalmi explores the relation between historiography and a mythic, metahistoric perspective on history. Although for the Jews of medieval Europe a "typological perspective" on the past—assimilating the past through older archetypes—was dominant, the 1492 expulsion brought about a change in the relationship between history and myth that results from the change wrought by the Holocaust.[5] Yerushalmi observes that "it is hard to escape the feeling that the Jewish people after the Holocaust stands today at a juncture not without analogy to that of the generations following the cataclysm of the Spanish expulsion. They, as we saw, ultimately chose myth over history" (99). Yerushalmi's analogy does not mean that history merely repeats itself but rather that both the expulsion and the Holocaust have dramatically altered the relationship between historical knowledge and collective memory. "Today Jewry lives a bifurcated life. As a result of emancipation in the diaspora and national sovereignty in Israel, Jews have fully re-entered the mainstream of history, and yet their perception of how they got there and where they are is often more mythical than real. Myth and memory condition action" (99). Alexy would not stray far from the same paradigm because she also considers her own story through what Gavriel Rosenfeld calls the "prism of preexisting historical precedents" ("A Flawed Prophecy?," 515), invoking the past to make sense of the present.

Alexy not only narrates her own and others' narratives of exile and transit in Spain, she also, as the subtitle of the memoir states, "discovers her spiritual heritage," ultimately choosing myth over history. One could say that with this invocation of the past the author inscribes her own story of conversion and exile within what David Roskies calls the "Jewish response to catastrophe." In this sense, crypto-Jews would function as an archetype, a trope that "could bridge the abyss left in the wake of the Great Catastrophe" (*Against the Apocalypse*, 10), and Alexy would replicate the gestures of the writers and artists of the nineteenth and twentieth centuries who, according to Roskies, "mixed symbol systems, juxtaposed sacred and profane, borrowed ferociously in order to face their ever-greater losses" (12). Yet Alexy's text is not equivalent, for example, to those of the "scribes of the ghetto" that Roskies analyzes. Rather, by invoking the past—specifically, the historical presence of Jews in Spain—Alexy situates her own story within the debates on historiography and collective memory that have marked Jewish perspectives on the past. Alexy's invocation of the past therefore allows her to claim her newly found Jewish identity at the end of the memoir: "The past and present have finally come together, inside and out. There remains still more to be done, but I know at last who I am, and my heart is at rest. My silver filigree mezuzah, which I bought in Jerusalem last year, is affixed to my front doorpost" (*Mezuzah*, 295).

The mythologization of the Marranos and the fusion of past and present reflect the author's effort to inscribe her own life story within Judaism. The story that Alexy narrates in her book is also a story of survival, and her re-creation of the Marranos within her text is an essential part of a survival strategy. Survival means not only having overcome a particular hardship, it also implies that others who underwent the same hardship perished. Ruth Leys explains that in the last decade a shift from a "culture of guilt" to a "culture of shame" has taken place (*From Guilt to Shame*, 6). Tensions between feelings of guilt and shame are apparent in Alexy's memoir, and the implications of both are visible elements in narratives of deliverance from the Holocaust in Spain.[6]

In *Memorias judías* the tension between guilt and shame over conversion from Judaism to Catholicism is also apparent. Berthelot herself comments that conversion at times was the price that needed to be paid to save one's life and the lives of loved ones (*Memorias judías*, 520). Avner, who came from Izmir in Turkey to Barcelona in 1931, agrees: "It is not a sin. Saving one's skin is what matters" (525). In the same breath, and not unlike Alexy, he also refers to the past, and more concretely, to the victims of the Inquisition: "Now, our ancestors did not feel this way: that is why they perished in the bonfires and all that" (525). The moral issue becomes apparent as the sacrifice of those who held on to their Judaism, no matter what the circumstances were, become an example to be followed.

Still, both Trudi Alexy and Avner did survive, and what others suffered in the Nazi concentration camps was considerably worse than what their families had to endure. The implications of these stories of survival nevertheless contribute to the complex articulation of the global memory of the Holocaust. Although the Alexys were not separated, as were so many Jewish families during the Holocaust, and nobody inflicted physical pain on them, placing them in a "hierarchy of suffering" should still be avoided. Such a hierarchy potentially prevents us from considering a story such as Alexy's in the broader context of understanding the Holocaust and its memory. As Rothberg argues, a hierarchy of suffering would not only be morally offensive, it also "removes that suffering from the field of historical agency (which is both morally and intellectually suspect)."[7] In other words, even if the experience of the individuals discussed in this chapter may have been substantially different from that of many others who survived the Holocaust, this does not mean that their story has no relevance within a larger understanding of the event and its consequences.

"Sepharad," the last of the three terms that I will be discussing in this chapter, also stands for far more than the Hebrew term for the Iberian Peninsula or for the lost, ancestral homeland. Trudi Alexy and her family, like many others, survived in and through Spain, not in and through Sepharad. Even so, understanding what Sepharad means is crucial for articulating the historical relationship between Spain and the Jews and for considering the ways in which references to events that preceded World War II by more than five centuries become part of stories of deliverance from the Holocaust in Spain. Memory and geography coalesce in understanding Sepharad. Any mention of Sepharad always evokes a discourse of loss and nostalgia for not only the forcibly converted and the expelled but also for Spanish politicians and intellectuals, who, in the early twentieth century, saw the reencountered Sephardic communities in the recently fallen Ottoman empire as an opportunity to establish a new imperial and pan-Hispanic enterprise (see Rohr, *The Spanish Right and the Jews, 1898–1945*, 30). Thus, the meanings attached to Sepharad—to its memory and its geography—also shifted according to changing historical circumstances.

Alexy, whose story is the main focus of this chapter, came from an Ashkenazi family, although her own story ends up being tightly interwoven with the different ways in which the Sephardic presence in Spain has been perceived through the centuries. Spanish philo-Sephardism in the early twentieth century did not preclude anti-Semitism. Only those Jews who were descendants of those who once shared the Iberian Peninsula with Christians and Arabs were considered worthy of salvation: the rhetoric of the period shows that a prolonged stay in Spain "purified" the Sephardim and differentiated them from the Ashkenazim. Such rhetoric has a genealogy—born in the fourteenth century, which undoubtedly evolved over time and according to different circumstances—that helps us understand that this alleged "superiority" is constructed.

Alexy does not mention the different ways in which Sephardim and Ashkenazim were perceived in Spain, nor does she go into detail about the intricate negotiations and the broken or half-broken rules and laws that made exile and transit possible. Rather, the author's main explanation for why surviving the Holocaust in Spain was possible, and why her conversion to Catholicism makes her feel guilty and ashamed, is that, centuries earlier, secret Jews once survived *as Jews* on the Iberian Peninsula. That the author invokes the past is less important than *how* she invokes it, because the same historical events—the establishment of the Holy Inquisition in 1478 and the 1492 expulsion—also appear in texts picturing Francisco Franco as the leader of a religious crusade that will finally restore order to all the disorder caused by the Republic and, more specifically, the Masonic-Bolshevist-Jewish conspiracy.

If one examines the ways in which these references appear in nationalist discourse during the Spanish Civil War, one finds that Jews were a discursive enemy of Francoist Spain. José María Pemán's "Poema de la bestia y el ángel" (1938) is the most obvious case; in this epic poem the author not only reflects contemporary anti-Semitic discourse but also makes Spain responsible for defending Western civilization from the "Beast": "the red and Semitic East," "the Synagogue," and "the Elder of Zion" (Rohr, *The Spanish Right and the Jews*, 78). Rohr explains how anti-Semitic rhetoric in Spain was an imitation and an adaptation of Nazi discourse (Franco was, after all, Hitler's ally) that constantly invoked the deeds of the Catholic monarchs and the forging of the Spanish imperial nation in 1492: "The myth of Reconquista was not only central to Nationalist thinking, it was also the lens through which it perceived the external world. Thus, Hitler's anti-Semitic campaign was labeled a crusade to save Europe" (66). Alexy's invocation of Spanish crypto-Judaism does not reflect that same "myth of Reconquista" that, as Rohr notes, informed the anti-Semitism of the Spanish right in the 1940s; however, the implications of the smooth fusion of past and present in her text need to be scrutinized.

Stories told from and about the complex circumstances that made exile and survival in Spain possible, stories that emerge from the interplay of "survival," "Holocaust," and "Sepharad," often end up being far more unambiguous than the actual conditions from which they emerge. Briefly, such elements as a mythical and timeless connection between all Spanish and/or all Jewish people, Franco's supposed ties to crypto-Judaism, and an unwavering connection between the Spanish past in relation to Jewishness (medieval anti-Jewish violence, the Spanish Inquisition, the expulsion) and the present, as though history were merely repeating itself with different actors, make for a coherent or even healing story of deliverance and redemption. As Alexy and the members of Barcelona's Jewish community work through the past, their narratives will always contain remainders that resist the drive to coherence.

Natalio and Rosalie, a married couple whose life stories appear in *Memorias judías*, add another dimension with regard to Franco's alleged role in protecting the Jews. Both explain that Franco had an important role in protecting the Jews. They agree that on separate occasions Franco was to have said that the "Jewish problem" had been solved in 1492, thereby, ironically, protecting the Jews who were residing in Spain in the 1940s. Natalio first states: "In a government meeting they had with the members of Falange, he gave a perfect answer: 'Spain has solved the Jewish question in 1492'" (Berthelot, *Memorias judías*, 534). Rosalie then adds that it "is the answer that Franco gave to Hitler in the meeting they had in Hendaye, when Hitler brought up the Jewish question" (534). Later in the same testimony, Natalio insists again that Franco's answer did help all Jews in Spain: "Franco did us a great favor when he said this: 'Spain solved the Jewish problem in 1492'" (534).

In addition to referring to the past, Natalio and Rosalie also personalize Franco's involvement with the Jews, a strategy that the Francoist government would use to provide a politically appropriate vision of Spain and its policies in the international arena after the end of World War II. Other life stories collected in *Memorias judías* also represent Franco's role as a personal choice. Régine R., who was born in Bulgaria in 1908 and came to Spain in 1932, states: "I have nothing against Franco. Franco has protected us and I owe a lot to Franco. . . . Franco has tolerated all of us and has never bothered us" (532). Luisa, Avner's younger sister, also arrived with her family from Izmir in 1931, and her words in support of Franco are even more ardent:

> We have to recognize that during Franco's rule, Himmler or some guy came, a German who asked about the Jews in Barcelona. And, apparently, the almighty God put this in Franco's heart and told him—this is what they say, I'm telling you—that there were not many Jews here, that there was no need to clean up. If it had been otherwise, they would have already picked them up and sent them to concentration camps, as they have done in France, as they have done in Germany or in Austria, unfortunately, and in so many other countries. (532–533)

As Luisa herself emphasizes, she is repeating a story she had heard, and she is aware that what she recounts is not exactly what happened; rather, they are stories told about these events. As the recent revelations mentioned at the beginning of the chapter have shown (and unlike the story Luisa tells), Himmler did receive a list of the names of all Jews residing in Spain.

Isaac P. was born in Italy in 1926; his parents were émigrés from Turkey. Isaac's older brother arrived in Barcelona in 1939 because the newly imposed racial laws prevented him from attending university in Italy; the rest of the family followed in 1942 and would remain in Barcelona until 1946. Isaac affirms that the notion that Franco himself actually saved the Jews is a legend. Berthelot asks Isaac about what exactly happened at the conference in Hendaye, and Isaac remembers a conversation with Ramón Serrano Suñer, whom he had a chance to meet through a friend when the former minister was already in his late eighties. According to Isaac, Serrano Suñer explained that the "Jewish problem" was not even mentioned during the meeting (544). Isaac openly acknowledges Franco's (and, by extension, the government's) contradictory policies and decisions: "With the Germans he was anti-Semitic, and with the English he was philo-Semitic. Where is the truth? Probably there is no truth" (544). The truth seems to be contained, as Berthelot points out, in the ambiguity. But narrating ambiguous stories can be a challenge—especially when someone, such as Trudi Alexy, aims to find her spiritual foothold by telling her story of exile in Spain.

Alexy's family was secular and, as mentioned earlier, as a young child she did not know that her family was Jewish. After conversion, she attended a Catholic school and then a Catholic university. The author's representation of secret Jews emphasizes her guilt and shame: others succeeded where she so miserably failed. She therefore covets the Marranos' "essential connection to their spiritual wholeness" (*Mezuzah*, 15). The secret Jews who appear in Alexy's text are a homogenous group that does not evolve over time, whose dignity becomes an example to follow.[8] Alexy briefly mentions that "a fair number [of Jews who chose baptism] actually became true converts"; according to the author, however, the "seductive appeal of Catholicism" in many ways explains why these converts did not secretly hold on to Judaism (17). Rather than exploring the intricacies of the conversions that took place both before and after 1492, Alexy invokes the past to construct heroic and undoubtedly seductive stories of subterfuge and resistance. Understanding why the author paints a very specific picture of Spain's secret Jews and why it is a constitutive part of her narrative is more relevant than determining the historical accuracy of the book. *The Mezuzah in the Madonna's Foot* is not a historiography but a text in which the author makes sense of a deeply personal and traumatic loss that occurred at a young age; her spiritual and emotional connection with the Marranos allows her to overcome the melancholia caused by that loss.

Although other family members, among them Alexy's maternal grandmother, perished in the Holocaust, neither Alexy nor her immediate family were deported to a concentration camp, precisely because the family first left Prague for Paris, converted to Catholicism, and found a relatively safe, even if temporary, home in Barcelona. Thus, instead of "Holocaust survivors," the term "refugees" would in many ways be more fitting for both the Alexy family's experience and their status, first in Spain and later in the United States. Yet the complex layers of meaning that "survivor" now conveys still help us understand Alexy's typological use of the Marranos and why such a typology is in many ways a byproduct of the coherent narrative Alexy articulates in her book. The testimonies Alexy unites in her book make Susan Rubin Suleiman's simile for understanding the experiences that are recorded in *The Mezuzah in the Madonna's Foot* suitable: "Like ashes after a fire, the survivor is a sign pointing to, or representing, something that 'once was'" (*Crises of Memory and the Second World War*, 213). Alexy's story and the ways in which she tells it reveal how complex and multiple such "signs" are. Originally, the term "Holocaust survivor," Suleiman explains, "designated only those who had been in concentration camps, whatever their age at the time; children who had survived in hiding, the vast majority, were not considered survivors, either by themselves or others" (180). Whether the Alexys are "refugees" or "survivors," the narrative of displacement, exile, and conversion in the memoir still intersects with what a Jewish family's survival meant in those years. Alexy repeatedly emphasizes the guilt and shame she feels as a consequence of surviving in hiding and because of her conversion to Catholicism.

> The shame over my apostasy [*sic*], not out of conviction but as an act of cowardice, hung over me like a dark cloud. I still saw myself as an impostor. My guilt had little to do with being a Jew or a Catholic,

per se. "Honor" and "standing up for the truth" were the real issues. My early childhood heroes had taught me that one suffers gladly for the truth and does not lie, even to save one's life. Taking the easy way out while so many others died remained as simplistically unforgivable as ever. (*Mezuzah*, 55)

Alexy's judgmental tone needs to be considered (her age at the time of conversion—she was eleven—will be addressed later). The author speaks of her guilt and shame interchangeably, which is common among narratives of survival. Rather than considering stories of survival and deliverance exclusively in terms of guilt or shame, we should take into account what Ruth Leys terms the tension between the "'moral' concept of guilt" and the "ethically different or 'freer' concept of shame" (*From Guilt to Shame*, 7). Because most of Alexy's memoir is about other survivors' and refugees' stories, one could say that *The Mezuzah in the Madonna's Foot* also reflects the very tensions Leys discusses. Alexy's thoughts on her own story and her own relationship to Jewishness reflect her guilt. Although the author burdens herself with moral judgments, she does not judge the other individuals she interviewed and whose stories she narrates in her book. Her guilt therefore reflects her sense of self, while her shame relates to her relationships with others.

Alexy's representation of secret Jews, however, would again place her in the realm of guilt because they stand for a bastion of morality against which she will measure her own story of survival in Spain. The Marranos who appear in the book represent the author's desired version of them. Rather than shifting from guilt to shame, a constant tension between the moral issue (guilt) and the ethical issue (shame) comes alive. This tension is essential to the specific narrative of deliverance she articulates in the book.

Alexy ultimately longs to find what she calls "the redemption of my disowned self" (*Mezuzah*, 20), a redemption that will occur once she gathers testimonies from other Jews who had experiences similar to hers in Spain, once she weaves a narrative of deliverance, once she retraces her own steps, and once all stories are told: "By 1988, I had to return to Spain to speak to them and to find what magical strength had sustained them during those terrible years" (66). Although the pronoun "them" refers to others who, like Alexy, found exile in Spain, the use of "magical strength" connects their experiences to those of the crypto-Jews. The "terrible" years therefore simultaneously invoke the years between 1391 and 1492, when most forced conversions to Catholicism took place as a result of the anti-Jewish violence, the years after the expulsion and the establishment of the Spanish Inquisition in 1478, and even the five centuries that span the period between the expulsion and the publication of Alexy's book. This lack of precision suggests that Alexy's representation of the Marranos is really far more related to what happened in the 1940s than in the five centuries that preceded World War II.

Although Alexy's book is not the most informative work on the history of the Marranos, it nevertheless reveals the ways in which the past attains new meaning in the present, specifically with regard to exile and survival in Spain. The current visibility of Jewish culture—or "what passes for Jewish culture, or what is perceived or defined as Jewish culture" (Gruber, *Virtually Jewish*, 5)—in Spain might be a unique opportunity to scrutinize the ways in which stories of deliverance came into being, to understand the composition of their different elements and to think of the "crises of memory" that Suleiman addresses. "How we view ourselves, and how we represent ourselves to others, is indissociable from the stories we tell about our past," states Suleiman at the beginning of *Crises of Memory*, as she reviews recent academic discourse on memory (1). She reminds her readers that "the emphasis on memory has been justly criticized not only because it can lead to dogmatism and kitsch but also to political instrumentalization of every kind, including some very bad kinds" (7). For Suleiman memory is about the stories we tell about our past and those that remain to be told. In the particular case of Alexy's use of the past, I would add that telling coherent stories also forms part of the "crisis of memory." Alexy articulates an idealized vision of the Marranos that effaces the actual lived experience of the individuals who practiced (or were accused of practicing) crypto-Judaism. This is not to say that *The Mezuzah in the Madonna's Foot* reflects the very bad kind of political instrumentalization to which Suleiman refers; however, questioning what lies beneath Alexy's romanticized vision of the Marranos can reveal the ways in which memories of deliverance from the Holocaust in Spain are articulated.

Alexy's text also opens up new questions in relation to the age of testimony and discourse on testimony, questions that Shoshana Felman and Dori Laub's *Testimony: Crises of Witnessing in Literature, Psychoanalysis, and History* in many ways introduced. In the chapter "An Event without a Witness: Truth, Testimony and Survival," Laub stresses that telling one's story is an intrinsic part of survival, as one of his interlocutors states: "We wanted to survive so as to live one day after Hitler, in order to be able to tell our story" (*Testimony*, 78). Laub, himself a child survivor, cofounder of the Fortunoff Video Archive for Holocaust Testimonies, and a psychiatrist who treats victims of trauma, including Holocaust survivors, concludes that the "survivors did not only need to survive so that they could tell their story; they also needed to tell their story to survive. There is, in each survivor, an imperative need to *tell* and thus to come to *know* one's story, unimpeded by ghosts from the past against which one has to protect oneself" (78).

Laub explains that the imperative of telling one's story of survival, which always coexists with the impossibility of telling this same story, is part of a therapeutic process (69). Laub's analysis can easily, maybe all too easily, be applied to Alexy's case; as a matter of fact, her journey back to Spain as an adult, her encounters with other refugees and survivors, and her mythical view of the Marranos can be interpreted as her response to the imperative (or at least to a version of it) that Laub mentions. Laub also argues, however, that these "buried truths" more often than not become a never-ending story, a melancholy story that can never have a sense of closure. He explains: "The imperative to tell the story of the Holocaust is inhabited by the impossibility of telling, and, therefore, silence about the truth commonly prevails" (79). These melancholy stories of the Holocaust cannot be told and at the same time need to be told. This paradox explains the indeterminate status of Alexy's memoir between history and myth and its reflection of the unresolved tension between guilt and shame.

Alexy's interwoven personal and historical narrative is not a private conversation between a survivor and a listener, as in Laub's experience. Nevertheless, Laub's argument (that survivors need to tell their story even though such stories are impossible to fully articulate) is also valid for understanding the underlying and unifying narrative in Alexy's book, in which a spiritual and idealized connection with Spain's secret Jews restores the losses that exile and conversion implied for Alexy.

Eva Hoffman, who has written a great deal on the legacy of Holocaust survival, even if not in the Spanish context, reminds her readers that although Freud "altered his theory [of mourning and melancholia] as a result of witnessing the First World War, he did not live to see the Second, and he may not have taken into account the kinds of losses from which it may be impossible to recover—losses, as after the Holocaust, not only of particular persons but of a people and a world" (*After Such Knowledge*, 72). For Hoffman, the task of mourning as considered by Freud in his 1915 essay is no longer possible, particularly for the "second generation, whose entire historical situation has placed it in the 'melancholic' position, whose fate it has been to live with a multitude of lost 'objects' that they never had a chance to know" (73). Stories of survival such as Alexy's therefore demand an engagement with melancholia. Melancholic remainders tend to defy narrative coherence even in such a text as Alexy's, which strives to achieve a certain sense of closure. One of the remainders is a lack of historical specificity; however, a more accurate representation of crypto-Judaism in her book would have made the spiritual connection impossible.

Alexy's vision of the struggles of converted Jews who continued to carry out their religious practices and traditions in secrecy since the late fourteenth century provides her narrative with a desired coherence. Thus, rather than discussing crypto-Jewish presence or voice in Spain, my analysis focuses on the symbolic meanings that Marranos attain in Alexy's memoir. Michael Gerli, who has widely published on the Spanish conversos, emphasizes the complexity and diversity of the converso condition:

> Conversos, like all other human beings, are the products of a myriad of different cultural practices and discourses such as class, gender, political economy, blood and even, as I shall propose, physical well-being and their relation to the structures of power and their society's systems for representing and signifying it. The cultural genealogy of conversos is therefore neither stable nor transparent, and in its very instability and opacity may contradict even the clearest family trees. ("The Ambivalent *Converso* Condition," 5)

Alexy does not take these distinctions into account; as a matter of fact, in her book conversos are lumped together with crypto-Jews. According to Francisco Márquez Villanueva, *converso* is a sociological term, not a religious one (*De la España judeoconversa*, 98). He also argues that the overlap between religion and politics led to anti-Jewish violence, which found its most virulent and deadly incarnation in the Holy Inquisition because it gave the Catholic monarchs complete control of the converso minority (110). Although secret Jews did convert to Catholicism at some point (most probably after 1391, when pogroms in different Spanish cities led to mass conversions), not all conversos lived as secret Jews. Even among them, explains Márquez Villanueva, it would be highly problematic to understand all behaviors and customs that differed from Christian ritual to be the same secret practice, transgression, or even outright defiance of the Catholic majority (106–107).

Conversos and secret Jews were anything but a homogenous group; there is no such a thing as a consistent converso or Marrano voice, and, as Mark Meyerson has pointed out, there were "other cacophonous converso voices, namely those recorded by the scribes of the Spanish Inquisition" ("Letters on 'Inflecting the *Converso* Voice,'" 180). Studying the texts that document the religious secrets that led to the torture chambers and pyres of the Inquisition is an immensely difficult but necessary task for understanding the complexity of conversions and their consequences in their respective contexts.[9] Alexy, however, needs the crypto-Jews to be a coherent and recognizable group; the kind of spiritual connection she establishes with secret Jews can only be built on the certainty of a group's particular identity. *The Mezuzah in the Madonna's Foot* therefore echoes the teleological view of history, in which a direct line joins the past and the present, that Nirenberg challenges in *Communities of Violence*. Alexy's book reflects such a discourse because she traces a transhistorical connection between her own experiences and that of the Marranos; she is not interested in specific interactions among crypto-Jews, other conversos, and the Christian majority. Rather, the Marranos attain a mythical or even archetypal value that in Alexy's book transcends the complex daily negotiations between minorities and majorities in medieval and early modern Spain. As Nirenberg's book and his article "Figures of Thought and Figures of Flesh" show, the kinds of connection that Alexy somewhat hastily establishes across different historical periods are far from unique in historical representations of Jews in Spain.

In the initial pages of her book, Alexy turns the Marranos into an organized community that neatly fits into her own spiritual quest in Spain: "The drama of the Marranos' dogged determination to cling to their way of life, holding fast to their beliefs and practicing their laws and traditions when being found out meant torture and death, symbolizes, for many, the importance of a connection to one's ancestral roots and the miraculous survival of the spirit, even in the most hostile of environments" (*Mezuzah*, 9–10). In the chapters that frame Alexy's research, the author establishes a long list of equivalences between her own story and that of the Marranos. The Inquisition and the Holocaust become, to borrow Nirenberg's metaphor, part of a "persecutory landscape" (*Communities of Violence*, 5). Alexy admits that the Marranos' steadfastness provides an example for the experience (and trauma) of conversion and exile during World War II. "Their stories of bravery and determination exemplify the spirit that has helped so many Jews to survive centuries of persecution, in constant danger and deprivation, with their humanity intact" (*Mezuzah*, 79). Statements such as this one, in particular the idea of an "intact humanity," reflect the strict moral standard that Alexy imposes on herself: she writes that she survived "by fraud" (14), that she should not be forgiven (14), that she was an impostor (39), and a "coward and a criminal" (40).[10] Alexy's having experienced exile and conversion as a young child partly explains both her stern morality and her view of the Marranos.

Although her experience was very different from that of those who were deported to death camps, the existing literature on child survivors is useful for understanding Alexy's story and the way in which she constructs it. Robert Krell defines a "child survivor" as "any person who was sixteen or younger in 1945" and then emphasizes the profound ways in which these traumatic experiences shaped the young survivors (*Child Holocaust Survivors*, 3–4).

A meaningful and coherent story (such as the one Alexy tells) is not going to turn these traumatic experiences into "secure" or "normal" childhoods, much less cure the wounds of the past; nevertheless, articulating such a story may alleviate the pain, even make it possible to live with a harrowing past. Krell notes that "for therapists who work

with child survivors and for those who document their stories, it is evident that recapturing memory and making sense of it is a *healing* enterprise" (7). In his own testimony, Dori Laub also emphasizes how his
childhood fantasies ended up forming a crucial part of his own survival
and resilience. Laub was in a concentration camp between the ages of
five and eight, and, as an adult, he remembers the fantasy world that
allowed him to survive his interrupted childhood:

> I developed a fantasy world and found other children my age with
> whom I played it out. We were going to build a huge army and in-
> vent new weapons with which we were going to be victorious against
> Hitler. I realize now that I never resumed a normal childhood or a
> normal life upon my return from the camp. Perhaps the rest of my
> childhood, and, indeed, of my life, was driven by the need to deal
> with what I had lived through in those early years. (Halter, *Stories of
> Deliverance*, 55)

The discrepancy between the events and the ways in which they were
(not) incorporated into memory would often lead to a complex identification process in relation to Jewishness for children who grew up
under similar circumstances. Suleiman's term "1.5 generation" for child
survivors of the Holocaust may apply in part to Laub and also Alexy.
"The specific experience of Jewish children was that they were persecuted because of an identity they could not even fully claim, since
disaster hit them before the formation of stable identity that we as-
sociate with adulthood, and in some cases before any conscious sense
of self" (Suleiman, *Crises of Memory*, 181). Members of this generation
are "child survivors of the Holocaust, too young to have had an adult
understanding of what was happening to them, and sometimes too
young to have any memory of it at all, but old enough to have *been
there* during the Nazi persecution of the Jews" (179). When her family
left France because of the imminent threat of deportation to a concentration camp, Alexy was eleven years old, which would place her in
the generation of those who were "old enough to understand but too
young to be responsible" (182).

Alexy's youth partially explains her escape into a fantasy world
through what she calls "magical thinking," which helped her make
sense of the unsettling events that were taking place around her. As

she explains, "magical thinking" originated in the books she enjoyed reading as young child:

> Although that world seemed no less tumultuous for the inhabitants of those pages than the one from which I was trying to escape, *their* reality relieved my anxiety by providing answers to questions I did not even know how to articulate. What mattered was that in *that* reality nothing happened by accident, everything had logical explanations and predictable consequences. Mysterious signs and random intuitions proved meaningful, even if only in retrospect. Those who were good were rewarded and those who were bad got punished—here on earth, or after death. Life felt more stable: I was convinced that whatever happened, no matter how unexpected or irrational, *someone, somewhere was in control.* "Magical thinking" (ascribing symbolic meaning to ordinary events, investing them with mythical relevance and power) became my religion, my spiritual security blanket. (*Mezuzah*, 13)

Alexy openly recognizes that this form of magical thinking was a survival strategy, which would explain her resilience—a term psychiatrist Boris Cyrulnik uses for the process through which an individual is able to resume normal development despite trauma or adverse circumstances. Her "magical thinking" provided her own experiences with coherence and meaning, both of which are fundamental aspects of children's resilience. "Undertaking the task of resilience means once again shedding light on the world and giving it back its coherence. The tool that makes this possible is called narration" (Cyrulnik, *The Whispering of Ghosts*, xvii). Using Hans Christian Andersen's traumatic childhood as a case study, Cyrulnik explains that a "bond and meaning" are what makes children, even severely traumatized children, resilient. As a child, "Little Hans" was able to overcome abuse, pain, and loneliness: "He kept company with swans, wrote stories, and had laws passed for the protection of other little ducklings" (37). Resilience, however, is not a "recipe for happiness." Instead, resilience is a "strategy for struggle against unhappiness that makes it possible to seize some pleasure in life despite the whispering of ghosts in the depths of our memory" (171). For Alexy, telling her own story and giving testimony are part of a mourning process, of giving up the ghosts of the past, as Cyrulnik would have it. Although she acknowledges that reality would eventually make the magic wear off (*Mezuzah*, 14), remainders of her "magical thinking" may explain the connection she establishes with Spain's secret Jews. Alexy is only able to make peace with her conversion to Catholicism once she incorporates her particular vision of the Marranos, a "meaningful kinship link" (12), into her narrative. Their presence in her memoir, to use Alexy's own definition of "magical thinking," suggests that "nothing happened by accident, everything had logical explanations and predictable consequences. Mysterious signs and random intuitions proved meaningful, even if only in retrospect" (13).

Alexy repeatedly writes about Spain as a magical place and also as a location where a Manichean world order still reigns: "Those who were good were rewarded and those who were bad got punished—here on earth, or after death" (13). Although for the young Alexy "Spain was sure to be a magical place where we would all be safe and where I would feel good again" (14), being baptized Catholic was an unforgivable crime for which she deserved punishment.[11] When the adult Alexy travels to Spain and then returns to the United States, she is at first transformed: she seems to have won her battle with depression. But "as the magic wore off," her melancholia returned (63). Her conversion remains a fraudulent act, a moral failure; the Marranos thereby become the moral bastion against which Alexy measures herself. Once Alexy discovers crypto-Jews, the magical world appears to be restored:

> The more I learned about the Marranos and their stubborn efforts to maintain their essential connection to their spiritual wholeness, the more I identified with them, or, perhaps, more precisely, the more I longed to be one of them. *They* had something deep inside that kept alive their link with one another and with their heritage, even under the most stressful circumstances. I, on the other hand, never saw myself as anything but a failed, flawed outsider during all the years I practiced Catholicism and long after I stopped doing so, cut off, forever banished from my own people because there had never been anything experiential in my own past to bind me to Jews. More than anything I longed to have what the Marranos had: a sense of *belonging*. (18)

Alexy projects this sense of belonging, even a sense of unity, on Spain's secret Jews—a notion that a quick review of the existing scholarship on crypto-Judaism could easily challenge. Yet Alexy's book, again, in spite of its subtitle and the narratives of other exiles she recounts, is not a history of crypto-Judaism but a personal reflection on exile, conversion, and the author's return to Judaism. Alexy moved to Spain when she was a young child; she saw Barcelona through a child's eyes: the chimneys on Gaudí's La Pedrera became a "fairyland playground" (45), and the curriculum at her Catholic school made her dream of "living the life of a missionary nun and dying a martyr's death in some exotic and dangerous land" (47). The narrator, however, is not a child but rather the adult Alexy who returned to Spain to carry out the research that allowed her to write the book. Her perspective on crypto-Jews is not the vision of a child who yearns for a magical, fairytale world: the grown woman who writes this book needs such a vision to articulate a coherent narrative of the past.

Alexy's narrative reveals the process by which the confusing and contradictory circumstances that she witnessed and struggled to understand as a young child begin to form part of a coherent story. The underlying issue is whether it is possible to discuss deliverance from the Holocaust in Spain without invoking the past. The challenge in narratives of deliverance is therefore to understand what invoking a symbolic past means without fusing the present and the past in a search for causality. A further challenge is to understand what gets left behind once survivors create coherent narratives of this period. What happens to the survivor's melancholia? What happens with the fragmented, incoherent remainders of memory that are left out of these narratives? The creation of coherence is a constitutive aspect of a survivor's engagement with a traumatic past, which demands an understanding of the mechanisms that make it possible to articulate coherent narratives. It is equally important to get a sense of what remains unsaid in such narratives as Alexy's.

In spite of the healing influence of the author's particular vision of the Marranos, epitomized, according to Alexy, in "their stubborn efforts to maintain their essential connection to their spiritual wholeness" (*Mezuzah*, 18) that she openly covets, the text's own aporias speak to the impossibility of closure that coexists with Alexy's attempts to find a sense of closure through the Marranos' collective history.

Alexy's use of Marranos is consistent throughout her book and reaches its apex in the chapter "My Marrano Soul: Matthew's Story," in which Alexy describes her encounter with "Matthew," who is a descendant of secret Jews, a researcher, and former priest. Matthew discusses his family lineage (from the Middle Ages on), constantly using the pronoun "we" when discussing his own family. Even Alexy finds his use of the pronoun a bit troubling. "He kept talking about Marranos as 'we,' yet he was obviously no longer under cover. Were he and his family Jews, Catholics, or Marranos?" (275). Questioned by Alexy, Matthew explains that this "we" is the result of his family's having been Jews, Catholics, and Marranos. "Thus confronted, Matthew revealed that all the other members of his family have remained Marranos, practicing Judaism in secret as their ancestors had five hundred years ago in Spain" (275). Matthew's identification as Jewish, crypto-Jewish, and Catholic unequivocally links him with the past: "As Secret Jews, during the early years, with the Church spying on us everywhere, we did the best we could under the circumstances" (276). The story of Matthew and his "Marrano soul" (278) embodies the lineage Alexy constructs in her book, as though at the end he redeems the author's spiritual quest. Alexy feels deeply, magically connected with Matthew: "I felt a connection to him and his people that went far beyond sympathy or care. Instinctively identifying with him as a spiritual brother, I decided to learn more about the Secret Jews he claimed were scattered throughout the Americas" (281). This is precisely Alexy's intention in her second book, a sequel to *The Mezuzah in the Madonna's Foot*. In *The Marrano Legacy*, she publishes the letters she exchanges with "Simon," a crypto-Jewish priest who resides in an unnamed Latin American country. As in the first book, Alexy constantly emphasizes her spiritual connection with these modern-day crypto-Jews.[12]

The Mezuzah in the Madonna's Foot ends with research on crypto-Jews in the American Southwest and a postscript in which the author narrates two journeys to Israel and a newly found sense of belonging: literally and symbolically, the Mezuzah is no longer hidden in the Madonna's foot but, as she writes, "affixed to my front doorpost" (295). In the epilogue, Alexy quotes King Juan Carlos I's address at the Sephardi Temple Tifereth Israel in Los Angeles in 1987. The author was eventually granted an audience with the Spanish monarch in 1991, and in her meeting with the king she was able to steer the conversation toward an apology for the 1492 expulsion, five years before the king's official apology in 1992. In response to Alexy's questioning, Juan Carlos I stated that he would not have issued the decree if he been the ruling monarch in 1492: "It is an unfortunate event in Spain's past that can be neither denied nor repressed" (298). Alexy also reproduces a letter she asked the king to write for her to include in the book and then finishes with an excerpt from Elie Wiesel's address at the ceremony in 1991 at which Juan Carlos I was awarded the Elie Wiesel Foundation Humanitarian Award. In his speech, Wiesel also immediately links present and past, the 1492 expulsion and the assistance that the Spanish government offered to Jewish refugees despite the complex circumstances in Spain in the 1940s. Like Alexy, Wiesel reports having felt a certain familiarity on Spanish soil during his first visit to the country: "In 1950, when I visited your still-tormented country as a young correspondent for an Israeli paper, I had an eerie feeling that I had been there before. Many places seemed familiar. I thought I 'remembered' events, names, experiences" (300, quoting Wiesel).

Wiesel's and Alexy's words make it seem as though the events initiated in 1391 invariably led to what they each recognized in Spain in the 1950s and 1960s. The inclusion of King Juan Carlos's letter and the comment about the Spanish monarch's agency over the past—"had *he* been the ruling monarch in 1492, he would not have issued that decree" (298)—emphasize that Alexy's book mirrors the "shades of genealogy that have proved so difficult to exorcise from our historical practices" (Nirenberg, "Mass Conversions," 41). Alexy's inclusion of Wiesel's speech and the king's words—and indeed her book as a whole—suggests that invoking a romanticized version of the more remote past ultimately provides coherence to narratives of deliverance from the Holocaust in Spain. But understanding what gets lost in this creation of coherence remains a crucial task. The need for coherence coexists with the incoherence of melancholy, with the "whispering of the ghosts," to use Cyrulnik's phrase, that echoes in every story of survival.

To speak of surviving the Holocaust in Sepharad is of course an anachronism. Alexy, the members of her immediate family, and the individuals whose life stories appear in *Memorias judías* survived in Spain, not in Sepharad, and they did so because of specific historical circumstances that changed quickly as the war years progressed, making it possible for her family to be fairly safe in a country that until the end of the war, despite its official neutrality, was allied with Nazi Germany. The author makes sense of the events, however, not by supplying detailed historical information but by articulating a spiritual affinity with Spain's secret Jews. Alexy mentions the family's use of entrance visas to Spain only once but does not explain the intricate combination of exit and entrance visas, *sauf-conduits*, forged documents, and substantial sums of money that in the 1940s were indispensable for exiles and the stateless in their attempt to flee Nazi-occupied Europe. One could say, again, that Alexy was a child when this happened and that she naturally would be more inclined to remember the handful of grapes one of the border agents offered her (*Mezuzah*, 43) than the documents that were necessary to cross the frontier.

It is the author's choice of myth over history in her identification with the crypto-Jews that allows her to tell her story in the first place. Thus, Alexy's book reveals the work of memory, underscoring the ways in which a survivor comes to terms with the past in the present. Thus, Alexy's idiosyncratic representation of the past both reflects and illuminates the historical contradictions that marked Jewish exile and transit in Spain during World War II. Understanding these contradictions is crucial in an era in which the Holocaust has become the reference point for mass violence and genocide worldwide. The phrase "globalization of the Holocaust" is used to discuss how a specific historical event has become, as Rothberg puts it, "a template of cruelty that can be used to foster understanding of the present and promote ethical and political action" (*Multidirectional Memory*, 264). The debate on this globalization should, however, also help critics to account for the ways in which the Holocaust transects and influences histories of those nations in which the Holocaust did not take place. Although these reasons alone underscore the importance of engaging with Alexy's story and with the ways in which she chooses to tell her story, we cannot forget that today most first-generation survivors (and many members of the 1.5 generation) are no longer alive. Alexy's story therefore also helps us understand the ways in which a thorny relationship with both the near and the remote past is bequeathed to future generations.

Three Responsible for the Fate of the World
Ángel Sanz Briz and Jorge Perlasca

In November 1944 the deportation of the Jews who remained in Budapest was imminent. Eleven-year-old Anna Königsberg feared for her life and her loved ones. One man, however, a "Signor Perlasca," said to be an ambassador and, as young Anna remembers, on whom "the fate of the world depended," saved her and thousands of other Jews from certain death in a concentration camp (*The Banality of Goodness*, 116). The Italian-born Perlasca worked out of the Spanish legation in Budapest, but he was not an ambassador; indeed, he was not even an actual employee of the legation. After Ángel Sanz Briz, chargé d'affaires at the Spanish legation, had left the Hungarian capital, Perlasca continued the undertaking that Sanz Briz had already set in motion, protecting Budapest's Jews from deportation. Thus, the young girl's words might best define who Giorgio (or Jorge) Perlasca was. Young Anna's hyperbole also exemplifies the ways in which rescue narratives attain shifting meanings in different national and historical contexts.[1]

Beyond describing the sequence of events that led to the rescue of around 5,000 Jews in Budapest through the efforts of the Spanish legation between the summer of 1944 and February 1945, this chapter examines the production of rescue narratives and the meanings that such stories attain in Spain in different historical moments from the early postwar years to the present. The term "rescue narrative" broadly refers to instances in which Jews were either protected or saved from deportation to a concentration camp. Rather than the victims, however, the protagonists of these narratives tend to be the rescuers, often honored as the "Righteous among the Nations," non-Jewish individuals who saved one or many Jewish lives during the Holocaust.[2] Although the events that led to the protection and even deliverance of the Jews are transnational and reveal complex constellations of citizenship and identity, the stories told about the rescuers emerge within a national or even nationalist context. In such stories as Alexy's, the survivors themselves make meaning of what happened; rescue narratives, however, tend to center more on the individuals (the righteous gentiles, the heroes) who made the rescue possible than on the survivors' experience.

One might question why an entire chapter of a book entitled *Jewish Spain* centers on events that did not take place within (or even close to) the Spanish borders and on the actions of two men who were not Jewish. One of them, Perlasca, was not even Spanish, but Italian. Examining the circumstances that facilitated the Spanish legation's protection of the Jews in Budapest will allow us to understand how the legend that the Francoist government protected *all* Sephardic Jews emerged. This legend remained for the most part unchallenged into the 1980s and even today reappears in historiographies and other narratives.[3]

Although Sanz Briz was not the only Spanish diplomat who was concerned with the fate of Jews in occupied Europe, the story that has risen around him is particularly relevant for attaining a nuanced understanding of the Spanish government's policies toward Jews, the options diplomats had, the types of transgressions their actions implied, and, finally, the emergence of the legend that Franco himself was concerned with the fate of the Jews and therefore ordered his diplomats to do what they could to help.[4] Because numerous accounts of the events in Budapest centering on both Sanz Briz and Perlasca are available, it is possible to compare the different versions and expose the fissures in history and memory—and, ultimately, to reveal the significance of representations and commemorations of Sanz Briz and Perlasca.

In fall 1944 the Spanish Ministry of Foreign Affairs ordered the chargé d'affaires in Budapest, Miguel Ángel Muguiro, to return to Spain, possibly because Hungarian and German authorities objected to Muguiro's publicly expressing his concern for the Budapest Jews. Muguiro had openly criticized the government's hostility toward Jews. Although historical information about his motives and sympathies is scarce, a chain of events that will eventually lead to Sanz Briz and Perlasca begins with this diplomat's actions.

Sanz Briz, who had been in Budapest for two years, now held Muguiro's position, and he began where Muguiro had left off: he issued

Spanish passports to Budapest Jews whether they were Spanish nationals or not; he provided protection letters (*Schutzbriefe*) that stated that the individuals holding them were under Spanish diplomatic protection; and in the name of the Spanish legation he rented safe houses where Jews resided—in dire conditions but in relative safety from the Nazis and the Hungarian Arrow Cross (modeled on the German Nazi party). Members of the Spanish legation were not alone in their concern with the fate of the Hungarian Jews. Such measures as setting up safe houses or procuring protection letters were initiated by foreign dignitaries from other neutral nations, among them the Vatican representative Angelo Rotta; Carl Lutz, the consul general of the Swiss legation; and Raoul Wallenberg, the well-known Swedish emissary credited with saving thousands of Jewish lives in Hungary. Rotta, Lutz, and Wallenberg were working in concert with the War Refugee Board and the World Jewish Congress. Although similar efforts to protect Jews had been undertaken in other parts of occupied Europe, the Hungarian case is particularly poignant because in many ways the Hungarian Jews were "the Nazis' last victims" (to invoke the title of Braham and Miller's study of the Holocaust in Hungary) as deportations of the Budapest Jews began in May 1944 and the Soviet troops took control of Budapest in February 1945.

By the end of 1944, the Soviet takeover of Budapest was imminent and Sanz Briz left the Hungarian capital. In 1991 Yad Vashem designated him posthumously as one of the "Righteous among the Nations."[5] His "successor," Giorgio Perlasca, the fake consul, was born in 1910 in Como, Italy. As a young fascist, he fought in the Second Abyssinian War and later alongside the Nationalists in the Spanish Civil War. His participation in the Spanish conflict allowed him to obtain an official document from the Francoist government that stated: "Dear Brother-in-Arms, no matter where you are in the world you can turn to Spain" (cited in Paldiel, *The Righteous among the Nations*, 318, and Deaglio, *The Banality of Goodness*, 56). In 1944, Perlasca was in the Hungarian capital for business, negotiating the purchase of livestock. After the fall of Mussolini and the German invasion of Hungary, Perlasca, now no longer a Mussolini supporter, found himself in an ambiguous legal position and unable to leave the country. Perlasca turned to the Spanish embassy, where, after examining the document promising him Spanish support, Sanz Briz eventually provided him with a Spanish passport. Giorgio had become Jorge. Perlasca's new nationality is one among many identity shifts at the time: the vast majority of the Budapest Jews under Spanish protection were neither Spanish citizens nor Sephardic. But Muguiro (and later Sanz Briz and Perlasca) was able to protect Jews because he informed the authorities that these individuals had a relationship with Spain. These relationships were sometimes real and sometimes fabricated. Historiographies, such as Avni's *Spain, the Jews, and Franco* and Rother's *Franco y el Holocausto*, provide evidence that these events did take place in Budapest—in other words, that the protection of the Budapest Jews is not a fiction. Nevertheless, fiction and imposture undoubtedly had a place in the sequence of events that would make the rescue narratives possible.

When the Red Army was closing in on Budapest in late November and Sanz Briz left for Switzerland, the Spanish legation would have closed its doors had it not been for Perlasca. He informed the authorities that Sanz Briz had merely gone on a diplomatic mission to Switzerland because, as Perlasca claimed, maintaining contact with the Spanish Foreign Ministry from Bern was easier than from Budapest. Sanz Briz had already actively protected a number of Budapest Jews, and Perlasca continued the task after his departure, producing more protection letters, even pulling individuals off trains that would take them to death camps, and challenging the German and Hungarian soldiers who threatened to take individuals away from the safe houses where they had found protection. The extent to which Perlasca and Sanz Briz shared this responsibility before the departure of the Spanish diplomat remains unclear; after Sanz Briz left, however, Perlasca served as Spain's "bogus consul" from December 1, 1944, to January 16, 1945. Once the Soviet army had invaded Budapest in 1945, Perlasca was able to return to Italy. The few remaining members of the Budapest Jewish community honored him shortly before his departure, but he did not receive any state-sponsored recognition in Italy, Hungary, Spain, or Israel until the 1990s. A campaign for public appreciation—initiated by a group of Holocaust survivors who had gathered in Berlin in 1987—began tracking down Perlasca, along with eyewitness reports and documents required for granting Perlasca the title of "Righteous among the Nations." Perlasca received the honor in 1989.

Although these events took place far beyond the Spanish borders and the Mediterranean shores, they nevertheless reveal the ways in which Jewish life and Spanish life intersect from World War II to the present. Accounts of what happened in Budapest between 1944 and 1945 appear in historiographies (Avni, Rother, Rohr) and in Enrico Deaglio's *The Banality of Goodness: The Story of Giorgio Perlasca* (1991) and Diego Carcedo's *Un español frente al Holocausto: Así salvo Ángel Sanz Briz a 5.000 judíos* (2000), as well as in numerous articles, for the most part written by journalists such as Deaglio and Carcedo. Sanz Briz and Perlasca are also routinely mentioned in more general works on the Holocaust in Hungary, as well as in texts centering on rescuers or the "Righteous," such as Martin Gilbert's *The Righteous: The Unsung Heroes of the Holocaust* (2004), Mordecai Paldiel's *Righteous among the Nations: Rescuers of Jews during the Holocaust* (2007), and Marek Halter's *Stories of Deliverance: Speaking with Men and Women Who Rescued Jews from the Holocaust* (1998). A look at these different materials conveys the facts about the rescue of Jews during the final years of World War II, but the different accounts do not always provide the same version of events or of the motivations and goals of Sanz Briz, Perlasca, the Spanish government, or Franco himself. The authors' diverse nationalities represent an additional factor that shapes the kind of rescue narrative they have produced: Deaglio is an Italian journalist and his book first appeared in Italy; Carcedo is Spanish, also a journalist, and his account of Sanz Briz's deeds was published in Spain; Belgian-born Paldiel is a Holocaust survivor himself and the former director of the Department of the Righteous at Yad Vashem, Israel's Holocaust authority; Polish-born Halter, also a survivor, is a novelist who currently resides in France. Deaglio's account has been translated into Spanish and English, but Carcedo's text is only available in Spanish.

Although a historian's documented research might provide a more accurate rendition of the events than, for example, the memories of an individual, only a comprehensive look at the different, if not contradictory, depictions of Sanz Briz's and Perlasca's actions will ultimately make it possible to understand the shifting meanings that the different versions of the events in Budapest attain.[6] These meanings also are involved with respective national histories. Once different versions of the events published in different parts of the world are read against one another, it becomes evident that Carcedo's account may be more informative about Spanish history than about the history of the Holocaust; the same can be said about Deaglio's account and Italian history.

Because details of the story remain ambiguous or unknown, it is very easy to articulate differing versions of the same events, in which either Perlasca or Sanz Briz might have ultimately been responsible for the protection of the Jews and would therefore deserve to be honored and commemorated. This is not to say that the different versions are mere fictions; rather, these accounts share a number of attributes with the historical novel. In his discussion of the rise of the historical novel in the nineteenth century, György Lukács argues that one of the purposes of this genre is to create a connection with the past: "What matters is that we should re-experience the social and human motives which led men to think, feel and act just as they did in historical reality" (*The Theory of the Novel*, 42). The connection that the reader of historical fiction has with subjects within his or her respective "historical reality" is crucial because the different accounts about Sanz Briz and Perlasca reveal more about the meaning of this particular reality (the Spanish consular protection of the Jews) than about reality itself. More often than not, Spain's and Italy's historical reputation is at stake in the different versions of the events.

It remains unclear whether Sanz Briz put Perlasca in charge of protecting Jews, either before or after his departure from Budapest, or whether it was Perlasca's own decision to do so, possibly without Sanz Briz's knowledge. In a letter that Sanz Briz wrote to Perlasca in 1945, responding to a missive he had received earlier from Perlasca, Sanz Briz expresses his surprise after finding out about the other's actions: "I did not know that you had taken care of the legation. Knowing you as I know you, I am sure that your love for my country inspired your acts."[7] In the same letter Sanz Briz also states that he alone was responsible for the protection of Jews in safe houses: "Do not forget that the decision to accommodate people in the buildings that were part of the legation was my own initiative. I had not received permission from Madrid, and I did it because of the terror that was reigning in the Hungarian capital." Sanz Briz advises Perlasca that he should not expect to receive any recognition for what he had done: "And don't you expect anything from anyone, neither your government nor any other will recognize the merit of your actions. You can be satisfied that you have done a good deed, and that you were able to ride out the terrible storm, where we all were innocent victims."

In a 1990 interview Perlasca himself provides yet another version of the events. He states that he issued hundreds of protection letters using a stamp with Sanz Briz's signature, and that Sanz Briz was not aware of this, as it was his job was to maintain relations with the local foreign affairs minister.[8] In a different segment of the interview, Perlasca again mentions the signature stamp, adding this time that he found it after Sanz Briz had left.[9] German filmmaker and journalist Nina Gladitz Pérez-Lorenzo, who also interviewed Perlasca, corroborates this version in a 1991 article ("Der Fall Giorgio Perlasca," 134). Enrique Vándor—who, together with his mother, Anny Koppel, and his brother, Jaime, survived in Budapest with the help of Perlasca's and Sanz Briz's efforts—remembers that Perlasca would sign the official papers with a stamp bearing Sanz Briz's signature (Berthelot, *Memorias judías*, 140). Jaime Vándor also mentions the signature stamp in an interview.[10]

Did Perlasca find the stamp, or did Sanz Briz give it to him? Although the existence and role of this stamp appears to be but a small detail, it still makes very different interpretations of the same events possible: if Sanz Briz left the signature stamp for Perlasca to use after his departure, then Sanz Briz might have made the decision for Perlasca; if Perlasca simply found the stamp on Sanz Briz's desk, then an element of chance is added to the narrative. Or, if Perlasca had already used the stamp before Sanz Briz's departure, possibly without Sanz Briz's knowledge, one could conclude that Perlasca's actions were completely clandestine, even though, given Perlasca's precarious legal and financial situation, this is less likely. Gladitz Pérez-Lorenzo argues that the merit was solely Perlasca's and that Spanish authorities and Sanz Briz himself purposefully misrepresented Perlasca's actions to enhance the international reputation of Francoist Spain. She contends that the role that Perlasca played in the protection of the Budapest Jews would have ultimately called into question the myth of Spanish benevolence toward Jews during the World War II. Indeed, Gladitz-Pérez Lorenzo suggests that the news about Perlasca, the "foreign adventurer and humanitarian," would radically challenge this myth.[11]

Corroborating or disputing any of the differing versions of the events in Budapest would be beyond the goals of this chapter, particularly because a testimony or an interview given almost half a century after the end of World War II will provide a very different perspective on the same event than a letter written in 1945 on the letterhead of the Spanish consulate in San Francisco. As mentioned in Chapter 2 in relation to testimonies about Jewish life in Barcelona, oral histories can be more informative about the meanings of events than about the events themselves. This does not imply that Sanz Briz, Perlasca, or any of the eyewitnesses purposefully misrepresent the truth; rather, they provide a series of events through which they lived with meanings that are relevant for the specific moment in which they address them.

In 1945 Sanz Briz, then a diplomat in San Francisco, might have had personal and professional reasons to hide his knowledge of Perlasca's role in Budapest after his departure, or he might not have actually been aware of what happened. When Perlasca received public homage in the United States in the 1990s and was asked to tell his story in interviews, he repeatedly put together the pieces of his now fifty-year-old story, which might have led him to provide a version of events in which he was entirely responsible for the protection of the Budapest Jews through the Spanish legation.[12]

As a matter of fact, Perlasca's actions were only indirectly related to the decisions the Spanish government made (or did not make) with regard to protecting Jews, and the government in Madrid was unaware of Perlasca's individual actions and transgressions (see Rother, *Franco y el Holocausto*, 381). This does not, however, mean (as some of the documents that the Francoist government later published imply) that Perlasca's work was irrelevant. Rather, Sanz Briz's and Perlasca's histories intersect to such an extent that any attempt to tell one story without the other's involvement will result in an inaccurate account. Indeed, because Perlasca never followed orders from the Spanish Ministry of Foreign Affairs, the myth of Spanish benevolence toward the Budapest Jews only holds once Perlasca's role becomes the glue that keeps everything together. At the same time, other accounts inflate Perlasca's role to such an extent that Spanish involvement becomes barely a footnote in the sequence of events.

The title of Enrico Deaglio's *The Banality of Goodness* is an obvious reference to Hannah Arendt's *Eichmann in Jerusalem: A Report on the Banality of Evil*. Deaglio finishes his book by stating that, had Perlasca been present at the Eichmann trial in 1961 (which led to Arendt's formulation of the "banality of evil"), Perlasca's testimony would "have been the proof that, even in the most impenetrable darkness, there exists—because it is part of the human spirit—the temptation of the irreducible, fabulous word-and-thought-defying 'banality of goodness'" (142). Perlasca's having confronted Eichmann himself in Budapest, as Deaglio reports, makes the reference to Arendt's work even more pertinent.[13]

The contradictions and inconsistencies in different accounts reveal that saving the Budapest Jews through the Spanish legation was possible because of the decisions both Sanz Briz and Perlasca made and because of the help they received from other employees of the legation and members of the Budapest Jewish community. The actions of the two men were not isolated; rather, they were part of a common effort in which other diplomats from neutral nations also played dominant roles. A very different rescue account—Tzvetan Todorov's analysis of sources that document the protection of Bulgarian Jews in *The Fragility of Goodness: Why Bulgaria's Jews Survived the Holocaust* (1999)—also echoes Arendt's title. Although Bulgaria joined the Axis in 1941, Jews from Sofia were relatively safe. In his analysis of the complex events that would eventually lead to the survival of Bulgarian Jews (excluding Thracian or Macedonian Jews, who were deported to the death camps), Todorov emphasizes the symbolic meaning that rescue narratives attain in national histories: "Memories conflict because the glorious role in the past—the role of the hero or, in other contexts, of the victim—constitutes a *precious symbolic capital in the present*, one that confers prestige, legitimacy, and, ultimately, more power on those who can successfully lay claim to it" (*The Fragility of Goodness*, 26; my emphasis). As Todorov shows, in the Bulgarian case it is impossible to determine who was ultimately responsible for the protection of Bulgarian Jews: specific political and clerical leaders, the Communists, as official narratives would have it, or the Bulgarian king. Todorov concludes his study with the following thoughts: "Looking back and reflecting on the rescue of the Bulgarian Jews, one comes to realize that no one individual or single factor could have brought it about. Only concerted action made it possible. We would like, perhaps, to be able to name an individual and declare him hero of heroes, the champion of good against evil; in reality the responsibility was shared" (40). Todorov refers specifically to the Bulgarian case; he is not talking about what happened in Budapest between 1944 and 1945. Nevertheless, his point remains relevant for Sanz Briz's and Perlasca's intertwined stories because stories about their actions appear in competing national histories that, ultimately, are not really about Sanz Briz and Perlasca, much less about the individuals whose lives were saved and those who were murdered. These are stories that involve the international reputations of two nations that did support Nazi Germany—one of them, Italy, had promulgated racial laws in 1938.

The interplay with Arendt's title appears, as it does in Deaglio's book, in the last paragraph of Todorov's analysis of the events in Bulgaria: "All this was necessary for good to triumph, in a certain place and at a certain time; any break in the chain and their efforts might well have failed. It seems that, once introduced into public life, evil easily perpetuates itself, whereas good is always difficult, rare, and fragile. And yet possible" (40). In the different versions of the events in Budapest, Perlasca and Sanz Briz each at times become the "hero of heroes, the champion of good against evil." In *Anatomy of Criticism* Northrop Frye classifies fictions by "the hero's power of action" (34), and many of the representations of Sanz Briz and Perlasca mirror his description of the epic and tragic hero: "If superior in degree to other men but not to his natural environment, the hero is a leader. He has authority, passions, and powers of expression far greater than ours, but what he does is subject to both social criticism and to the order of nature. This is the hero of the high mimetic mode, of most epic and tragedy, and is primarily the kind of hero that Aristotle had in mind" (34). Rescue narratives in general are not necessarily fictitious, but they do correspond to specific structures of recognizable narratives, structures that inform the ways in which stories about a "hero of heroes, the champion of good against evil" are told. In the particular case of Francoist Spain, rescuing and protecting Jews in occupied Europe also became "precious symbolic capital in the present," as the ensuing analysis of the myth of Francoist benevolence toward Jews will reveal.

From the Keys to Sepharad to Repatriation:
Myths about Spain's Protection of the Jews

When prompted about the Spanish government's relationship with the Jews during World War II, Ramón Serrano Suñer, Francisco Franco's brother-in-law, second in command during the Spanish Civil War and minister of foreign affairs from 1939 to 1940, repeatedly stated in a 1997 interview that the government ordered all its embassies to protect Sephardic Jews as though they were Spanish nationals.[14] A number of circumstances might explain why, at the age of ninety-one, the former Nazi supporter, who during World War II was the unofficial spokesperson of Spanish anti-Semitism, provided this specific explanation in the interview; however, his words do reflect the legend that the Spanish government attempted to deliver Sephardic Jewry from the Holocaust.[15]

The shifting use of the terms "Sephardic Jews," "Spanish Sephardim," "protégés," and "Spanish nationals" in documents produced by the Spanish government partly explains the origins of this legend.[16] Although the Francoist government did protect a limited number of Spanish nationals in Nazi-occupied Europe, this does not mean that the protection was extended to all Sephardic Jews. Some confusion about Primo de Rivera's royal decree of 1924 might also contribute to the ambiguous uses of the terms. As mentioned in the introduction, the decree was issued so that the Sephardim who were under Spanish consular protection in the former Ottoman Empire could apply to become Spanish citizens. The new citizens would reside in the young nations that emerged after the empire's fall. By 1930, however, the decree had expired.

As early as 1943, the Spanish government, through its embassies, began spreading the myth about the nation's benevolence toward Jews. Although a select number of diplomats did help protect Jews, there is considerable discrepancy between what actually happened and how these events were represented and disseminated by the Spanish government and its official channels. As Rohr observes, Spain's motive for publicizing this legend clearly had opportunistic roots, at times based on anti-Semitic notions of Jews and their power: "Using the Jews to improve Spain's image abroad had a compelling attraction. The idea of reaching a 'Gentleman's agreement' with the worldwide

Jews to present a positive image of Spain abroad, particularly in the United States, was a logical consequence of the overestimation of Jewish power in Francoist thought that derived from the Protocols of the Elders of Zion" (*The Spanish Right and the Jews*, 153). Briefly, the myth that the Spanish government exhausted its resources to help the Jews, and that Francisco Franco himself was personally invested in saving the Jews, can be traced back to the anti-Semitic fabrication that international Jewry controlled all media and propaganda (154).

In the late 1940s Spain's international image was indeed a thorny issue: after all, the dictatorial government was in place because it won a war with Hitler's and Mussolini's help. In July 1948, only two months after the foundation of the State of Israel, the Sección de África y Próximo Oriente of the Spanish Ministry of Foreign Affairs produced a document aimed at informing the world of what Spain had allegedly done for the Jews. The document is biased and incomplete: the depiction of Jewish life in Spain before 1492 is idealized to such an extent that references to the expulsion do not even appear. Although the document does contain a report on the rescue of Sephardim in Romania and France, neither Salonika nor Hungary, where far more could have been done to protect the Jews, is mentioned.[17] This first report was soon supplemented with a second one, titled *Spain and the Sephardi Jews*, this time produced by the Office of Diplomatic Information, also in 1948 (see Avni, *Spain, the Jews, and Franco*, 181; Rother, *Franco y el Holocausto*, 399). In an English translation of this document (cited in the Introduction), published and distributed by the Spanish embassy in Washington, D.C., the conflation—one that indeed already appears in documents produced shortly before the end of World War II—of "Spanish Sephardis" and "Sephardis" (terms used in the document) is evident, suggesting that Spain had protected all Sephardic Jews, regardless of their nationality (see Rother, *Franco y el Holocausto*, 399).

Two press releases from 1943 focus on the repatriation of Jews who were also Spanish nationals, but, rather than providing accurate information, both texts reiterate recognizable stereotypes about the Sephardim, including the cliché of their endless nostalgia for the lost homeland of Sepharad.[18] The weight that both texts put on language is remarkable: what ultimately provides a connection between the Jewish refugees and the Spanish is the former's use of Judeo-Spanish—sadly ironic, considering that Ladino was a "casualty of the Holocaust" (Rodrigue, "The Ottoman Diaspora," 884). A press release about repatriated Jews from France—and anticipating more refugees from Greece—states that Spain has welcomed the newly arrived Jews, emphasizing that they speak archaic Spanish from the fifteenth century, which ultimately makes the Sephardim Spanish, or at least Spanish enough.

> Other trains with refugees are expected. The Spanish people have received them affectionately, talking to them. They were amused by the ways in which they spoke that old Castilian, with archaic terms, that for some Spaniards today is difficult to understand. But it is possible to have general conversations between the Spaniards who speak the Castilian of the twentieth century and those that return with the speech used in the fifteenth century, when they left Spain. (Quoted in Salinas, *España, los sefarditas y el Tercer Reich*, 119)

Another press release also refers to Greek Jews and reiterates the same stereotypes, even mentioning the commonplace image of the keys that the expelled Sephardim took with them, expecting to use them again once they returned to the lost homeland. The text also emphasizes that the repatriated Jews are, first and foremost, Spanish.

> Today ancient horizons return. And as proof that they never stopped being Spanish, and that the eternal Iberia traveled with them to all corners of the world and accompanied them in all their suffering, they bring back to the land they left five centuries ago the keys to the homes they left and to which they have, without a doubt, the right to return. Cover up this marvelous adventure? No, those that find out about it will discover that tradition, devotion to the vernacular, love for one's land and one's home are stronger than all persecutions and can triumph over all menaces. (Quoted in Salinas, *España, los sefarditas y el Tercer Reich*, 120)

Both documents affirm that the Jews' "Spanishness" was what ultimately made their deliverance from the Holocaust possible, which goes hand in hand with the notion that a prolonged stay in Spain had "purified" the Sephardim, a myth that Franco himself had repeated in the 1940s. In the study that reproduces the press releases, Salinas implies that what happened to the Sephardim between 1492 and 1943 has been forgotten; only their connection with Spain is brought to the forefront, so that their Jewishness is erased, vanishing in history and memory. The message that comes across in these documents slightly differs from the official position of the Francoist government. If, as both documents suggest, the government rescued the Sephardim because they were considered Spanish, then the argument that humanitarian reasons ultimately led to the Spanish protection and rescue of Jews (an argument put forth in the document that the Office of Diplomatic Information published) no longer makes sense. If the Francoist government protected Jews in occupied Europe solely for humanitarian reasons, then the Jews would not need to be Spanish or speak Ladino to be worthy of protection and deliverance. The two press releases, as well as the continuously shifting terms—Sephardic Jews, Spanish Jews, Spanish nationals, and protégés—in other contexts, reveal that the actual motivation to save Jews was constantly reinvented or adjusted, contingent on whatever suited the present moment and was politically expedient.

When the historians at the United States Holocaust Museum and Memorial were investigating Giorgio Perlasca's case in the early 1990s, Nina Gladitz-Pérez Lorenzo, who also interviewed Perlasca, sent a long report and copies of documents she had obtained at the archives of the Spanish Ministry of Foreign Affairs to the U.S. institution. Gladitz-Pérez Lorenzo also includes some of the same information in her 1991 article "Der Fall Giorgio Perlasca" (The case of Giorgio Perlasca). In the letter and the article Gladitz-Pérez Lorenzo argues that Perlasca, not Sanz Briz, was responsible—and should be honored and compensated—for saving more than 5,000 Jews in Budapest. Among other materials that corroborate her argument, Gladitz-Pérez Lorenzo also includes "A Diplomat's Bag Opens Up for a Journalist," an article from June 1949 published in the Spanish daily *El Heraldo de Aragón* with the subtitle "Spain Has Been the Courageous and Fairminded Protector of Sephardic Jews in Hungary, Confronting Racists, and Communists." In the article Sanz Briz himself, without ever mentioning Perlasca, narrates a version of the events that took place in Budapest. At the end of the article, Sanz Briz reiterates the same cliché about the Sephardim—that they use an untouched and archaic language, making them more Spanish, and, as the other texts suggest, more human:

> The difficult part for us was that many were in need of protection: but I know to what an extent what was done can be qualified as super-human. An entire apartment block was taken by the Spanish lega-tion and turned into a safe asylum for those poor people, who first expressed their dread and later their gratitude in that same language that their ancestors used in Toledo around the fifteenth century, old Spanish words that at that point sounded to my ears not like a cold literary evocation but like the very human heartbeat of Spanish life in our finest centuries.

In addition to the facts that Sanz Briz states in the article (to which Gladitz Pérez-Lorenzo very much objects), particularly that he was himself responsible for the rescue, the text reflects the same clichés that also appear in the two press releases and that continue to inform the perception of—and, at times, the scholarship on—the protection of Jews in occupied Europe.[19] Further, Sanz Briz seems to imply that *all* the protected Jews were Sephardim, which, following Rother's analy-sis, seems unlikely. As a matter of fact, the historical Sanz Briz made the effort to protect Ashkenazim and Sephardim, and their supposed Spanish origin or relationship with Spain was often fabricated. Thus, in this interview Sanz Briz becomes a very different hero than he actually may have been. Not only are his own terms (the "superhuman" effort) self-promoting, suggesting that he is constructing himself to be the type of leader Frye describes as the hero of the "high-mimetic mode, of most epic and tragedy" (*Anatomy of Criticism*, 34). The romanticiz-ing terms Sanz Briz uses also suggest that his heroism confirms part of the dominant narrative that the Francoist government circulated, namely, that Sephardic Jews deserved to be saved because they were more Spanish than Jewish. Ironically, the other version, in which the Francoist government's order to protect Jews was motivated by a hu-manitarian ethos, vanishes.

When Federico Ysart's *España y los judíos en la segunda guerra mundial* (Spain and the Jews in the Second World War) was published in 1973, the rhetoric had not changed. Rother explains that Ysart's re-search is biased: documents that might have put the Spanish government's actions in a negative light are not mentioned in the book. Ysart also criticizes the actions of other neutral nations so as to make Spain appear in a more positive light than other countries (Rother, *Franco y el Holocausto*, 19). José Antonio Lisbona explains that the Spanish Ministry of Foreign Affairs commissioned Ysart to write a book about Spain's policies toward Sephardi and Ashekanzi Jews during World War II that would emphasize "the humanitarian task that was carried out in spite of the adverse conditions for the negotiations that had to be done" (*Retorno a Sefarad*, 120). Although not officially a government publication (the book was published by Dopesa, a private publishing house, and even received the Ensayo Mundo award), Ysart's book reflects the version of events that had become official by the late 1940s, in which the diplomats were motivated by humanitarianism and Christian charity and never needed to challenge the Francoist government to carry out their actions.

Ysart's language, however, in many ways betrays the official version because the text continues to suggest that what made the Sephardim warrant protection and deliverance was their Spanish heritage in terms of language and culture. Ysart begins with an anecdote that illustrates Spain's alleged benevolence toward Jews. Max Mazin, president of the Hebrew Association of Spain, recalls eyewitness accounts of Civil Guard members' risking their own lives to save elderly and infirm Jews, as well as children, who were crossing the Spanish-French border illegally: "Years later eyewitnesses have told me how at other borders, this time sea limits, members of the Civil Guard ventured into the waters to carry to shore Jewish children, elderly, and disabled, who were arriving on Spanish shores illegally under the protection of night, in makeshift boats that often sank in the sea" (Ysart, *España y los judíos*, 10).[20] In the lines that follow, Mazin further underscores Spain's role in dark times: "Spain's name is one of the very few lights that shine in the long and dark night that the Jewish people lived during the tragic Nazi years" (10). Conveniently placed at the beginning of the text, the anecdote, provided by a Jewish source, sets the tone for the rest of the work.

Ysart begins his book with a brief reflection on the historical relationship between Spain and the Jews. He proposes that the humanitarian impulse to save lives is ultimately explained by Jews' having once resided in Spain. His discussion of a special bond between Spain and the Jewish people echoes the first document produced by the "Sección de África y Próximo Oriente," in which convivencia was idealized and the expulsion completely ignored: "Nothing else in Europe compares to the medieval coexistence of Jews, Moors, and Christians; elsewhere the Hebrews were always an element that was foreign to the national essence" (14).

According to Ysart's romanticizing terms, Jews' having once lived in Spain created a special sensibility that again links the past with the present. Ysart's depiction of the Jewish community in Salonika (like the press releases quoted earlier) is filled with clichés about Ladino.

> The peculiar sound of Greek contrasts with the language of other men and women in the corner of Macedonia. One could say that their words sound softer, whistlelike, as though they had been used and worn out. These are old words, which maybe a veteran of the Spanish war would recognize right away. Half the population speaks that strange language, Ladino, introduced since the early fifteenth century by Spanish Jews. They are in the Toledo of the Orient, where for centuries old Castilian has miraculously survived, and with it, an entire way of life, peculiar in those latitudes. (61)

Ysart's slant becomes even more obvious when he drops a number of Sephardic family names: "Castro, *Bahamonde*, Capuano, Carazo, Fernández, *Franko*, Pardo, Toledo, Serrano" (61; my emphasis). The implication that the Spanish dictator's surnames (Franco and Bahamonde) indicate a Jewish or crypto-Jewish ancestry is anything but subtle. But this is not a new idea: Franco's supposed crypto-Jewish origins are in many ways part of the legend of the Spanish dictator's personal investment in saving the Jews. At the World Jewish Congress held in Atlantic City in 1944, Juan de Cárdenas, the Spanish ambassador in New York, attempted to convince Rabbi Maurice Perlzweig, head of the British wing of the World Jewish Congress, of Franco's alleged Jewish origins. It was also during that congress that a "resolution was passed acknowledging Spain's assistance to Jewish refugees" (cited in Rohr, *The Spanish Right and the Jews*, 153, and Rother, *Franco y el Holocausto*, 393).[21] This myth was also spread among Jewish communities, as the testimony of Holocaust survivor George Horovicz reflects: "I heard somebody say that if [Franco] were in Germany he would have been taken for a Jew, because he had a very small percentage of Jewish blood in him, even though he was a strong Catholic. You will find that in Spain nothing happened to Jews. He did not send one person back."[22] In the 1975 *New York Times* obituary for the Spanish dictator, the possibility of Franco's Jewish origins is also mentioned: "It is widely believed, although skirted officially, that Sephardic Jews were among his ancestors."

Although the names Ysart lists may have been surnames of converso families, this does not necessarily mean that Franco's family was crypto-Jewish or, if it were true, that it had anything to do with Spain's policies (or lack thereof) toward Jews during World War II. Ysart's namedropping does signal, however, the mythologization of Franco and his role in saving Jews. Ysart also reiterates the endless nostalgia for Sepharad; he even mentions the legendary keys to the lost homes: "There was not a family that did not know its exact lineage in the kingdom of Sepharad. Many kept in their crammed storage spaces the keys to a distant home that would die with their memories, forever living in the refrains, advice, and a thousand popular sayings that still sound on the shores of the Mediterranean" (*España y los judíos*, 61–62). As in texts from the 1940s, the trite image of the keys suggests that the Sephardim were rescued more for their perceived unconditional love for Spain than for humanitarian reasons. Ysart's chapter on Hungary also includes an account in Sanz Briz's own words of the events in Budapest. Perlasca, however, is not mentioned. Ysart's book reproduces part of an interview with Sanz Briz conducted by Isaac Molho and published in Jerusalem in 1964. The interview could easily lead to the conclusion, although proven to be inaccurate, that Sanz Briz was ultimately following orders that were purportedly based on Franco's personal investment in the fate of the Jews.[23]

Chaim Lipschitz's *Franco, Spain, the Jews, and the Holocaust* (1984), which is coincidentally the only source for Spanish history that Deaglio cites in his biography of Perlasca, contains an interview held with the dictator himself. Franco states that the ultimate reason for saving the Jews was "an elementary feeling of justice and charity" (165). Lipschitz makes Franco responsible for the protection of the Jews, even though later sources (Avni, Marquina Barrio and Ospina, and Rother) have shown that this was not the case. As a matter of fact, Marquina

Barrio and Ospina consider the book to be "an excessively hagio-graphic work of Franco's politics" (*España y los judíos*, 222). Lisbona explains that the sources were translated and manipulated by the Span-ish Ministry of Information and Tourism and the embassy in Madrid to create a narrative that would be attractive in the international arena (*Retorno a Sefarad*, 120).

Briefly then, the myth of the Francoist protection of the Jews is built on two opposing ideas: that Jews were saved because they were more Spanish than Jewish and that Jews were saved for humanitarian reasons. In the next section of the chapter the different ways in which this myth appears in representations and commemorations of Ángel Sanz Briz and Giorgio (or Jorge) Perlasca will become evident.

Sanz Briz and Perlasca

Rather than passing judgment on what the historical Sanz Briz and Perlasca (who did, in fact, save an important number of lives, taking considerable risks to do so) might have believed, I am concerned with challenging the versions of events that were used to depict and justify an international image of the Francoist government as a humanitarian and benevolent regime.

Very few Jews (possibly none) who were also Spanish nationals re-sided in Hungary during World War II, making the circumstances there very different from the situation in France or Greece (see Rother, *Franco y el Holocausto*, 363). In 1944 the Spanish government was well aware of what the deportation of Jews to concentration camps in Eastern Eu-rope meant. An eyewitness report, written by two survivors who had managed to escape from Auschwitz, had come to Sanz Briz's attention. The diplomat informed the Spanish government about the atrocities that were taking place in the concentration camps. It remains unclear, however, whether it was Sanz Briz's decision to inform the government, or whether he did so following a request from the local Jewish leader-ship, as Martin Gilbert contends in *The Righteous*.[24] Gilbert argues that information about the mass murder of Jews led Sanz Briz (not Franco or the Spanish government) to do what he could to protect the Buda-pest Jews. Despite official documents produced and disseminated only a few years later that claim otherwise, the Francoist government did not take any extraordinary measures to protect Jews, even though Spain was aware of the atrocities in Auschwitz by 1944.

Although Sanz Briz later received orders from Madrid to protect Jews, these were not a consequence of his report on Auschwitz or, again, of Franco's concern. Alarm about the fate of Hungarian Jews came from the Jewish communities in Tangier and Tétouan. In Tangier the local Jewish leadership had asked the Spanish high commissioner in May 1944 to convey a petition to the Spanish capital, asking for permission for 500 Jewish children to emigrate from Hungary (see Rother, *Franco y el Holocausto*, 364).[25] The Moroccan Jewish communities had committed themselves to covering the costs of rescuing the children. Although the Germans did not agree to authorize the exit of the 500 youths, Sanz Briz was ordered to expedite 500 visas for Jewish children younger than eleven (365). Because Germany did not allow the transit to Spain, the children remained in relative safety under the protection of the Red Cross. Another group of Jews then petitioned for visas to Tangier, and this group of 700 also ended up being protected by the Spanish legation in Budapest (366). In the end 1,200 lives were spared at no real cost, monetary or otherwise, to Spain, even though the government ultimately took advantage of these events, using the protection of the Budapest Jews to improve the country's international reputation (367).

Although Spain did not participate in the initial international protests against deportations of Jews, Sanz Briz did attend a meeting called by Vatican representative Angelo Rotta on August 21, 1944. In addition to Sanz Briz, diplomats from Sweden and Portugal signed a document denouncing the deportations of the Budapest Jews. When the Arrow Cross seized power in Hungary in September 1944, Leon Kubowitzki, the leader of the rescue department of the World Jewish Congress, addressed the Spanish ambassador in the United States, Juan de Cárdenas, asking for protection of Budapest Jews. At this point the minister of foreign affairs, José Félix de Lequerica, instructed Sanz Briz to help the Jews, first Sephardim who were Spanish nationals, then all Sephardim, then all Jews (370).[26]

Summarizing the events that took place in Budapest, Rother underlines the following three facts: (1) protecting the Budapest Jews was not a Spanish initiative; (2) Francisco Franco never intervened directly or personally in the protection of the Jews (even though Sanz Briz himself would claim so in the 1949 interview published in *El Heraldo de Aragón* and again in the 1964 interview with Isaac Molho); and (3) the Spanish legation became involved in the rescue of the Jews much later than the Swiss and Swedish legations (370). Sanz Briz's individual actions and personal initiative helped to save more than 3,500 lives (378).

Although Carcedo's *Un español frente al Holocausto* reproduces these facts, it also reiterates many of the recurrent myths about the protection of the Jews. The constant commonplaces and clichés that cement the legend of Spanish benevolence toward Jews also appear repeatedly in Carcedo's text. Carcedo resolves the contradiction of the period (the dictatorial government implemented a brutal repression in Spain and simultaneously defined the protection of the Jews in occupied Europe as humanitarian and charitable) by implying that the Francoist government itself was humanitarian and acted on principles of Christian charity. Carcedo emphasizes, as the Franco regime did, that religion, not race, defined who was Jewish in Spain; the violent political repression that took place in postwar Spain is not discussed in the book.[27]

Carcedo begins with the description of a book burning that Sanz Briz witnesses. Although the book burning did take place in Budapest on June 16, 1944, it is uncertain whether Sanz Briz actually saw it or had any of the following thoughts:

> The diplomat, still unpleasantly surprised by the destruction of that treasure of culture and knowledge, who felt that his known capacity for self-control was getting tangled in his vocal chords and that his sympathies for the efficiency and discipline of the German regime were turning into hatred, took a while to notice that bibliographic wonder on which, even if he moved very little, he might end up stepping. The book fallen by his feet was entitled *Mishneh Torah*, and its author was the Spanish sage, of Jewish religion, Moses Maimonides. (*Un español frente al Holocausto*, 27)

The reference to Maimonides, who in Sanz Briz's thoughts becomes "the Spanish sage, of Jewish religion" is noteworthy because this apparently chance encounter with the book allows Sanz Briz to emphasize Maimonides's Spanishness—a significant gesture in a text in which the contradictions of the situation are constantly dodged by under-lining the idea that in Spain Jews were considered not a separate race (as in Nazi Germany) but a separate religion.[28] Sanz Briz affirms this notion more than once: "Spain has never been a racist country and the regime at no point succumbed to the temptation of the Reich to become one" (80).

The book burning that opens Carcedo's text connects the events in Budapest with the history of Jews in Spain and the history of the Inquisition. The depiction of the event is a literary trope, leading back even to Don Quixote's burned library and to a famous statement (often cited in relation to Nazi book burnings and the Holocaust) from Heinrich Heine's 1821 play, *Almansor*. After witnessing the burn-ing of Arabic manuscripts in Granada ordered by Torquemada, one of the characters warns that, where they have burned books, they will end in burning human beings.[29]

Sanz Briz's witnessing and reflecting on the book burning provides coherence and context to the kind of character Sanz Briz becomes in the text. Carcedo's Sanz Briz is a model citizen; he is self-possessed, educated, and compassionate, especially when it comes to children.[30] His being a patriot but not an ideologue dilutes the ties between the Francoist government, to which he is loyal, and the Nazi regime, thus distancing the Spanish dictator from the brutality of Hitler's Ger-many. When Mme. Tournée, the secretary of the legation, warns Sanz Briz that many of the local Jews "fear that Franco and Hitler are the same," the chargé d'affaires responds: "That's ludicrous!" (171). Sanz Briz also affirms that, although the Catholic monarchs expelled the Jews in 1492, they cannot be considered the führers of the Iberian Peninsula. In a conversation with the Swedish emissary Raoul Wal-lenberg, Sanz Briz explains who the Sephardim are and why they speak Spanish, emphasizing the same clichés about memory, language, and unconditional love for Spain: "And they hold on to many keepsakes of Spanish culture. Some even still own the keys to the homes that their great-great-grandfathers had to abandon 450 years ago" (131). To Wallenberg's response that "there were already führers on the Iberian Peninsula four centuries ago," Sanz Briz counters: "Those were dif-ferent times. I think that is an inappropriate claim" (131). Although the exchange might suggest that Sanz Briz refutes the hasty connection between the expulsion of the Jews and the Holocaust, he actually trivializes the expulsion. He adds the following to his clarification to Wallenberg: "Back then the Jews were expelled from many countries. And it was a peaceful expulsion. Also very detrimental for the Spanish economy. The proof that they did not suffer persecution is that they still feel an immeasurable love for Spain" (132).

In addition to distancing Franco from Hitler, Carcedo depicts Sanz Briz as very detached from Francoist Spain and from daily events within Spanish borders. In an interview with the Hungarian minister of foreign affairs, Gabor Kemeny, Sanz Briz emphasizes: "All Spanish are equal before the law. And, on the other hand, protection is a Spanish tradition that has its origins in our humanitarian vision of life" (225). To himself, Sanz Briz justifies his actions as based on "exceptionally humanitarian reasons" (207), situating himself within an apocryphal Spanish tradition, a transparent and blatantly nationalist fiction in which "Spanish" and "humanitarian" become one and the same. A close look at the political repression that under Franco's orders was taking place in Spain during the same years certainly makes whatever "humanitarian" ethos the Francoist government might claim highly dubious. This version of events also alternates with the other justification for the protection of the Jews, that the Sephardim were more Spanish than Jewish and therefore more deserving of protection than the Ashkenazim.

The first time two Sephardic Jews appear in Sanz Briz's office asking for Spanish papers, the diplomat is immediately intrigued by their use of Ladino: "At first it was difficult to understand the old Spanish, maybe similar to 'fabla,' that imitation of Spanish that playwrights liked so much, but once he got used to it, he found it charming" (54). Echoing the points mentioned in the 1943 press releases cited earlier, Sanz Briz reflects on Judeo-Spanish: "They still speak Spanish. Old Spanish that barely evolved, but Spanish. It can be perfectly understood" (131). As in the earlier texts, Ladino is reduced to a charming and literary form of expression, set in a remote past. Muñoz Molina's Señor Salama also comes to mind: although he barely remembers Salama, one of the intellectuals who visits the Spanish Atheneum in Tangier does recall (in an extremely condescending and paternalistic tone) his "flowery talk" (*Sepharad*, 117–118). Sanz Briz, arguing that the twentieth-century discrimination against Jews can by no means be compared to what happened in Spain five centuries earlier, also voices the myth that the Sephardim will always have an eternal and endless love for the lost homeland Sepharad. Briefly, Carcedo's Sanz Briz suggests that the great injustice and horror of the Holocaust was not that Jews were being deported, tortured, and murdered but that Jews who spoke and felt Spanish were being deported, tortured, and murdered: "It was unacceptable, he thought, that people who spoke Spanish and who still felt Spanish after so many centuries of diaspora would be treated with such truly inhumane cruelty. This was done to the Jews because they were merely considered to be of a different race" (*Un español frente al Holocausto*, 23). Carcedo's text underlines the idea that, despite Franco's alliance with Hitler, neither racism nor anti-Semitism ever existed in Spain. In the book Sanz Briz also points out that repatriated Jews could lead a peaceful existence in Spain because "the Spanish law does not discriminate based on religion or race" (59).

The book draws its coherence from this depiction of Spain's attitudes and policies toward the deportation of Jews. Although it is true that racial laws were never passed in Spain, the Spanish government never intended to allow exiled and repatriated Jews to settle in Spain, as becomes clear in a 1943 letter from Minister of Foreign Affairs Francisco Gómez de Jordana:

> We cannot let [Jews with Spanish nationality] settle in Spain because it does not suit us and [Franco] does not authorize it. Yet at the same time we cannot abandon them in their current situation and ignore the fact that they are Spanish citizens as this could bring about a press campaign against us overseas, particularly in the United States, and result in serious international difficulties. In light of this situation, we have considered bringing them in groups of one hundred. Only after one group leaves Spain—going through the country like light goes through glass, without a trace—do we allow a second group, which in turn would be evacuated to let others come. With this system it is clear that in no case will we allow the Jews to remain in Spain. (Rohr, *The Spanish Right and the Jews*, 147)

Although Sanz Briz does not seem to be aware of these policies, Carcedo does discuss the hurdles that the Spanish government established so that Jews would not settle in Spain (*Un español frente al*

Holocausto, 105). Carcedo supplies information that such historians as Avni and Rother have put forth; thus, the book is not historically inaccurate. Nevertheless, the author's characterization of Sanz Briz, without being hagiography, does reproduce the same myths and clichés that sustain the legend that Franco protected all Jews for humanitarian reasons. Carcedo's depiction of Perlasca as a secondary character, if not a caricature, reveals additional bias in *Un español frente al Holocausto*.

Although Perlasca was a Franco supporter and possibly even a life-long Franco admirer, Carcedo overstates his devotion to Franco. Almost every sentence Perlasca proclaims is punctuated with the words "¡Viva Franco!" (114, 116, 123, 124). Even though he appears to be inspired by Sanz Briz's efforts to protect the Jews, he is also naive, especially in contrast to the serious, intelligent, and compassionate Sanz Briz. When Perlasca asks for a Spanish passport for himself, he refers to the Sephardim as those Jews who "speak a very strange Spanish" (193). In other accounts Perlasca already began to resist anti-Semitism before leaving Italy, after witnessing a child's being mistreated by German soldiers. In Carcedo's version, however, Perlasca's involvement results from his encounter with Sanz Briz at the Spanish legation in Budapest, in which Perlasca admits: "I did not used to like the Jews, but because I did not know them, because of the propaganda against them that was hammered into us. Now I feel more and more sorry for them, and I can empathize better with them. I would like to do something for them. This is not right" (195). In response, Sanz Briz offers Perlasca the opportunity to collaborate with the Spanish legation and even mentions a small salary (195). Perlasca remains, however, a secondary character in this book, and only reappears briefly in the epilogue: "after Sanz Briz left, he assumed the responsibility of protecting the Jews in the safe houses; he even told the Hungarian authorities that he was the new chargé d'affaires from Spain" (274). Carcedo's book, after all, is about Sanz Briz, and the Spanish diplomat becomes responsible for the deliverance of thousands of Jews, despite what most historiographies reveal—that the responsibility for the protection of the Budapest Jews was shared, and not only by Sanz Briz and Perlasca.

When accounts about Sanz Briz are compared with accounts about Perlasca, the most controversial question is: Who was ultimately responsible? Who was the hero of heroes, the champion of good against evil" (Todorov, *The Fragility of Goodness*, 40)? In accounts that center on Perlasca, especially Deaglio's and Gladitz-Pérez Lorenzo's, the more astute Perlasca makes Sanz Briz aware of what is going in Budapest and not vice versa, as Carcedo's book would have it. In *The Banality of Goodness* Perlasca yells at Sanz Briz when he hesitates to help him obtain Spanish papers: "'Can't you see what's happening in this city?' I said. 'Can't you see that they're murdering women and children, that they're torturing people and putting innocent people in jail?' Sanz Briz, as a good Latin, understood" (Deaglio, *The Banality of Goodness*, 67). Perlasca also explains that "Sanz Briz then asked me to stay on at the embassy office and help out with the effort to protect the Jews" (67). When Sanz Briz's departure from Budapest at the end of November is imminent, he advises Perlasca that he will be able to procure the necessary documents for him to leave Budapest, and that he should depart from the Hungarian capital as soon as possible. "Don't do anything special," Sanz Briz advises him. "Wait for the right moment and then come away. Think about it. I'm leaving tomorrow morning" (77). Deaglio explains that Perlasca was not initially sure whether he should also leave, but after visiting one of the safe houses the following morning, he promised the suffering inhabitants that he would stay in Budapest and help protect them from the Nazis and the Arrow Cross. He then managed to convince the Hungarian authorities that Sanz Briz had not left Budapest for good but had gone on an important diplomatic mission, and that he, Perlasca, was now in charge (79).

According to Deaglio's text, Sanz Briz did not instruct Perlasca to take charge of the legation; the decision was solely Perlasca's. Sanz Briz's 1945 letter, in which he expresses his surprise to learn what Perlasca had done, would confirm this. Deaglio states that, after Sanz Briz's departure, Perlasca "nominated himself as the Spanish representative" (2), and he credits Perlasca with the rescue of 5,000 Jews. Deaglio also writes that once the war was over, Perlasca "returned home and took up his former life, until someone remembered him and tracked him down" (2). In Deaglio's version of events (and Gladitz-Pérez Lorenzo's as well) it appears that Perlasca was uninterested in fashioning himself as a hero, but more recent accounts, particularly an article by Emiliano Perra, suggest that, on the contrary, Perlasca was very keen on being recognized for what he had done in Budapest.

Although understanding Perlasca's motives and actions after the war is difficult, if not impossible, the discrepant versions of what Perlasca did—or did not do—show that the hero's humility is in many ways part of the fabric of the hero's story.

In Mordecai Paldiel's version of events, however, Sanz Briz put Perlasca in charge, and the same idea comes across in Gilbert's text.[31] Paldiel writes: "Perlasca was presently invited by Ambassador Sanz Briz to join his staff, and specifically to deal with Jews who claimed Spanish descent and were sheltered in Spanish protected houses" (*The Righteous among the Nations*, 318). Gilbert affirms that Sanz Briz put Perlasca in charge of the safe houses in the city, but when it comes to Perlasca's decision to remain in Budapest, his text is more ambiguous: "On November 30 the head of the Spanish Legation, Angel Sanz Briz was ordered to leave Budapest for his safety. His friend Giorgio Perlasca, the Italian whom he had earlier put in charge of the Spanish 'safe houses,' became the Spanish Chargé d'Affaires, taking the Spanish name Jorge. In this capacity he issued three thousand protective documents on the writing paper of the Spanish Legation" (*The Righteous*, 400).

Yet another version of Perlasca's story appears in Marek Halter's *Stories of Deliverance*. Halter centers on the ways in which Perlasca outmaneuvered and defied the Germans, even Eichmann himself, and the Hungarians but without explaining how Perlasca came to join the Spanish legation. He writes: "At this time Giorgio Perlasca was acting out of his own initiative, 'squatting' in some way in the Spanish Legation using official documents and seals to fake up those famous refugee cards which allowed Jews in Hungary to escape the Nazis" (*Stories of Deliverance*, 281). Halter's version also implies that the legation was in a chaotic state even before Sanz Briz's departure. By making Perlasca alone responsible for saving 5,200 Jews in Budapest, rather than confirming any national narrative, Halter aims to commemorate the individuals who helped Jews to survive the Holocaust: "This memory of the Just, will it not be our one hope and, who knows, our last chance?" (xvi).

Rother writes that, after receiving his passport in 1944, Perlasca offered to help Sanz Briz protect the Jews of Budapest. The ambiguities begin right away: Sanz Briz only mentions Perlasca indirectly in his correspondence, and Perlasca does not appear in Sanz Briz's final report, sent to the Ministry of Foreign Affairs from Bern (*Franco y el Holocausto*, 379). But according to the interview given to Gladitz-Pérez Lorenzo and the interview available at the United States Holocaust Memorial Museum, Perlasca was the one calling the shots all along. Perlasca, posing as a Spanish diplomat, did in fact sign the protest note against the persecution of Jews that diplomats of neutral nations published in November 17, 1944, and again on December 23 (Sanz Briz had previously signed two other notes). Rother writes that it is plausible that, even before Sanz Briz left Budapest, Perlasca was the one who actively went to the safe houses and confronted the Hungarian and German authorities who were threatening Jews under Spanish protection.[32]

Rother acknowledges that Sanz Briz could not report about Perlasca's activities in public, even if he might have wanted to do so, because Sanz Briz was not authorized to name Perlasca, or anyone, as chargé d'affaires before his departure. It also is possible that Sanz Briz did not write about the Italian in his reports because he did not actually have the right to provide Perlasca with Spanish papers. Thus, including Perlasca's actions might have posed political and professional risks. Nevertheless, it is difficult, if not impossible, to establish whether Sanz Briz purposely concealed Perlasca's efforts to enhance his own reputation.

Different portrayals of Perlasca also fit within specific Italian myths, most prominently, the notion that the Italians were "good people," or *brava gente*, who did all they could (especially when contrasted with the Germans) to protect the Jews. This myth has been circulating since the end of World War II, and even provided the title for a 1964 film.[33] Davide Rodogno challenges this version of history, arguing that the myth "is absolutely useless for explaining Fascist Italy's policy toward the Jews in the Balkans" ("Italiani brava gente?," 214). Deaglio suggests that the myth could provide a partial explanation for Perlasca's story: "It would fit well with the self-image of Italians: 'brava gente' (good people), people so humane that their humanity needs no rational elaboration but comes from the gut and springs forth—despite all the orders, uniforms and ideologies to the contrary—at the mere sight of someone being humiliated or abused; people endowed with innate theatricality and psychological intuition" (*The Banality of Goodness*, 3). If, as Rodogno argues, "the claim that 'the Italians' as a people did not betray the Jews to the Germans for humanitarian reasons simply cannot be sustained" ("Italiani brava gente?," 235), Deaglio's portrayal of the "hero" also becomes questionable. Nevertheless, Deaglio depicts Perlasca as surpassing the myth: "But what Giorgio Perlasca did is unique and astounding. He didn't have a role; he created it for himself" (3). Perlasca's actions were no doubt exemplary; nevertheless, the myth of Italians as good people plays as much part in the way Perlasca is commemorated today as the myth of nostalgia for Sepharad does in accounts about Ángel Sanz Briz.

Emiliano Perra provides a different version of Perlasca's story in an article about the Italian reception of the miniseries *Perlasca: Un eroe italiano*. Perra explains that Perlasca did attempt to tell his story and tried to receive recognition for his actions in Italy and Spain for decades: "Immediately after the war, he sent reports of his actions in Hungary to the governments of Spain and Italy, as well as to a local newspaper. In 1948 he met with leading Christian Democrat politicians . . . in the hope of obtaining public recognition, but none of these attempts proved successful" ("Legitimizing Fascism through the Holocaust?," 99). In a 1970 letter to a retired diplomat, Perlasca (who was financially struggling) "lamented the silence and failure to acknowledge his contribution on the part of the Spanish and Italian governments alike" (99). None of these instances is mentioned in other accounts about Perlasca; he is always portrayed as modest, secluded, and completely isolated from any possibility of receiving international commemoration until the late 1980s. Perra's analysis confirms that, if a story of an individual who risks his life for others is exemplary, a story of an individual who does all that, never expecting anything in return and remaining silent about his deeds because of his modest nature, is even more appealing.

Don Quixote Confronts Hitler

Although the events take place far away from Spanish borders and involve individuals who are not Spanish, references to Spain's ultimate honorable caballero, Don Quixote, appear frequently in accounts about what happened in Budapest. As mentioned earlier, in Carcedo's *Un español frente al Holocausto* Sanz Briz suggests that his own deeds are part of a Spanish and humanitarian tradition (207). To underline the humanity and generosity of all Spaniards, he refers to Don Quixote:

> Spain, you know it as well as I do, is a nation that has always been characterized by its generosity. The mythical figure of Don Quixote often reflects our ways and our behavior. And now we will once again have the chance to demonstrate this. The actions of the legation in a foreign country are limited; we cannot interfere in another nation's affairs. But the legation and, in particular, its members all have a humanitarian duty toward our fellow citizens that we should not forget. (169)

Carcedo is not the first writer to make a reference to Don Quixote when discussing the Spanish protection of the Jews. Ysart's chapter on Spanish diplomats' protection of Jews in the Balkans is titled "Quijote frente a Hitler" (Quixote confronts Hitler). After a biased account of the events in Bulgaria, Romania, and Hungary, Ysart turns to the protection of the Budapest Jews and concludes: "Spain has accomplished its humanitarian mission, and with the arrival of the Soviet forces, its official representative had to leave for Bern. But Don Quixote had triumphed on a new front of an uneven battle which, in the most difficult years of its recent history, it fought against Hitler and the long and powerful sails of its Third Reich" (151).

Haim Avni challenges Ysart's depiction of Spain and its diplomats as a "Don Quixote" facing Hitler. He concludes his chapter on the creation and circulation of the myth of Spain's and Franco's benevolence with a reference to the errant knight: "The Franco regime did not want a Jewish community established either in La Mancha or in any other part of Spain, and so it could never become the modern Don Quixote it pretended to be" (*Spain, the Jews, and Franco*, 199). Yet it is not always clear what the figure of Don Quixote exactly stands for in these accounts. In both Ysart's and Carcedo's texts, Don Quixote symbolizes the Spanish spirit—honorable, humanitarian, and, even if unorthodox, always on the side of good, fighting "the long and powerful sails" of evil.

In Carcedo's book, Perlasca himself alludes to Cervantes's hero; after Sanz Briz offers him the assistance of the legation, Perlasca proclaims: "You are a Don Quixote, Don Ángel, thank you so much!" (116). The references to Don Quixote are nonetheless skewed; the errant knight is used to highlight both Sanz Briz's and Perlasca's courage, even their heroic spirit, but Quixote's madness is not considered. Although both men's actions could be considered mad because they took risks that could have cost them their lives, in all accounts Sanz Briz and Perlasca always appear to be lucid and in control of their actions and decisions. Even Perlasca becomes Don Quixote. The Spanish version of Deaglio's *Banality of Goodness* includes an essay by Jaime Vándor, whose testimony also appears in *Memorias judías*. Jaime Vándor, who was born in Vienna as Helmut Jacques Vándor and later emigrated to Hungary, received, with his mother and brother, one of the Schutzbriefe that Perlasca procured and also resided in one of the group homes that were under Spanish protection. He remembers Perlasca as "a Quixote who was respected, because he exuded confidence and because of his handsome appearance. He was a useful and efficient caballero, tireless and he did not discriminate when helping the most vulnerable" (99). Although the term *caballero* can mean both "knight" and "gentleman," the former might convey better Vándor's original meaning. The Perlasca that Vándor remembers, the Perlasca who saved his and his family's life, fought against the odds in an unorthodox but firm and passionate manner.

The references to *Don Quixote* signal the profound ambiguity of these narratives. The errant knight becomes an appropriate trope because Alonso Quijano might be another ambassador responsible for the fate of the whole world.[34] Don Quixote was, after all, determined "to redress grievances, right wrongs, correct injustices, rectify abuses and fulfill obligations" (Cervantes, *Don Quixote*, 30). The constant references to *Don Quixote* also hint at the frequent impostures, the different forms of subterfuge, that made it possible for Spanish diplomats to save Jewish lives. The stories of deliverance of the Budapest Jews through the Spanish legation include identity shifts, such as the sequence mentioned earlier in which Giorgio becomes Jorge and later the "consul" Perlasca, as well as the slippages among Sephardim, Spanish Sephardim, Spanish nationals, and protégés. A year before his death, Perlasca, the false ambassador and true impostor, received the medal of the Order of Isabella of Castile, the same monarch who signed the expulsion edict and forged the nation where the errant knight continues to ride—a nation of impostors, kingdom of subterfuge, of invented and false identities, where maybe only men like Perlasca can become ambassadors responsible for the fate of the whole world.

The constant references to Don Quixote reveal an additional aspect of these rescue narratives. The narrator of Cervantes's novel, we need to remember, translates the text from the original *aljamiado*, the Romance vernacular in Arabic script, written by a Moor, Cide Hamete Benengeli. This fictional author, as William Childers notes in *Transnational Cervantes*, "displaces the idea of any essentialized cultural identity or preordained order to which the text could correspond" (70). *Don Quixote* emerges from the extremely contradictory and sedimented society on the Iberian Peninsula in the years that followed the reconquest of Muslim Spain, the expulsion of the Jews, and the conquest of the Americas. These were the years, briefly, when certain processes of religious and ethnic identification, which could have been evident, concealed, or falsified, acquired a whole new set of shifting meanings, often with devastating consequences for individuals and communities as a whole. If, as Childers argues, Cide Hamete Benengeli's presence in the text destabilizes "narrative authority" (70), then one may argue analogously that references to Don Quixote destabilize the rescue narratives that I have discussed. If Cervantes's novel is, as Menocal argues in *The Ornament of the World*, "in part a postscript to the history of a first-rate place, the most poignant lament over the loss of that universe, its last chapter, allusive, ironic, bittersweet, quixotic" (263), then Don Quixote himself (like the figure of the Marrano in Alexy's text) becomes a traveling signifier, used to provide meaning and coherence to accounts of events as complex and contradictory as the consular protection of Jews in occupied Europe.

Last but not least, the references to Don Quixote also reveal inadvertently what might be the darkest aspects of these rescue narratives. Both Sanz Briz's and Perlasca's stories have an important entertainment value: they are adventure tales of self-made heroes, who are humble and therefore human. The stories of those who were rescued and those who perished on the long march all the way to Auschwitz vanish behind these heroic tales.

Four   History's Patio
Spanish Colonialism in Morocco
and the Jewish Community

Toward the end of Ángel Vázquez's 1976 novel, *La vida perra de Juan-ita Narboni*, the protagonist reflects on Tangier, the city where she was born and which she would never leave. For Juanita Narboni, Tangier is "a city where we are not completely Christian, not completely Jewish, and not completely Moorish. We are what the wind wants us to be. A mélange" (378). Juanita continues pondering on the culturally diverse city, which, with the exception of Spanish occupation from 1941 to 1945, maintained an international status until Moroccan independence in 1956: "We had Jewish friends, who asked Saint Anthony for a boy-friend when they were single, and Muslim friends who talked about Miriam—the Virgin Mary—and the Archangel Saint Gabriel, and Christians . . . who invoked Aixa Kandisha because they wanted to kill their husbands" (378).[1] The character's reference to the wind ("we are what the wind wants us to be") evokes a whimsical relationship with cultural and religious identity, but throughout the novel the Tangier wind constantly aggravates Juanita, suggesting that interactions among Christians, Jews, and Muslims in Tangier are not merely the result of chance. The second part of the quotation intimates that among the women in Tangier a gender-based affinity mitigates religious and cul-tural difference. But both Vázquez's novel and Farida Benlyazid's 2005 film version show that, in spite of Juanita's fond memories of Tan-gier's golden era of cultural and religious pluralism, these differences remained in place for the duration of the colonial rule, administered by Spain, France, and Britain between 1923 and 1956.[2]

123

The characters in the novel and in Benlyazid's film are trapped in the interstices of the colonial relationship that Morocco and Spain shared in the past and that in the present remains unresolved. The

Jewish community in the Protectorate, the northern Moroccan zone that Spain would control between 1912 and 1958, forms part of this relationship.[3] In literary representations of the Protectorate, a tension between philo-Sephardism, which defined Spanish colonial attitudes toward Moroccan Jews in the nineteenth and early twentieth centuries, and anti-Semitism, which would rise during World War II, becomes evident. This tension and its impact on both contemporary meanings of "Jewish Spain" and the debate on the "recovery of historical memory" will be explored in the pages that follow.

The first part of this chapter centers on the depiction of the Protectorate in an issue of the magazine *Vértice* (a publication of the Falange Española de las J.O.N.S.) from August 1938, during the Spanish Civil War.[4] Although the bulk of the magazine portrays an idealized Spanish-Muslim brotherhood in Morocco, rationalizing Spanish colonial rule and the participation of Moroccan soldiers in the Civil War on the Iberian Peninsula, one story, Luis Antonio de Vega's "Itinerario lírico de Sultana Cohén," focuses on the Jewish community, specifically on a Jewish woman, in the Moroccan city of Tétouan. The appearance of Vega's piece in one of the Falange's publications certainly determines the ideological inclination of the text. Despite the political tendencies of the publication, however, "Itinerario Lírico de Sultana Cohén" is not devoid of inconsistencies and contradictions. The brief text narrates the story of Sultana Cohén, who, during the 1859–1860 African war, falls in love with General Prim, the leader of the Spanish army.[5] When the Spanish leave the Moroccan city, Vega hints that Sultana Cohén commits suicide. All that is left of her is her "itinerary," her route following Prim and his troops when they leave Tétouan. In 1938, when the article was published, the Jewish woman's presence is a ghostly remainder of an exotic and distant past; for contemporary visitors Sultana Cohén's "lyrical itinerary" has become a leisurely tour of the city.

Vega's text, published during the Spanish Civil War, reiterates the racial and gendered categories that in the past were used to justify Spanish colonialism in Morocco. In the different narratives about the Protectorate, Muslims and Jews are portrayed either as meek, submissive, and always vulnerable to the worldly charms of the Spanish invaders or as sultry temptresses. Meanwhile, Muslim men, formerly the enemies of Spain, are now part of an imbalanced and invented "brotherhood" that is "grounded in a shared language and religion, while the grandiloquent phrase 'spirit of the race'—all but an oxymoron, given the racial theories of the time—began to gain purchase" (Martin-Márquez, *Disorientations*, 49).[6]

Vázquez's acid prose challenges the rigid forms of identification that justified the Spanish colonial enterprise in Morocco and that have marked Spain's contradictory relationship with the Jews in the twentieth century. The second part of this chapter therefore discusses Vázquez's novel and Benlyazid's 2005 film adaptation. Although Vega essentializes the Jewish woman as an exotic other dwelling in a remote Moroccan past, Vázquez's novel and Benlyazid's film version reflect on Tangier's cultural and religious pluralism. Rather than idealizing a defunct but harmonious convivencia as an example to be followed in the present, the novel and the film offer a critical view of the history of Tangier and Spanish colonialism in Morocco. Both reveal that the cultural and religious diversity of Tangier in the first part of the twentieth century operated within a colonial and therefore profoundly gendered context. Benlyazid's film goes one step further by adding two sequences that center on intimate relationships among Christian, Jewish, and Muslim women, showing how these potentially liberating relationships remain structured by colonialism; thus, a "sisterhood" does not become an alternative to or liberation from the Spanish-Muslim brotherhood. Both the film and the novel end with a mad and terribly lonely Juanita wandering around a Tangier she no longer recognizes after independence. In her story, and in the multiple stories of women in the Protectorate, national and religious identification is not (despite Juanita's claims) merely up to the whims of the wind but contingent on the history of colonialism. By focusing the analysis specifically on representations of Jewish women in Spanish Morocco (representations that are deeply intertwined with the shifting nature of Spanish colonialist rhetoric in different moments of the nineteenth and twentieth centuries), this chapter reveals the contradictions that mark Spanish colonialism in North Africa. These contradictions are intrinsically connected to "Jewish Spain" and endure today.

Spain and Morocco: An Invented Fraternity

Spain and Morocco share an intricate web of relations, often in contradiction with one another, rather than a single postcolonial relationship that evolves neatly in the aftermath of colonialism. Because, as Ann Stoler writes in *Carnal Knowledge and Imperial Power*, "the dichotomy colonizer/colonized is a historically shifting pair of social categories" (13) and because colonial rule in Morocco was always contingent on Spain's relationship with other European colonial powers, representations of Moroccan Jewish women also shift according to the specific, instrumental role they play in the narratives that inform Spanish colonial rhetoric in relation to Morocco. As historian Dipesh Chakrabarty has argued in *Provincializing Europe*, colonized nations were commonly confined to the "imaginary waiting room of history" to rationalize the colonial enterprise. This waiting room of history became, according to Chakrabarty, "justification for denial of 'self government' to the colonized" (9).[7] Vázquez's novel and Benlyazid's film version show that, in the case of Spanish colonialism in Morocco and, more specifically, women's lives in the Protectorate, we may not be dealing with history's imaginary waiting room but with history's imaginary patio: a space that is only apparently secluded, a space that at first glance seems to make gender-based affinities flourish but that ultimately turns out to be structured by colonialism and its gendered hierarchies.[8] Thus, rather than making an ahistorical statement about the Jewish-Muslim relationship in Morocco and in Spain or even looking for "evidence of a rosy Jewish-Muslim symbiosis" (Nirenberg, "What Can Medieval Spain Teach Us about Muslim-Jewish Relations?," 18), it will be more fruitful to consider how these different relationships shaped the representations of the Moroccan Jewish community in different forms of "high" and "low" culture in Spain.

From the nineteenth century onward, and for the duration of the Civil War and World War II, Spanish attitudes toward Jews in Morocco oscillated between paternalistic philo-Sephardism and virulent anti-Semitism, mirroring similar trends on the peninsula. The government of Marshal O'Donnell represented the 1859–1860 war as a "crusade against infidel Moors"; indeed, the roughly 6,000 Jews living in Tétouan at the time actually benefited (even economically) from the invader's presence (see Rohr, *The Spanish Right and the Jews*, 11, 12).[9] Hazel Gold observes that the war led to a "reencounter with the Sephardic community in Tétouan" ("Illustrated Histories," 92), resulting in an increased interest in all things Jewish in Spain. While both Jews and Muslims appeared in nineteenth-century political and cultural writings about Morocco, philo-Sephardist discourse of the period tended to present more favorable images of Jews than of Muslims. Sixty years later, however, in the context of the Spanish Civil War, the "godless ones" (Albet-Mas, "Three Gods, Two Shores, One Space," 593) were no longer Muslims but the heathen Republicans, discursively collapsed together with Jews, communists, and atheists. Sebastian Balfour explains that "reduced to its quintessential character, the Spanish 'Other' was Communist." Balfour continues: "Apart from Islam, historically anti-Spanish identities—Jewishness, freemasonry, liberalism, atheism, Protestantism, and so on—thus became boiled down to a single category in the rhetoric of the Nationalists. It was a useful concept for mobilizing support, not only among traditional sections of the Spanish population but also among Moroccans, for whom these identities were a threat" (*Deadly Embrace*, 284).

The shifting representations of Jewish communities in relation to the role that the colonial metropolis needed them to play become particularly apparent if we consider Francisco Franco's own biography and his radically contradictory statements about Moroccan Jews.[10] In an article that was published in the "Revista de tropas colonials" in 1924, Franco describes the small Jewish community of the city of Xauen in northern Morocco. According to the text, the Jews of Xauen were ecstatic when the Spanish colonial troops arrived to liberate them from the Muslims. "That day, when the wretched, humiliated Israelites were shedding tears of joy and, with their typical accent and their old Castillian vocabulary, were cheering Queen Isabella, the good queen" (quoted in Rohr, *The Spanish Right and the Jews*, 68).[11] Years later, when Franco was an ally of Nazi Germany, his rhetoric in relation to the Jews shifted radically. In a speech made in Madrid on May 19, 1939, to celebrate the Nationalist victory, he warned that the "Jewish spirit, which permitted the alliance of big capital with Marxism and which made so many pacts with the anti-Spanish revolution, could not be extirpated in a day" (68). Franco's rhetorical shift from Orientalist paternalism to downright aggression demonstrates how rapidly attitudes about Jews changed in relation to the developments of the Spanish Civil War.

The Nationalists' dominance in the Protectorate represented a serious threat for the Jewish community. Moroccan Jews, who, in the philo-Sephardist discourse of the past, had functioned as agents of Spanish colonialism, now became the target of Nationalist violence because they were believed to support the Republic (see Rohr, *The Spanish Right and the Jews*, 85). The same Jewish communities that Spanish colonial forces purportedly protected from the Muslims in the nineteenth-century conflict were used to ease the relationship between Spanish Catholics and Moroccan Muslims during the Civil War.

According to Abel Albet-Mas, between sixty and seventy thousand Moroccan mercenaries fought for the Nationalist army ("Three Gods, Two Shores, One Space," 592). A combination of coercion, economic compensation, and never-fulfilled promises led young Moroccan men to fight in this army, often as cannon fodder; "they were considered 'easy to manipulate,' because of their limited cultural resources outside their own world" (597–598). The Nationalist propaganda machine also used vilified images of the Moroccan soldiers as a rhetorical weapon, images that Republican cultural production not only reproduced but also disseminated.

An anecdote that Balfour mentions in *Deadly Embrace* further illustrates how rapidly the interactions among Catholics, Muslims, and Jews changed in the specific context of the Moroccan soldiers' participation in the Civil War. According to Balfour, "after the first colonial troops had been transported to the mainland, Catholic women supporters of the Nationalist cause in Seville embroidered the image of the Sacred Heart onto the tunics of Regulares mercenaries. It is possible that the Moroccan soldiers, coming from a culture also steeped in superstitions, hoped the image might turn into a shield against enemy bullets just as it had always been a symbol of protection for Spanish Catholics" (281–282). More intriguing is how the rhetoric of "crusade" was applied instrumentally according to different contexts: "Franco is supposed to have told a small inner circle of generals and fellow officers with whom he was having supper that the same Moroccans had told him that a long time had gone by since they had been allowed to kill Jews. That is to say, they were happy to be wearing the emblem of the heart of a Jew because they were starting to kill them." Balfour notes that, although this may have been a told as a joke, it is not "a surprising one in view of the close bonding between Africanists and Regulares and their shared anti-Semitism" (282).[12]

Reproducing shifting circumstances, then, Jews and Muslims became friend or foe from moment to moment. The "slipperiness of the concept of the Moroccan Other" (198) suggests that representations of the Jewish other are just as slippery. As Martin-Márquez's extensive study shows, and as a close reading of Vega's "Itinerario lírico de Sultana Cohén" should corroborate, invocations of the past play a crucial role in any portrayal of encounters and disencounters among Catholic Spaniards, Jews, and Muslims in the Spanish Protectorate.

Sultana Cohén's Vanishing Presence

Luis Antonio de Vega (1900–1977) was one of the most prolific authors of Orientalist verse and prose set in the Protectorate, as well as a staunch supporter of the Nationalists during the Civil War. He arrived in Morocco to work as a teacher and eventually became the director of Arabic schools in Larache. He also wrote a series of "Moroccan Songs" in which he "adopts the voice of a Moroccan woman who anxiously awaits the return of her beloved" who has left for the war in Spain (Martin-Márquez, *Disorientations*, 232). Recognizing Vega's "efforts to 'ventriloquize' Moroccan women," Martin-Márquez (referring to Ann Laura Stoler's *Carnal Knowledge*) emphasizes "the fundamental importance of the regulation of gendered identities and sexual desire for the colonial project" (233). This ventriloquism is particularly apparent in the "Moroccan Songs" with Vega's tendency to "put words in Moroccan women's mouths" (243). In "Itinerario lírico de Sultana Cohén" he uses the same strategy. An earlier version of Sultana Cohén's story precedes the 1938 text: the ballad "Romance de Sultana Cohén" opens Vega's *Romancero colonial*, published in 1934.[13]

In Vega's poetry and prose, the representation of Muslim and Jewish women serves different functions, which in the end contributes to the propagandistic message that comes across in a 1938 story in *Vértice*. "Itinerario lírico de Sultana Cohén" stages the cultural paradoxes that are part of Spanish colonial intervention in Morocco. The instrumental role that the Jewish community in general (and Jewish women in particular) plays in the colonial discourse of the period becomes apparent in the text. The brief narrative recounts Sultana Cohén's ill-fated love for General Prim, the leader of the Spanish forces during the 1859 war. When the Spanish troops leave Tétouan, an infatuated Sultana Cohén follows the troops led by Prim; the text suggests that she drowns herself in a river. Vega's piece evokes past legends of ill-fated love between Christian men and Jewish women, from the well-known story of Alfonso VII and "la fermosa" Raquel (first narrated by King Sancho IV of Castile to his son Fernando in *Castigos e documentos para bien vivir*, a document from the late twelfth century, later fictionalized by Lope de Vega in *Las paces de los reyes y judía de Toledo* in 1617) to Gustavo Adolfo Bécquer's "La rosa de la pasión." These are stories of doomed interfaith love that end unequivocally with the Jewish woman's death, whether she had desired to convert to Christianity or not.[14]

These texts are worth mentioning because Vega works within a specific tradition that had evolved since the Middle Ages, one that in the particular context of Spanish colonial rule in Morocco in the 1930s serves him for transporting the Jewish community to a remote past, accessible only through a strongly gendered and colonial nostalgia. Gold has argued that in nineteenth-century literature, Jews—who were for the most part absent from Spanish society—do appear in literary texts as "always elsewhere, territorially and temporally" ("Illustrated Histories," 93). In Vega's prose, nineteenth-century Tétouan becomes a distant and exotic past, appropriate for Sultana Cohén's story. At the end, all that is left is the ghostly memory of her "itinerary," which has now become the blueprint for a leisurely tour of Tétouan as it was in the 1930s, but where the Jewish community is no longer present.

In "Itinerario lírico," published in a Falangist magazine, and in the reactionary discourse of the period, Morocco is the location where a Spanish-Muslim brotherhood, although always under Spanish control, materializes. Moroccan Jews stood in the way of that brotherhood and had to conveniently vanish from the Protectorate. Aimed at a conservative, middle-class audience, *Vértice* appeared in Barcelona between 1937 and 1946, in Spanish, with summaries in French, German, Italian, and

English. The magazine was the Falange's most significant publication (others were *Y*, *Revista para la mujer*, *Fotos*, and *La ametralladora* [Machine gun]), and possibly the most important magazine among the Nationalist publications. Although the influence of the early twentieth-century avant-garde remains evident in the magazine's visual elements (including cover images, photographs, and graphics), its artistic virtues do not disguise its ultimate purpose: propaganda.[15]

The issue in which Sultana Cohén's story appears features the title *En Marruecos* (In Morocco) at the bottom of the cover, with the image of a cone-shaped, veiled face in the center (Figure 3). Only the woman's serious but alluring eyes are visible. A small Star of David is set inconspicuously on top of the first "e" in *Vértice*, taking the place of the accent. The woman's veiled face suggests seduction and mystery, while the geometrical shape of the veil conveys the avant-garde influences of the journal. The cover image also reveals the gendered nature of this propagandistic representation of Morocco. With the exception of Sultana Cohén's story, the remaining articles and photographs that center on Morocco in the issue feature men: Moroccan and Spanish soldiers. Women are invisible in Spanish Morocco unless they are confined to a remote and romanticized past.

Communicating the goals of the Spanish presence in Morocco is a thorny endeavor. The realities of Spanish rule in Morocco clash with the lofty rhetoric of ancestral fraternity that unifies both nations, as Martin-Márquez explains: "While a horrifically violent colonial discourse and practice was transferred from the protectorate to the peninsula over the course of the 1930s, Spanish texts set in North Africa during this period became suffused instead with a dreamy Orientalism that exalted and eroticized fraternal relationships between Spaniards and Moroccans" (*Disorientations*, 206).[16] As the Civil War progressed and the virulent anti-Semitism in Nazi Germany intensified, the Jewish communities in Morocco, formerly represented as the victims of Muslim violence during the 1859 intervention and later in the Rif War, would soon join Spain's list of (new) ancestral enemies.

The August 1938 issue of *Vértice* as a whole—and Vega's text specifically—reveals the transformation of Moroccan and Jewish female subjects into static figures that justify Spanish colonial rule and, at the same time, the promotion of the "crusade" against Republicans,

Figure 3. Cover of *Vértice*, August 1938. Designed by Antonio Lara de Gavilán ("Tono"). Private Collection.

Jews, and atheists. Although the ideological goals of the magazine are unequivocal, the contradictory and shifting roles that Muslims and Jews will play in its rhetoric will become apparent with a close analysis of Vega's text, which clearly displays the "dreamy Orientalism" that Martin-Márquez mentions.[17]

The articles as well as the extensive use of photography in the magazine aim to document Morocco's voluntary collaboration in the war: the tone of the writings is celebratory and fraternal. The photo essays underline the idea that Moroccan collaboration was the result of neither coercion nor economic incentives. The images show Moroccan and Spanish soldiers participating together in military parades. Photographs of the secretary of foreign affairs, Ramón Serrano Suñer (whose outspoken anti-Semitism is mentioned in Chapter 3) and Colonel Juan Beigbeder (who in 1937 became the high commissioner of the Protectorate) greeting the troops and the local leadership also appear in the issue. A photo essay titled "Moros en la guerra" (Moors at war) shows Moroccan men drinking tea and sharing their hookahs with Spanish soldiers. Images of men in battle are also present, although devoid of violence.

The magazine also includes a "conversation" between Serrano Suñer and Dionisio Ridruejo (a regular *Vértice* contributor). Nothing in the text is surprising; the same colonial rhetoric about the Spanish-Moroccan brotherhood appears over and over. Although coercion, terror, economic incentives, and illusory promises of independence explain the presence of Moroccan mercenaries in the Nationalist army, the idea that comes across in the essay is that a universal destiny of brotherhood brought the groups together. Francisco Franco himself is called a "Moor" in the text, a tremendous contradiction considering that he represented himself as the divinely chosen leader of a crusade. Catholics and Muslims are presented as unified by their religious devotion, turning the nonbelievers (Republicans) into their greatest antagonist. Religion, as Ridruejo's text reveals, unites the Moroccan and the Spanish people, and Franco's "semidivinity" made this possible: "Franco is a religious myth, Franco is semidivine. His blessed appearance is awaited, and in all mosques of Islam people pray for the man who has chartered ships for pilgrimages to Mecca. His portrait has made its way to these sacred grounds, and when people talk about him, they refer to him as 'The Sun of Morocco.'" The manipulation of symbols of division and hatred from the past into symbols of unity becomes particularly blatant when the author invokes the figure of Santiago Matamoros, the saint usually associated with killing Moors during the Reconquista, often artistically rendered in the act of slaughtering the Moorish enemy. In this text, the Moor-slayer performs a new miracle: Catholics and Muslims are no longer enemies but brothers.[18] Ridruejo writes: "Like a miracle that Santiago himself made possible—who after being a warrior was again an apostle—the once hostile flags of the crescent moon mix, and with such loyalty, with the banners of the cross, with the arrows that came to Granada, with Clavijo's insignia, and with the banners of Lepanto. Ramón Serrano Suñer has witnessed the indisputable evidence of a fissure in history in Morocco, and now he travels up to Santiago to proclaim this at the apostle's feet." Depicting the Moor-slaying patron saint of Spain as now actually performing the miracle of engendering Catholic-Muslim brotherhood allows for a sort of pseudosyncretism in which Christians remain in a position of superiority (after all, the saint was the one who performed the miracle). The articles and photographs provide a message that, given the historical context, is hardly surprising: Spanish rule in Morocco and the participation of Moroccan soldiers in the Civil War are a given, a natural consequence of an ancestral union between the two nations, a colonial union in which Spain, of course, always kept the upper hand. The role that Moroccan Jews play in this representation of Morocco becomes apparent in Vega's "Itinerario lírico de Sultana Cohén."

Vega begins by setting the story at the end of the African war in 1860. In Vega's idiosyncratic version of this chapter of Spanish-Moroccan history, General Prim becomes a treacherous leader of a Masonic conspiracy under British leadership, ultimately weakening Spanish rule in Africa. Despite his treason, the young Jewish woman falls fatally in love with him and follows him to her death. Although the text could easily be dismissed as a sentimental and superficial version of history, it reveals the specific ideological program that *Vértice* disseminated: Freemasons and Jews are conspiring traitors.

The 1859 intervention supposedly saved Moroccan Jews from their Muslim countrymen, but the Moroccan-Spanish brotherhood that marks colonial rhetoric in the 1930s, in addition to a surge of anti-

Semitism that resulted from Franco's alliance with the axis, leaves no room for Jews in Morocco. Thus, what remains after Sultana's unrequited love for General Prim is the more successful (love) story of Spanish-Moroccan brotherhood. Sultana Cohén—and, by extension, the Jews of Morocco—leaves behind a nostalgic, bittersweet memory that will not stand in the way of Spanish-Moroccan fraternity. The last part of Vega's story is a precise description of the road Sultana Cohén takes as she follows the Spanish troops' withdrawal. This is her "itinerary," which now has become nothing but a stroll through the city. "It is recommended," Vega writes, "that all those who come to Tétouan for the first time follow the same path that every afternoon the little girl from Oran took during the first occupation."[19]

Vega's story of unrequited love displays the deep inner workings of colonialism and gender as well as a nostalgic vision of an idealized past that in this particular context echoes the *cursilería* that Noël Valis has traced in Spanish culture from the nineteenth into the twentieth century.[20] In Valis's understanding of the term, "Itinerario lírico de Sultana Cohén" is *cursi* because of its over-the-top sentimentality and exceedingly baroque prose. The actual "lyrical itinerary" through Tétouan, following Sultana Cohén's ghostly traces, ends up forming "a phantom topography of desire" (*The Culture of Cursilería*, 244). Even though Vega's text appeared during the Civil War, it anticipates the kind of rhetoric that the Francoist regime would disseminate. As Valis observes, "behind the shield of 'National Catholicism,' a façade of national, political, and religious unity, Francoism defensively drew up barriers against both the outside world and internal dissent, stressing Spain's exceptionality and uniqueness. Ironically, the result was often far less grandiose and much more banal, indeed cursi, than intended, as a warped and retrograde, Victorian-style mentality suffocatingly took over" (5). I emphasize the cursilería of Vega's text because in "Itinerario lírico de Sultana Cohén" the author situates Moroccan Jews in the past, only accessible through a *cursi* form of nostalgia.

Even though the historical events Vega describes precede the publication date of "Itinerario lírico" by roughly seventy years, his representation of the Jewish woman, along with the kind of cultural stereotypes he evokes in the text, leaves the impression that Sultana Cohén's Tétouan belongs to a remote and distant past. Sultana Cohén is an ornament in the beginning of the text, and she will be the shadow of an ornament by its end. Vega's making her the "ornament of the blue Jewish quarter" is not surprising. The Orientalist and cursi descriptions are accompanied with a nostalgic perception of Sepharad, which, as discussed in earlier chapters, remains common in contemporary Spain: "Sultana Cohén was the daughter of a goldsmith, and her family was from Oran. The words of a childish and hesitant Spanish sounded in her throat, and with sad eyes she gazed at the limited landscape of the mellah" ("Itinerario lírico"). Vega's discourse espouses the commonplace that all Sephardic Jews speak an archaic form of Spanish, unchanged despite exile and displacement.

The portrayal of Sultana Cohén also emphasizes her innocence and helplessness. The description of her use of Spanish as "childish and hesitant" infantilizes her, underlining the idea that Moroccan Jews, and Jewish women in particular, are at the mercy of their Islamic enemies and in need of the protection of Spanish colonial power. The Spanish invaders therefore become the welcome saviors: the Jews of Tétouan, who meet in the home of Sultana's father, want the war to continue so that the Spanish can free them from the Muslim oppressors, "becoming a council of good Hispanism [*buena hispanidad*] around a large table situated in the center of a patio covered with red tiles." The author's reference to the *buena hispanida* of Tétouan's Jews is no coincidence. Because they display this buena hispanidad, the Sephardim from Tétouan become less Jewish and more Spanish, but never Spanish enough: Spanish philo-Sephardism in the early twentieth century did not preclude anti-Semitism. Only those Jews who were descendants of those who once shared the Iberian Peninsula with Christians and Arabs were considered to be worthy allies for Spain: the rhetoric of the period shows that a prolonged stay in Spain "purified" the Sephardim, differentiating them from other Jews.[21] The "superiority" of the Sephardim invoked in the 1940s corresponds to the notion of hispanidad that also appears in Vega's text.

General Prim, leading the troops in the 1859 war, cannot be a hero for Vega: he was a progressive leader in the nineteenth century, a protagonist of the Glorious Revolution that aimed to end Queen Isabella II's conservative rule. His legacy is therefore at odds with the kind of reactionary propaganda that *Vértice* propagated. By making him a Freemason, Vega turns Prim into a traitor. Evidence suggests that Prim might very well have been a Mason, but proving this is not relevant in the context of Vega's story. Rather, considering that the text was published in 1938, the general's alleged freemasonry links the love story between Sultana Cohén and General Prim with the "Judeo-Masonic-Bolshevist conspiracy."[22] During the Second Republic and earlier years of the Francoist dictatorship, this so-called conspiracy "enabled the various right-wing groups to focus their attention on a group of imaginary enemies and served as the unifying agent that held them together" (Rohr, *The Spanish Right and the Jews*, 38). Bearing in mind that *Vértice* was, after all, a publication of the Falange, the General's freemasonry immediately signals that he is the enemy and that Sultana Cohén, despite her sweet grace, falls for one of her kind: a traitor.

The protagonist of Vega's text does not differ much from the representations of Jewish women that appear in Pedro Antonio de Alarcón's neo-Catholic writings on Morocco. Martin-Márquez points out that Alarcón, in his *Diario de un testigo de la guerra y de África*, argues that "qualities that are repulsive in Jewish men are the opposite in the women, for 'in women weakness is always enchanting and cowardice is attractive'" (*Disorientations*, 111). As a matter of fact, Alarcón appears briefly in Vega's story, when Sultana encounters him in Tétouan; coincidentally, he is waiting for "the arrival of another Hebrew girl" ("Itinerario lírico"). The text suggests that Jewish women are meek, naive, and, as earlier texts also imply, always ready to give up tradition and faith for the love of a Catholic Spaniard. This certainly seems to be the case for Sultana Cohén; the general's mere appearance enchants her: "General Prim comes by the Jewish quarter, on his way to the Alcazaba. . . . Sultana shivers like a shrub shaken in the strong wind, and her gaze tangles in the beard of the Spanish general." Vega's baroque intertwining of the woman's gaze with the general's beard and his description of her shivering like shrubbery in the wind are unashamedly cursi and underline the woman's passivity and vulnerability.

Sultana Cohén's infatuation with the general makes her realize that she actually yearns to be a Christian, a desire that emulates anti-Semitic tales of earlier periods, such as Lope de Vega's play *Las paces de los reyes y judía de Toledo* and Bécquer's legends. As Sultana Cohén gazes at the sky, she reflects: "Oh, little Jewish star, . . . who could make you a Christian!" A reference to a star also appears in Bécquer's legend, "The Passion Flower," a tale in which Sara Levi, the most beautiful Jewish woman in Toledo, falls in love with a Christian and is crucified by her own father in a morbid reenactment of Christ's passion and martyrdom. In Bécquer's legend the strikingly beautiful woman whose eyes shine like "a star in the night sky" ("La rosa de la pasión," n.p.) finds salvation and redemption through the Christian man she loves. In both texts Jewish women fall for gentile men, and both women are semantically and thematically linked with a star: Sultana Cohén gazes at the night sky and identifies with the star, the "estrellita judía," and yearns to be a Christian; Sara Levi's eyes shine like a star in the night; she will eventually find salvation through the Christian man she loves.

In Vega's piece, the love story between Jewish woman and Christian man displays nostalgia for an Orientalized past and simultaneously erases the woman from the Moroccan scenery. Even for the Jews of Tétouan, the Spanish withdrawal is to be blamed on conspiring Freemasons, such as Prim: "The Spaniards are leaving! The Queen has sold Tétouan to the Emperor! It was not the Queen! ("Itinerario lírico").[23]

Although Prim's responsibility for the military disappointment in Morocco is clear in Vega's text, the reference to Sultana Cohén's suicide is veiled. The clearest hint that Sultana might intend to drown herself for love is her combing her hair before leaving her home to follow the withdrawing Spanish troops: "The girl from Oran combs her locks for the last time, paying homage to the gallant beard." As the general leaves, she follows him all the way to a bridge, where she admires him one last time: "Sultana follows the riders and Spanish infantry, dressed the color of pomegranates, and by the bridge the river speaks to her with its music. She stops by the Jewish stream, holding on to her heart: 'General Don Juan Prim has a gallant beard.'" An actual union between the Jewish woman and the Spanish man (treacherous as he might have been) is unthinkable. The two characters never even get close enough to touch. This love story is not only cast in a remote past: its fulfillment was never an option to begin with. Daniela Flesler recognizes a comparable trend in a very different context. In her analysis of the representation of love affairs between immigrant men and Spanish women in contemporary Spanish film and fiction, the romance always fails as well: "Even though these texts strive to show positive images of immigrants, they reveal, through failed romance plots, a profound anxiety about racial/cultural contagion and miscegenation" (*The Return of the Moor*, 131). The kind of anxieties about race and culture that this failed romance plot reveals are apparent at the end of Vega's text.

The text breaks after "General Don Juan Prim has a gallant beard," thereafter becoming a brief pseudoethnographic description of everyday life in the Moroccan city. The traces of Sultana Cohén's unrequited love for the general turn into a site for tourists: "Sultana Cohén's shoes from Tafilete leave a romantic trace for Moroccan tourism" ("Itinerario lírico"). At the end of the text, Vega returns to "the Tétouan of Prim and Sultana, graceful, lyrical, immutable." The love story, and with it the Jewish woman's presence, is only a pretext for what really is the "love story" between Morocco and Spain: "And with joy the Moroccan and the Spanish people, who understand and love each other, unite in one and the same glorious embassy." In this representation of the Spanish-Moroccan fraternal union, the Jewish woman (who for love yearned to become a Christian) is merely ornamental, a trite image of the past. Vega thereby attempts to elide the conflict between Spanish philo-Sephardic discourse and the discourse of the Moroccan-Spanish brotherhood. A close reading of the text reveals that colonialism ultimately connects the two discourses written during the Civil War and its immediate aftermath. Vázquez's 1976 novel and Benlyazid's film, which will be discussed in the next section, allow us to examine more specifically the interactions (and their meaning) among the three cultures in Tangier. Benlyazid's film version of Vázquez's novel displays the colonial tensions that frame that coexistence as well as the consequences of colonialism that persist in the contemporary relations between Spain and Morocco.

Tangier's Wretched Life

Ángel Vázquez (Tangier, 1929–Madrid, 1980) grew up in Tangier as the son of an abusive father who would soon after his birth leave his mother, Mariquita Molina (who appears as a character in *La vida perra de Juanita Narboni*). A self-taught writer who was exposed to Tangier's cultural effervescence and its diverse population at an early age, he received the prestigious Planeta award in 1962 for his novel *Se enciende y se apaga una luz* (A light turns on and off), after having already published short stories and the novella *El cuarto de los niños* (The children's room, 1956). In 1964, he published *Fiesta para una mujer sola* (Celebration for a lonely woman), which, along with his short stories, has been recently reissued, as has *La vida perra de Juanita Narboni*.[24] Vázquez, however, remains marginal in the Spanish literary canon, despite the reprinting of several of his works, Benlyazid's film, and words of praise from none other than Juan Goytisolo himself, who has repeatedly listed Vázquez as an unfairly forgotten author.[25]

Not unlike Goytisolo, Vázquez was a complicated and irreverent personality, as Trueba notes in her introduction to the Cátedra edition of *La vida perra de Juanita Narboni*. Vázquez described himself as "self-taught, polyglot, classless, and a lonely alcoholic, . . . 'a giant queen' . . . with no faith in God, selfish and no confidence in myself. Homosexual, alcoholic, drugged, kleptomaniac" (quoted in introduction to *La vida perra de Juanita Narboni*, 17). Some of these attributes could also apply to Vázquez's most memorable character, Juanita Narboni.

Her "wretched life" spans from 1914, when she is still a young child (even though her actual age is not mentioned) to the 1970s, when, in a decolonized Morocco, Juanita slowly descends into a maddened solitude. But more than the plot, the main character's frenzied, abrasive, disenchanted, irreverent, yet at the same time hilarious, narrative voice is what makes this novel so interesting and even indispensable for understanding the Spanish-Moroccan relationship and the Jewish community of Tangier in the twentieth century.

Tangier and the surrounding region had suffered conquests by the Phoenicians, Romans, Visigoths, Arabs, Portuguese, and British. After the Anglo-Moroccan agreement of 1856, Tangier became the diplomatic capital of Morocco. Representatives of France, Spain, and Britain ratified Tangier's international status in 1924, which was, however, interrupted by the French capitulation in 1940. Taking advantage of France's weakness, Spanish Nationalist troops marched into Tangier, and the city formally became part of the Spanish Protectorate in 1941. During these years, and as long as the alliance with the Axis lasted, Spain hung on to unfulfilled German promises that it would be given increasing colonial control over North Africa. Spanish troops were forced to withdraw from Tangier shortly after the Allied victory.

In the late 1930s and early 1940s, the Jewish community numbered between 12,000 and 14,000, including the 2,000 refugees from Eastern Europe who had begun arriving in the 1930s and continued throughout the 1940s. Even though these are considered to be the "golden days" of Tangier, the Spanish Civil War and World War II would have a dramatic impact on the city's diverse population. Repression in Morocco against Republican sympathizers became fierce once Tangier was incorporated into the Protectorate; at the same time, a steady flow of Jewish refugees with stories not altogether different from Antonio Muñoz Molina's fictional Isaac Salama (discussed in Chapter 1) continued to arrive in the North African city. Vázquez worked for the Holländer family, who were, like the fictional Salamas, Hungarian Jews who had escaped to Tangier with Ángel Sanz Briz's help.[26]

In a brief preface to his novel, Vázquez discusses his use of *yaquetía* (or Haketia), a fusion of Spanish, Hebrew, and Arabic that up to the mid-twentieth century was spoken mostly in Tangier, mainly by the Sephardic population. Juanita Narboni is not Sephardic (her mother is Andalusian; her father, a British citizen from Gibraltar), but she and her circle of mainly female friends from Tangier express themselves in a sort of lingua franca that in any case would come very close to Haketia. Vázquez describes the unique language spoken in international Tangier as "old Castilian mixed with Hebrew, sprinkled with Arabic, French, and Portuguese" (*La vida perra de Juanita Narboni*, 119). In the novel the language becomes, as the author notes, a "memory language" (*lenguaje recuerdo*) (119). Even though the author claims that this vernacular, spoken mainly by women in Tangier, is both popular and authentic, the word *recuerdo* strongly hints at the author's reconstruction of memory (and language) in the text. In other words, rather than taking the characters' use of Haketia for granted as a "popular" and therefore "authentic" portrayal of life in Tangier, Vázquez's text consciously recreates a lifestyle and a period that, like Juanita Narboni's life, is vanishing in the wind.

In addition to telling Juanita's story, the novel portrays the life of the author's mother and her circle. Many historical characters appear in the text, along with historical anecdotes characteristic of Tangier's international glamour and worldliness in the 1930s and 1940s. With the conscious re-creation of a "memory language," the novel displays how individuals in Tangier (whether Jewish, Muslim, or Catholic; male or female; gay, straight, or bisexual; sane or mad) clash with stereotypes and crumbling representations of otherness. Thus, the novel defies any notion of a fixed identity, a concept absolutely crucial for maintaining and justifying Spanish colonial rule over Tangier and the Protectorate as a whole.

According to Juan Goytisolo, the novel is impossible to categorize: it does not correspond to any preexisting theoretical scheme and cannot be assigned to the specific national context of the twentieth-century Spanish novel.[27] Goytisolo's *Don Julián* also takes place in Tangier, and it was the author's stay in the Moroccan city that partly inspired his novel, as he recalls in *Disidencias*: "It is hard to live in a city like Tangier, facing the nearby presence of the Spanish coast, without evoking the legendary figure of Don Julián and dreaming of a grandiose 'treason,' like his. I was detached from the official values of the country to such an extent that the idea of my country's profanation, its symbolic destruction, was with me night and day" (quoted in Gould Levine, introduction to *Reivindicación del conde don Julián*, 15).

Although Goytisolo's textual and aesthetic strategies in *Don Julián* demolish "the myths and institutions of sacred Spain" (introduction to *Reivindicación*, 62) and even the Spanish language itself, Vázquez speaks from a location literally and figuratively marginal to the "harsh homeland, the falsest, most miserable imaginable" (Goytisolo, *Count Julian*, 3) that Goytisolo's prose tears apart in his novel. *Count Julian* emerges from what Goytisolo calls the "posthumous or involuntary participation" (304–305) of authors he admires, such as Américo Castro and Guillermo Cabrera Infante, and of others he despises. The only woman in his list is Teresa de Ávila. Vázquez, however, was an avid reader of women authors, particularly Teresa de la Parra, Lydia Cabrera, and Mercè Rodoreda, as well as—and these might be his strongest influences—Katherine Mansfield and Virginia Woolf (see Trueba, introduction to *La vida perra de Juanita Narboni*, 25). Although the differences and affinities between Vázquez and Goytisolo could be the subject of a much longer and quite different analysis, the following discussion will focus on the crucial roles that female protagonists play in *La vida perra de Juanita Narboni* and the influence of women writers on Ángel Vázquez.

The "memory language" in the novel is spoken by women and among women; in the preface to *La vida perra de Juanita Narboni*, Vázquez mentions that he writes emulating "my mother and her group of friends, Jewish and Christian" (120). They are the ones who spoke the language that Benlyazid reproduces in her film version. Although Vázquez suggests that his language reflects women's lives in Tangier, the characters by no means reflect the kind of "ventriloquism" that marks Vega's representations of Muslim and Jewish women. Juanita Narboni has nothing to do with the submissive Sultana Cohén or the Jewish women who appear in Pedro Antonio de Alarcón's texts. Juanita is a contradictory, bigoted, and sexually repressed character; she simultaneously voices the most archaic forms of patriarchy, her own sexual repression, and her desire for liberation.[28]

Discussing her sister's and her own reputation in Tangier, Juanita first claims that they are deeply respected but in the same breath confesses, crudely, as she oftentimes does, that this is not true: "We are the *señoritas* Narboni. And the whole world respects us because we don't owe anything to anyone and because we can walk in these streets with our heads up high. We walk on a straight path. At least I do. Oh, what a load of shit. We all know what they say behind our backs" (*La vida perra de Juanita Narboni*, 153). Her comments about her Muslim servant, Hamruch, are just as incongruous; Juanita never stops expressing her love, her need, and her contempt for Hamruch in an amalgam of complex sentiments: "And here I am, cleaning up father's shit and taking care of him in his final moments, with that pathetic Hamruch, with that blessed woman, she's been more of a sister to me than anyone, like a daughter, and like a mother for all of us" (326).

Juanita's constant thoughts about desire and sexual repression are particularly apparent early in the novel. Together with her sister and a few friends, Juanita visits a movie theater, but while the other women manage to sit together, Juanita can only get a seat next to a Moroccan man. His virile presence immediately absorbs her: "A man he is, and what a man! What a beast! He has touched my hand, and his skin feels as though he has scales" (135). She cannot stop looking at him, thinking of him, even smelling him: "when I look at him, I look at

him because I do not want to, because if I really wanted to look . . ."
(136). She feels attracted to the man but at the same time represses
her desire, forcing her own thoughts (and, consequently, her repressed
desire) to move elsewhere: "And I do not even want to look you in the
face. I sense it, that face, that face made of sea. How mysterious poor
people are! The sea is blue! That is enough for me" (136).

Much more can be said—and has been written—about Juanita's
voice, whose complexity Benlyazid's film—with Bellod's screenplay,
Mariola Fuentes's performance, and the film's setting in Tangier—
faithfully depicts. The film *La vida perra de Juanita Narboni* includes
a number of brief yet telling scenes that reveal the director's engagement with women's issues in her native Morocco, her commitment
to feminism and multiculturalism, and her reflection on the current
postcolonial relationship between Spain and Morocco.

The Moroccan director received the novel from the author himself
in the 1970s. Vázquez's portrayal of Tangier through Juanita Narboni's
"wretched life" so moved Benlyazid that, once the MEDEA program
provided her with necessary funds, the director no longer hesitated to
film the novel that for her "made the Tangier of my childhood come
alive" (Benlyazid, "El cine dirigido por mujeres," 224).[29] The director
herself considers Juanita's life to be mirror of life in Tangier: "Juanita
becomes Tangier's mirror. A city of parties and dances matches her
youth, with the glitter of the city's golden age. An abandoned and forgotten city, feeding only on memories, matches her old age."[30]

In the few scenes Benlyazid adds to the otherwise very faithful film
adaptation of the novel, it becomes clear that the Moroccan filmmaker's version also makes a statement about the postcolonial relationship between Spain and Morocco and the ways in which conflicts
among Christianity, Islam, and Judaism influence women's lives in Morocco. The director herself describes her oeuvre—which also includes
the acclaimed *A Door to the Sky* (1989) and *Women's Wiles* (1999),
which is based on an Andalusian tale—in the following terms: "Simply
said, I work on time, memory, the women's universe, and the citizen's
commitment, and I also leave space for my multicultural imaginary"
(Benlyazid, "El cine dirigido por mujeres," 224). The specific issue of
multiculturalism is important in Benlyazid's adaptation: the film shows
that Tangier's multicultural population and international status might

provide an alternative to constructions of "otherness" (both Muslim and Jewish) that have marked the Spanish-Moroccan relationship. Colonial rule, however, radically interrupts and undermines this alternative vision.

Although Vega's texts display the construction of gendered, colonial subjects as static figures that are instrumental in Spanish colonialism in Morocco, Benlyazid's film challenges the gendered colonial hierarchies, very much in place in the "paradise" of Tangier in the 1930s and 1940s, by displaying the domestic, intimate sphere within which most of its plot takes place.[31] Benlyazid's film and, in particular, the depiction of Juanita Narboni and her relationships with the two women who are closest to her, her Sephardic friend, Esther (Nabila Baraka), and her Muslim maid, Hamruch (Salima Benmoumen), reveals that understanding intimate relationships within a domestic sphere can be as instructive about coloniality and postcoloniality as any study of the battles that have taken place between Morocco and Spain.

The previous section has shown how a Jewish woman becomes an ornament within a romanticized and cursi version of the Moroccan past that bears no relationship to the Spanish-Moroccan relationship in 1938, whereas Benlyazid's film highlights Tangier's multiculturalism while also underscoring a yet unresolved colonial past. With her film version the director establishes a connection between Tangier's diverse history as a "multicultural fact" and a "multicultural project." Ella Shohat and Robert Stam differentiate between these two categories in the following terms: the multicultural fact "references the obvious cultural heterogeneity of most of the world," while the multicultural project "entails a profound restructuring of the ways knowledge is produced through the distribution of cultural resources and power" (*Multiculturalism, Postcoloniality, and Transnational Media*, 7). According to Shohat and Stam, "a radical version" of the multicultural project "calls for reenvisioning world history and contemporary social life from a decolonizing and antiracist perspective" (7). Thus, the added scenes in Benlyazid's film do not represent the idealization of a harmonious convivencia in Tangier from a woman's perspective. Rather, they reveal how important an essentialized other (whether Jewish or Muslim) has been in the history of Spanish colonialism in Morocco and how decolonization is really only possible once this same discourse is dismantled.

The first telling sequence that the Moroccan filmmaker adds takes place after the memorial service for Juanita's mother. Juanita hosts the wake, and her mother's Catholic friends are saying the rosary. A song in Arabic interrupts the women's prayer, a song that takes Juanita back to an event that occurred a few days before her mother's death, when the clumsy Juanita stumbled on the way to the cinema, breaking the heel of her shoe. A crazed-looking old beggar laughs at her and sings in Arabic "a life is going to fall," as if presaging her mother's death. After her guests dutifully say the rosary, Juanita is visibly shaken when she thinks she is hearing the beggar's voice singing the same melody. Startled, Juanita asks who is singing. Juanita's sister, Helena, tells her that the voice belongs to Hamruch, even though it sounds like the same voice that Juanita heard after she stumbled and fell earlier. Juanita screams at the absent Hamruch, desperately trying to maintain her authority over the servant, who moments earlier, after Juanita reprimanded her for serving the tea at the wrong time, had already taunted her employer, saying that she was crazy and that she needed a husband. At this point, a certain tension between the two women becomes evident, a tension that at the same time cannot be dissociated from the great need Juanita has for Hamruch. The film establishes that both women are unequally and yet permanently bound to one another.

After Juanita's guests leave to go shopping, Juanita's Sephardic friend, Esther, arrives; instead of accepting Juanita's tea and pastries, Esther pulls a bottle of liquor out of her purse. The women quickly move to the patio, where they will share the bottle and gossip about life in Tangier and about their sisters. As usual, Juanita complains about her sister's modernity, admiring and censuring Helena's liberation from tradition. Eventually, the camera shifts briefly to Hamruch. She sits on the floor in a corner of the patio, cleaning vegetables. Although she remains present throughout the sequence and is privy to the women's conversation, they do not include her. When Esther asks Juanita to sing, she chooses a traditional Andalusian song, and the singing is interrupted again with a brief shot of Hamruch. Esther now asks Juanita to sing something more cheerful, and both women break into "El paipero," a traditional Sephardic song.

The camera travels again to focus on Hamruch, who sits with a sullen expression behind a low wall that divides the patio and partially covers her. It only becomes clear now how close Hamruch has been sitting to the two other women: they have shared the space all along, but in the first part of the sequence Esther and Juanita are barely aware of Hamruch's presence. For a brief instant the three women share the same frame, but Hamruch remains at the margin until the song is over and Juanita, suddenly noticing her servant's presence, asks her: "Hamruch, why the long face?" Hamruch, showing her resentment toward Juanita, who had scolded her earlier, says: "You sing, I don't." To which Juanita responds: "Do you want to drink with us? Just a little sip?" Hamruch replies: "Don't be silly." At this point an obviously tipsy Juanita gets up and insists that Hamruch should now dance with her. She begins shaking her hips in what looks like a clumsy parody of traditional Moroccan dance and shouts out, "habibi, habibi [my love, my love]." But when they are joined by Esther, who unlike Juanita does know the words to a traditional northern Moroccan song, the expression on Hamruch's face changes: they both know the lyrics of the song and clap their hands. It is clear that Esther, the Jewish woman, has become a liaison between the other two. Now the three women are dancing and singing together on Juanita's patio, suggesting that this all-female space has the potential to become liberating, but only up to a certain point. The relation between gender and space is significant, as it is in the director's first film, *A Door to the Sky*, which as Shohat and Stam suggest, "offers a positive gloss on the notion of an all-female space, counterposing Islamic feminism to orientalist fantasies" of the harem (*Unthinking Eurocentrism*, 165).[32] Although the songs in Spanish, Judeo-Spanish, and Moroccan Arabic underline Tangier's tricultural heritage, the gendered nature of the space where the songs are performed, as well as the fact that this scene will be followed by the Spanish invasion of Tangier in 1940, reveals that Benlyazid is not portraying an ahistorical form of female convivencia on Juanita's patio, which also becomes history's imaginary patio.

Esther's role as an intermediary between Juanita and Hamruch—a role that Moroccan Jews often played before colonialism and that, with colonization, led to the establishment of new hierarchies and conflicts between the Jewish and Muslim populations—further shows how "history's imaginary patio" becomes a space of nostalgia more than a space of liberation. As Rohr writes, Franco himself depicted Moroccan

Jews not only as allies but also as beneficiaries of Spain's colonial ambitions in North Africa. Emily Benichou and Daniel Schroeter's book on Jewish communities in North Africa, however, reveals that "the Jews did not necessarily 'choose' to identify with Europe. Rather, Europe, in effect, chose them: the imposition of colonialism and modernity on the Maghrib directly led to the ultimate detachment and uprooting of Jews from these societies" (Benichou and Schroeter, *Jewish Culture and Society in North Africa*, 11). Esther simultaneously resists but also accommodates to the traditional role assigned to Jews in colonial North Africa. As she mentions later in the film, Esther feels "Moroccan," differentiating herself from Juanita and her colonial inhibitions. But the film also shows that the three women, Juanita, Hamruch, and Esther, constantly negotiate their forms of identification within a colonial and gendered system, built on fixed and essentialized forms of identity and otherness.

As the scene's montage suggests, historical developments in Tangier radically interrupt the potentially liberating project that had been initiated on Juanita's patio. After a fade-out, a shot of a raw fish on a wooden plate appears on the screen. The words "14 de Junio de 1940" appear on the image. "Ay, I don't like dead fish," sighs Juanita. "It seems as though they look at you with rancor," she adds, while the camera remains fixed on the fish. Before the shot moves up to show Juanita, we hear Hamruch's voice alerting Juanita that Franco's troops are invading Tangier. Throughout the scene, the film's constant allusions to an already vanishing multicultural world remain; as Juanita says to Hamruch: "What is the matter with you? As if you had seen Aixa Kandisha!" The reference to the demonic seductress Aixa Kandisha, a figure from Moroccan folklore, signals Tangier's multiculturalism, which will be threatened with the Spanish invasion of Tangier. Both women move out to the balcony, and when a neighbor confirms that Spanish troops are marching into the streets of Tangier, the camera remains fixed as Juanita and Hamruch look at each other. This sequence represents a radical break with the scene on the patio in which Esther was a liaison between Juanita and Hamruch. Esther's absence now emphasizes that the Francoist invasion of the Moroccan city will radically hinder the liberating possibilities that once seemed within reach. The earlier sequence ends with a symbolic union among women that has the potential to challenge both colonial rule and conflict among the three religions. Juxtaposed with this sequence, the dead fish could symbolize rancor but also atonement. In this sense the singing and dancing on the patio would be a carnival, followed by Lent (when no meat, only fish, is consumed) and atonement. Carnival has thematic importance in the novel: it was during a carnival celebration that Juanita, wearing a Pierrot costume, discovered that her fiancée is homosexual. Juanita's patio was never an ahistorical theater of convivencia.

The relationship between Hamruch and Juanita will remain colonial and hierarchical in spite of how much Juanita needs Hamruch, and yet how little Juanita knows about her servant. This becomes clear at the end of both the novel and the film. In the 1970s, after decolonization, Hamruch stops coming to Juanita's home one day. An aged and decayed Juanita wanders off in a Tangier she no longer recognizes, looking for her faithful servant. Her search is futile: Juanita does not know where Hamruch lives; she does not even know her surname, nor does she know her children's names. No matter how much these two women shared in the forty years they spent together, their relationship remains at the same time profoundly unequal and absolutely indispensable for Juanita's survival. She descends into madness after Hamruch, the sole companion who remained with her through the years, disappears from her life.

This sad ending of Juanita and Hamruch's relationship (and the wretched ending of Juanita's wretched life) further proves that the scene on the patio is only an apparent liberation. Vázquez's novel and Benlyazid's film reveal that three cultures coexisted in Tangier—as they did, centuries earlier, in Spain—but in an unequal manner, shaped by colonialism. By juxtaposing the moment of female solidarity among the three women with the image of the dead fish, Benlyazid reveals the ways in which history itself disrupts those moments in which such a multicultural project (led by women) might have been possible. Benlyazid's camera questions the gendered colonial hierarchies between Spain and Morocco that have constrained the lives of women in the twentieth century and that persist today. Her work critically interrupts the constructions of otherness (and of barbarism) that were indispensable for Spanish colonialism in Morocco and elsewhere. Although the fleeting depiction of the three women dancing and singing together might suggest a coherent and even joyful story of Muslim-Jewish-Christian convivencia and harmony, history (the Spanish invasion of Tangier in 1940) cuts through the scene on the patio, suggesting that it is, more than a space of liberation, a space of nostalgia.

Esther's role as the intermediary further reveals the fissures in the imaginary sense of harmony and wholeness. Not only is Esther absent from the scene, her role is further complicated by her having a Muslim lover. The next scene in which Esther appears takes place in 1965, after Moroccan independence, and long after Helena has left Tangier. In this particular scene, Esther and Juanita attend a traditional Moroccan wedding. The bride is the daughter of Idriss (played by Abdellah Mountassir), an upper-class, French-educated Muslim, who has been Esther's lover for many years. We witness a few scenes from the lavish wedding, in which both Juanita and Esther exchange pleasantries with Idriss's wife, and Esther, once again, dances comfortably and with pleasure with the other Moroccan women while Juanita remains on the side.

After the wedding scene, in one of the few flashbacks in an otherwise linear film, we see a younger-looking Juanita and Esther on the beach.[33] At this point Esther confesses that she has been in love with Idriss since she was fourteen, when they both attended the lycée together. To Juanita's outcry ("But he is a Moor and you're Jewish!"), Esther calmly explains to Juanita: "Our families have been here for centuries. We are not like you, you don't interact with the Moors. In a way, I do feel Moroccan." Esther can do what Juanita cannot: she can feel Moroccan, while the British and Spanish Juanita is unable to do so.[34] Esther, like Juanita's sister, Helena, is sexually liberated. She has taken charge of her desire and control over her body, a choice that Juanita simultaneously envies and censures.

Although Esther may have been liberated enough from colonial inhibitions to engage in a romance with Idriss, the relationship remains clandestine. Esther's departure from Tangier is a consequence of decolonization and also ends the romance. Thus, Esther's relationship with Idriss reveals, as do the relationships that Flesler studies, "a profound anxiety about racial/cultural contagion and miscegenation" (*The Return of the Moor*, 131). Juanita Narboni's wretched life remains completely removed from even the mere possibility of such a romance.

As mentioned earlier, Juanita expresses her desire for the Moroccan man who sits next to her in the movie theater but then immediately censures herself for it. In the film, and after Esther's confession on the beach about her affair with Idriss, Benlyazid uses music to fuse the flashback with the wedding. As Juanita still visibly ponders the juicy piece of information Esther has just given her, a song from the wedding plays, returning the women to 1965. At this point, Esther will inform Juanita that she will spent the night with Idriss, their last night together; she is about to emigrate to Canada with her siblings, leaving Juanita lonelier than ever. She returns to the wedding festivities by herself, with American pop music playing and the guests happily twisting their way into a modernity that has no room for Juanita and her memories.

In Benlyazid's take on Vázquez's novel, Juanita Narboni's Tangier becomes an alternative to violent strife and conflict among the three cultures in the Mediterranean world, comparable to the ways in which convivencia has commonly been perceived. The film, however, goes one step further: the poignant representation of Juanita's solitude and bitterness cannot be divorced from the colonial and condescending attitude she displays toward Moroccans in general and toward her servant, Hamruch, in particular.

It becomes clear that Tangier's "golden era" is neither harmonious nor an example of the tolerance of difference. Indeed, the coexistence of Christians, Jews, and Muslims in Tangier and in the Protectorate as a whole often becomes a projection or mirror image of the nostalgically invoked convivencia on the Spanish shore of the Mediterranean. Américo Castro, whose research established the groundwork for an understanding of how contemporary Spain is the result of interactions among the three cultures in the Iberian Peninsula, examined Judeo-Spanish culture and language early in his career. Samuel Armistead observes that "Morocco must have had a profound effect upon don Américo; his experience in the *mellahs*, in the *juderías*, must have provided him with vivid perceptions and must have set him to thinking of medieval Spain from new and original perspectives. His subsequent re-evaluation of the Spanish Middle Ages should be considered in light of his Moroccan experience" ("Américo Castro in Morocco," 77). Briefly, Armistead argues that what Castro discovered in northern Morocco in 1922–1923 could be the origin of his argument in *España en su historia*.

In an article from 1922, Castro also suggests that the Judeo-Spanish (or Haketia) spoken in Morocco could provide clues about the Spanish spoken in the fifteenth century or, as Castro writes, "in the times of the Catholic monarchs" ("Entre los hebreos marroquíes," 146). That the expelled Jews took their language with them and that the language survived but was also transformed in the different locations of the Sephardic diaspora are well-known facts. The novel and the film, however, add another dimension, suggesting that Spanish North Africa (and the international zone of Tangier) became the displaced and deterritorialized location of convivencia before Moroccan independence. The Protectorate would therefore become history's imaginary waiting room—and history's imaginary patio. The invented fraternity that marks Spanish colonialism in Morocco might also provide further clues for understanding *cainismo*, the fratricidal impulse that such authors as Ana María Matute and Manuel Rivas have depicted in their literary representation of the Spanish Civil War. Only now the brother to be killed might be the "other" brother, from across the Mediterranean, the Jewish or Muslim "brother," a historical construction that was indispensable for the justification of colonialism in Africa. I do not mean to imply that the debates over purity of blood in the sixteenth and seventeenth centuries are merely reiterated in twentieth-century Spanish culture. Rather, close readings of the literary and visual culture that Spanish colonialism in Africa produced should provide new clues about how to understand the cultural imaginaries of representations of the Spanish Civil War and current debates on historical memory. The instrumental roles that Jewish communities and Jewish women in the Protectorate play within this imaginary are therefore not only part of what mapping Jewish Spain today entails, these roles also represent a fundamental part of recovering historical memory of the Spanish Civil War and Francoist repression. The stories of Spanish and Moroccan "brothers" have been told; this chapter has aimed to trace where the "sisters" in these stories have gone.

Five   Touring the Remainders of Sepharad
From Heritage Travel to the
"Ruta Walter Benjamin"

This chapter returns to the opening moment of *Jewish Spain* to consider once again the three plaques at 1 Carrer de Marlet: the original plaque that dates to the early fourteenth century, the plaque with the mistranslation of the original Hebrew that was affixed during a nineteenth-century restoration, and the explanatory sign that was placed on the building in 2007. The three signs show the ways in which perceptions of a Jewish past and present come together in multiple palimpsests, as do Barcelona's former major synagogue Shlomo Ben Adret on 5 Carrer de Marlet, only a few steps from the building with the historical signs, and the structure that today hosts the Casa de l'Espai Call (Centre d'Interpretació del Call), located on the Placeta de Manuel Ribé. This chapter focuses on the multiple meanings of the remainders and ruins of Sepharad that are visible—or that have been made visible—in contemporary Catalonia.[1] The chapter will center on what the recovery of Jewish heritage means for the Jewish quarters in Barcelona and Girona and for sites of exile at the Spanish-French border, mainly the border town of Portbou, where philosopher Walter Benjamin, fleeing from the Nazis and Vichy France, took his life. The inauguration of Dani Karavan's monument "Passages" in 1994 has helped to turn this border town into a memorial to the different forms of exile, displacement, and defeat that came about at the French-Spanish frontier between 1939 and 1945.

Although a leisurely walk through Barcelona's and Girona's small Jewish quarters can also be a tour of the cities' urban palimpsests, specific sites at the border—such as the Museu Memorial de l'Exili (Exile Memorial Museum, or MUME) in La Jonquera and the signposts placed in locations in Portbou—show that the border itself has palimpsestic features.[2] The term "palimpsest" commonly refers to a parchment or vellum from which an earlier text has been erased or scraped to make room for a new inscription; because the remnants of the older text are sometimes still visible, the palimpsest has become a useful image within poststructural and postcolonial theories.[3] Andreas Huyssen argues that a recognition of the palimpsests in urban settings invites a critical reading strategy in which "literary techniques of reading historically, intertextually, constructively, and deconstructively at the same time can be woven into our understanding of urban spaces as lived spaces that shape collective imaginaries" (*Present Pasts*, 7). Thus, this chapter centers not only on the spaces themselves but also on the ways in which they are depicted, transformed, and rewritten in a number of texts that serve to guide tourists and visitors: signposts and historical markers, pamphlets published by museums, and scripts for guided tours that with varying degrees of success have an effect on the forms of memory that these sites evoke.

"Memory is never shaped in a vacuum; the motives of memory are never pure," writes James Young in *The Texture of Memory* (2). Municipal governments, tour operators, and individuals have turned the medieval structures that have remained in place throughout the centuries into walking tours of Catalonia's Jewish past. Their motives range from economic (attracting tourists) to civic (managing the restoration of the city center) and personal (exploring one's ancestry). The Memorial Democràtic, a commission that the Catalan government administers, has taken charge of making the few traces of the exile routes that remain both visible and accessible. The roughly seven-kilometer Ruta Walter Benjamin from Banyuls-sur-Mer (Rousillon) to Portbou (Catalonia), marked with signposts on the French and Spanish sides, is the most famous example. Benjamin's untimely death in Portbou and Karavan's stirring monument have sparked many essays and works of art; two documentary films, Manuel Cussó-Ferrer's *La última frontera* (The last frontier, 1991) and David Mauas's *¿Quién mató a Walter Benjamin?* (Who killed Walter Benjamin?, 2005); and an opera, Brian Ferneyhough's *Shadowtime* (2004).[4]

Although touring a medieval Jewish quarter where shelter, food, and drink are always close by might be a far more popular option than trekking across the Pyrenees, these very different sites (the Barcelona and Girona Calls and the Ruta Walter Benjamin) turn the remote and the recent Jewish past into a specific, present-day experience. As Young suggests, more than sites of collective memory, these are sites where memory becomes *collected* because the different memories that come together are neither homogenous nor consistent. Young explains that he is concerned with "the many discrete memories that are gathered into common memorial spaces and assigned common meaning" (*The Texture of Memory*, xi). He then adds: "If societies remember, it is only insofar as their institutions and rituals organize, shape, even inspire their constituents' memories. For a society's memory cannot exist outside of those people who do the remembering—even if such memory happens to be at the society's bidding, in its name" (xi). The different ruins of Sepharad—whether in the Jewish quarters of Barcelona and Girona or on Jewish escape routes as a whole or in Portbou as a border-crossing site—do not provide a clear and unequivocal vision of the past. Instead, these ruins and the discourse that surrounds them render visible the multiple and often contradictory negotiations of what the past means for different individuals and collectivities.

The connections between these two very different types of sites (restored medieval Jewish quarters and signposted World War II border crossing routes) might seem arbitrary at first or, worse, might appear to reflect the kind of teleological view of history in which both the 1492 expulsion and the Holocaust are connected and part of a uninterrupted narrative. There are three reasons, however, for treating both kinds of site in this chapter: (1) the sites themselves and the texts written about them often evoke the deeply flawed, linear narratives that stubbornly continue to appear and that are critiqued in earlier chapters; (2) despite their having originated in two radically different moments in history, these sites remain the sole traces of a Jewish presence in public spaces in Catalonia; and (3) no matter what period in the past these sites attempt to reconstruct or preserve, they are more instructive about what "Jewish Spain" means for the contemporary heritage traveler or memory tourist than they are about their significance within their respective historical contexts.

Touring Sepharad Today

The distinctions between traveling and tourism have been widely discussed in such fields as anthropology and sociology. The history of tourism in Spain is also very much part of a process of defining a national identity, a process that is both open-ended and uneven. Justin Crumbaugh's *Destination Dictatorship: The Spectacle of Spain's Tourist Boom and the Reinvention of Difference* argues convincingly that tourism needs to be taken seriously in the context of twentieth-century Spanish history and, more specifically, the history of Francoism.[5] The history of state-sponsored tourism in Spain dates back to 1905, when King Alfonso XII signed a decree creating a national commission in charge of attracting foreign visitors to Spain (Afinoguénova and Martí-Olivella, *Spain Is (Still) Different*, xiii). Leisurely travel to Spain preceded the creation of this commission, and it is worth noting that in the nineteenth century journeys to Spain became a literary trope in the work of Romantic writers, among them Washington Irving (*Tales of the Alhambra*, published in 1832) and Prosper Mérimée (in the 1845 novella, *Carmen*). Although Spain's most notable tourism slogan, "Spain Is Different," dates back to 1929, tourism acquired a specific political meaning with the creation of the Ministry of Information and Tourism in 1951, symbolically opening the gates to modernity, to economic development, and to a refiguration of Spanish national identity.[6]

Tourism, in Spain and elsewhere, is anything but static; it shifts according to cultural, economic, and social transformations in both the guest and the host countries. Tourism, as Afinoguenova and Martí-Olivella show, should be understood as being as much about power as it is about national identity. The authors recognize that tourism is "a powerful state-guided force validating the territorial and cultural entity known as 'Spain'" (*Spain Is (Still) Different*, xiv). Thus, studying tourism in Spain is an eye-opening endeavor in relation not only to the history of the Francoist government from the early 1960s to the transitional period but also, as this chapter will show, to the changing meanings of all things Jewish in contemporary Catalonia and contemporary Spain. Memory tourism does not reveal what Jewish Spain once was or is today but what it is envisioned be in the context of the nation's cultural development and promotion.

Possibly the most obvious distinction between tourism and other forms of travel is the opposition between the authentic (travel) and the inauthentic (tourism).[7] Tourism may have been initially understood to function as a "quest for authenticity" (Rojek and Urry, *Touring Cultures*, 11); that is, tourism was to provide a means of escaping the daily routine of work and conventional life—touring unknown grounds would provide a way of finding again one's true subjectivity. The Spanish government's 2011 television advertisements for tourism certainly play on this. Under the rubric of "I need Spain," the ads (filmed by acclaimed director Julio Medem) show young, attractive, and multiethnic individuals and families visiting beautifully shot sites in urban and rural Spain, while a voiceover says that one does not need fast food, GPS, Internet chats, or other technological innovations that have made life easier but at the same time less "authentic." One indeed needs Spain, however, because traveling in Spain will provide visitors with access to real feelings, a communion with the landscape, art, food, and, more than anything, the friendly and fun-loving Spanish people—and, finally, communion with oneself. These recent ads shore up the notion that the contemporary tourist still needs to find herself or himself and that a version of what the "authentic" self or "authentic" experience is will ultimately be what renders any form of leisurely displacement (call it "travel" or "tourism") worthwhile.

Rojek and Urry concede that such locations as Las Vegas reveal that tourist sites "are increasingly using extravagantly inauthentic accessories to attract tourists" (*Touring Cultures*, 11). One does not need to look at the excesses of Las Vegas or Disneyland, however, to grasp that tourism nowadays has often become synonymous with simulacra and inauthenticity. Rather than trying to locate the exact line that divides the so-called authentic from the simulacra, establishing once and for all where traveling ends and tourism begins, we should look instead for other variables that allow us to understand where travel shifts into tourism and why this shift is relevant. This does not mean that visitors who tour the Call in Barcelona or Girona are going to be confronted with nothing more than a miniature Las Vegas or, to use George Ritzer and Allan Liska's term, a "McDisneyization" of Jewish cultural heritage.[8] Rather, tourism oscillates between a quest for the authentic and the perfect simulation that, at least temporarily, fills the gap for an authenticity that can neither be restored nor recreated. Or, to put it in Barbara Kirshenblatt-Gimblett's terms, "tourists travel to actual destinations to experience virtual places (*Destination Culture*, 9). As mentioned earlier, the goal of this chapter is not to explain the intricacies of Jewish life in medieval Barcelona or Girona but to understand what the "heritagization" (as Flesler and Pérez Melgosa call the phenomenon in "Hervás, Convivencia and the Heritagization of Spain's Jewish Past") of these spaces means today in relation to Jewishness. The term refers to the contemporary production of Jewish heritage in Spain as a visible and easily accessible destination.

Ruth Ellen Gruber's *Virtually Jewish* establishes the ways in which Jewish heritage tourism in Europe today in many ways functions "without Jews." Gruber argues that "Jewish culture—or what passes for Jewish culture, or what is perceived or defined as Jewish culture—has become a highly visible component of the popular public domain in countries where Jews themselves are practically invisible" (*Virtually Jewish*, 5). Gruber does not include the Iberian Peninsula in her study, but her argument remains largely relevant for understanding the motivations and effects of the current recovery and marketing of Jewish sites. Barcelona and Girona are, of course, not the only cities in which the reconstruction of the Jewish quarter (or judería) is a thriving and also economically profitable enterprise.

Flesler and Pérez Melgosa recognize an "underlying ambivalence to the enterprise of marketing the Spanish Jewish tradition for the purposes of tourism" ("Marketing Convivencia," 69). The reconstruction of Jewish-heritage Spain partially reflects a trend that has been common in other parts of Europe for the past two decades. In Spain, however, the Jewish population has been absent for more than five centuries, so that all things "virtually Jewish" need to be examined bearing in mind the mass conversions that took place in 1391, the complex forms of identification that are at the heart of what Michael Gerli calls the "ambivalent converso condition," the 1492 expulsion, and the causes and effects of crypto-Judaism. In medieval, early modern, and contemporary Spain, absence and presence can never be absolutes; touring the ruins of Sepharad also means touring the shades of absence in presence and those of presence in absence.

According to Gruber, because these Jewish quarters are more virtual than real, there are problematic consequences for the interaction between different populations, among them the different Jewish communities in Europe. Gruber explains that her terms "virtual Jewish world" and "virtual Jews" derive from the virtual worlds and communities of cyberspace, which "people can enter, move around, and engage in . . . without physically leaving their desks or quitting their 'real world' identities" (*Virtually Jewish*, 21). The problem, as Gruber poses it, is that a "Jewish space" is filled with the perpetuation of what a specific—even desired—"Jewish presence" should look like.[9] Gruber explains that this process takes place when virtual Jews, "perform . . . Jewish culture from an outsider perspective." She then adds: "In doing so, they may take over cultural and other activities that would ordinarily be carried out by Jews. In other cases, they create their own realities that perpetuate an image of Jewish presence" (11). A virtual Jewish space in Barcelona or Girona, however, would undoubtedly speak to different historical circumstances than one in, for example, Berlin or Prague.

In Spain, as Flesler and Pérez Melgosa show, the remainders of a Jewish presence are very few and have undergone radical transformations over the centuries: "In fact, many of these sites act as a wishful fantasy, supposedly showcasing a Jewish quarter that is more virtual than real, since there is not a Jewish population inhabiting it, and most traces of this 'Jewishness' have been systematically transformed or destroyed" ("Marketing Convivencia," 74). These wishful fantasies, whether just whimsical or downright dangerous, perpetuate old stereotypes.

In many ways the promotion of Jewish heritage in Spain today is monopolized by "Caminos de Sefarad," created in 1992 as "a tourist route through a cluster of cities that had had a significant Jewish presence before the 1492 expulsion" (67) that would later become "Red de Juderías de España: Caminos de Sefarad."[10] Flesler and Pérez Melgosa point out that the Jewish quarters that are often exhibited today as spaces of coexistence and racial harmony were actually created to separate and visualize differences between Christians and Jews.[11] An appropriate analogy would be to restore and showcase the Berlin wall as a symbol and site of the tolerant coexistence of capitalism and communism in the second part of the twentieth century.

This is not the only contradiction that is part of the marketing of convivencia for touristic purposes. It also takes place in a vacuum because the (very small) Jewish population in Spain, roughly 40,000 individuals, has for the most part not been involved in the different heritage tourism endeavors. As a matter of fact, it is not the specifically "Jewish" aspect of these restored medieval quarters that makes them so appropriate for the promotion of tourism but rather that they have come to symbolize the period of convivencia, underscoring commendable aspects of Spain's national identity. Flesler and Pérez Melgosa explain that in the marketing of Jewish heritage sites in Spain "the notion of *convivencia*, the presumed peaceful coexistence among Muslims, Jews, and Christians in the Iberian Middle Ages, became the dominant way to understand that period and was promoted as a sign of Spain's intrinsic knowledge of democracy and of its inherent racial and cultural tolerance: a multiculturalism *avant la lettre*" (63). Ironically, an examination of the different medieval sites in Catalonia and the controversies that surround them reveals contentious debates over who owns the (Jewish) past, suggesting that the present is not one of convivencia and tolerance but of conflictive meanings and, at times, the kind of historical (or even ahistorical) hodgepodge displayed in the plaques at 1 Carrer de Marlet.

Barcelona's Call

Although the city is more famous today for its modernist architecture, cuisine, trendy locales, Mediterranean coastline, and world-class soccer team, Barcelona holds an important place in Jewish history. Jewish life in Barcelona dates back to the ninth century. The "Disputation of Barcelona" of 1263 might represent the zenith of the interactions between Jews and Christians because life for the Jews of the Call became increasingly complex after this date. Rabbi Moses ben Nachman, or Nachmanides (who was actually born in Girona) faced convert Pablo Christiani for a theological debate organized by Ramon de Penyafort, King James's confessor. Even though Nachmanides appears to have emerged as the rhetorical victor, members of the Dominican order eventually forced him to leave the Iberian Peninsula.[12]

The Jewish community was attacked and destroyed in 1391, and Jews would remain largely absent from the city until a small number of Jewish migrants arrived in the early twentieth century, mainly from the former Ottoman Empire.[13] Today, both the vestiges of the Call and the Jewish community in Barcelona are relatively small, and yet in the past decade, especially since 1992, when the Red de Juderías/ Caminos de Sefarad was established, Barcelona's Jewish quarter has acquired more importance, especially with regard to heritage tourism. Ben Frank's *A Travel Guide to Jewish Europe*, which dates back to 1992, devotes only one paragraph to the Call, and some of the information he includes is inaccurate: "The main street of the quarter is still called 'Calle del Call' or 'Carrer del Call,' 'the quarter of the kahal.' In Catalan *call* is the equivalent of the Hebrew *kahal*, 'community'" (228). While the speculation that the word *call* comes from *kahal* might seem fitting, most scholars agree that *call* is actually a derivation from the Latin *callis* (street), used as early as the ninth century to refer to the actual street where Jews resided in medieval Catalonia. The more accepted word for "community" was *aljama*.

Today, three initiatives compete for attention in relation to Barcelona's Jewish past. The first is the already mentioned Casa de l'Espai Call, a center for interpretation under the auspices of Museu d'Història de Barcelona (MUHBA), the city's history museum. The second is Associació Call de Barcelona, led by Miguel Iaffa, the owner of the building that hosts the synagogue Shlomo ben Adret. According to the historians of MUHBA, the space is not in fact the old synagogue and is therefore not part of the city tours that Casa de l'Espai Call sponsors. Iaffa himself, however, tells a very different story, as will be seen. Last but not least, Dominique Tomasov Blinder, an Argentinian-born architect and long-time Barcelona resident, founded the Urban Cultours project, which organizes tours and programs focusing on "all aspects of Judaism in Barcelona."[14] Tomasov Blinder herself gives regular tours of the Call to both locals and visitors. Of course, there is also a long list of smaller operators, tour guides, and virtual heritage tours that offer a visit to the Call as part of their itinerary, but these three are the ones that are exclusively devoted to the city's Jewish history.

Although the three organizations share the same space (roughly eleven streets) for their itineraries, and although the stories they tell about the city's past are undoubtedly related, a comparison of the three raises questions of who has the right and the responsibility to tell the story of Barcelona's Jewish past. Rather than privileging any one of these representations of Jewish Barcelona as the most accurate, I am interested in addressing the questions that arise once these three initiatives are seen not in competition with but in relation to one another. Rothberg's critique in *Multidirectional Memory* of the notion of competitive memory (discussed in the Introduction) also resonates in this context. Ultimately, the similarities and radical differences among the three initiatives do reveal that the heritage itineraries in Barcelona's Jewish quarter are part of a process and a production, as Barbara Kirshenblatt-Gimblett defines it: "By production, I do not mean that the result is not 'authentic' or that it is wholly invented. Rather, I wish to underscore that heritage is not lost and found, stolen and reclaimed. It is a mode of cultural production in the present that has recourse to the past" (*Destination Culture*, 150). Heritage travel and memory tourism are therefore about the present and from the present; heritage travelers and memory tourists might think that they are touring the past, when in actuality they are touring a production of the past.

The Associació Call de Barcelona, led by Miguel Iaffa, a charismatic Catalan-Argentinian Jew, centers on the rehabilitation of a particular space, the major synagogue on Carrer de Marlet that is today called Shlomo ben Adret.[15] Iaffa purchased the space in 1995, when it was still in ruins, and turned it into a small museum that also hosts religious services. In the brochure for sale at the synagogue, the space itself is described as a "relic of Catalan and Jewish cultural heritage. Jewish, because we stand before a synagogue located in Barcelona's old Jewish Quarter. Catalan, because the stones of the old Synagogue form part of the region's historical memory" (Romeu Ferré and Iaffa, *The Former Major Synagogue of Barcelona*, 2–3). The tone suggests that, by entering the building, one also enters the past: "We'll enter through a tiny door on Marlet Street. We must bow our heads. In this way, we honor the memory of a devastated community" (5). The booklet, then, in addition to providing historical information as such texts are meant to do, also aims to establish a link between past and present, implying that the rehabilitation of the synagogue functions as the continuation of an interrupted past. "This extremely old synagogue has just experienced a rebirth. Although some details are still lacking, we possess the most important one: your presence here, which carries on the tradition" (7). The tone implies that the goal of this association is to honor the past and make it alive in the present, but the question that arises is whose present it is. The free tours that MUHBA offers through Casa de l'Espai Call do not include a visit to this synagogue; a recent travel guide, *Rutas por las juderías de España* (Routes in Spain's Jewish quarters), sponsored by the Red de Juderías and published by El País-Aguilar, states that the building is not actually a synagogue: "Right on Carrer de Marlet, a certain building is showcased today as the main synagogue of Barcelona, while according to researchers it is more likely that the space was the women's vestibule, or the *sinagoga de las donas* (women's synagogue). The space is used for prayer services" (*Rutas por las juderías de España*, 76).[16]

Iaffa himself, however, questions the purposes of the government-sponsored Casa de l'Espai Call. In a 2006 interview with *El País*, he expresses his doubts about the Casa de l'Espai Call, still incomplete at the time of the interview: "They [the municipal government] have not told us anything, and this is regrettable from a historical perspective." Iaffa explains, unintentionally echoing Gruber's argument: "They want Judaism without Jews and without a past."[17] In Iaffa's view, the city's promotion of Jewish heritage tourism is evidence of the kind of "non-Jewish embrace of the Jewish phenomenon" that Gruber criticizes in *Virtually Jewish* (8). Gruber argues that, elsewhere in Europe, "many who so tightly embrace Jewish memory and Jewish culture, who profess themselves interested in 'bringing back to life' what was destroyed in the Holocaust, have manifested little apparent interest in the local living Jewish present" (10). The Jewish public spaces to which Iaffa refers were not destroyed in the Holocaust, as were the sites Gruber discusses; they were destroyed more than five centuries earlier. "Bringing back to life" the Barcelona Call is therefore a more complex process that entails, quite literally, unearthing layer upon layer of history. Although we might never know whether the Shlomo ben Adret was once a synagogue, the conflict over this space shows that the heritage traveler and memory tourist will always encounter, consciously or not, differing views of the past.

Like Iaffa, Dominique Tomasov Blinder has also criticized the lack of a Jewish perspective in the representation of the past in municipal government initiatives. The U.S.-born Argentinian and long-time Barcelona resident began providing tours of the Call in 1997, when she created Urban Cultours. As with the pamphlets that the other two organizations publish, the Urban Cultours website includes information about Jewish life in medieval Barcelona, but it is the only one that also covers Jewish life in the present, including information about currently functioning synagogues, and where to purchase Kosher food and celebrate Jewish holidays. For Tomasov Blinder and Urban Cultours, touring the Barcelona Call is anything but a static endeavor; rather, it is a constant negotiation between past and present and between municipal authorities and local Jewish communities.

In her guided tours of Jewish Barcelona, Tomasov Blinder places the emphasis on her own background (she is Jewish, an architect, and has studied the city's history, including its Jewish history). For her, the recovery of the city's past needs to include a Jewish element, as she explains in an interview: "I want to give a Jewish voice to the explanation of the Jewish past—and to connect it with the Jewish present. Many in Spain cannot see any connection. We are considered a species separate from our history. The authorities are not interested in talking to us. They say: 'It is our history, not yours. It has nothing to do with religion'" (quoted in Levin, "Whose Heritage?," 23).

Unlike the MUHBA tour guides, who follow a set script, Tomasov Blinder offers her tours as a dialogue, weaving in her own story and her identification with Judaism with the visitor's questions. This identification is central to her commitment to the preservation of Jewish heritage. Tomasov Blinder and David Stoleru cofounded the "Zakhor Study Centre for the Protection and Transmission of Jewish Heritage" in 2008. The goal of this organization is to provide civil society, the scientific world, universities and research centers, public entities, and Jewish communities with a Jewish dimension to the reading and analysis of Jewish history. The organization has been particularly active in efforts to ensure that Jewish remains buried at the Montjuïc cemetery would be handled properly and according to Jewish tradition, thus clashing with the scientific and municipal authorities in charge of examining the bodies found at the necropolis, which is more than a thousand years old.[18] Like the Call, the burial ground at Montjuïc undoubtedly has different meanings for the different individuals and communities that coexist (or hardly coexist) in Barcelona.

Both Iaffa's and Tomasov Blinder's initiatives precede the Espai Call. The Barcelona history museum's "answer" to their more independent endeavors certainly capitalizes on the past, even though Iaffa might question whose past that is. The actual structure that today hosts the Casa de l'Espai Call dates from the sixteenth century, although some of the building materials stem from earlier eras, including the window frames from wood that most probably had once framed a door. A niche in the structure may once have held a mezuzah. And on the façade at the back of the building, the remains of a Hebrew inscription can still be detected.

According to legend, the house once belonged to a Jewish alchemist who cursed his own home after selling a powerful love potion to a Christian nobleman who, unbeknownst to the Jewish man, needed the potion to cast a spell on the alchemist's own daughter. But the city's records show that a weaver named Jussef Bonnhiac used to reside at this address; his home was burned down during the anti-Jewish riots in the late fourteenth century and was later restored. In the mid-twentieth century it was used as a garage. In spring 2008 the Casa de l'Espai Call opened its doors to the Barcelona public. The stated goal of the institution, which is managed by the city's history museum, is to familiarize visitors with Jewish life in Barcelona from the ninth to the fifteenth century.

On entering the building, visitors are immediately confronted with its unearthed history: glass floors allow a good view of what was once the building's water reservoir. But exactly whose and what kind of history we are invited to visit or gaze at remains a question. The alchemist's house is a palimpsestic building not only because of its material structure but also because it is impossible to disentangle what the building is and once was from the legends and stories that have given the structure its appealing patina.

Even though the Casa de l'Espai Call is a center for the interpretation of the history of the Jewish quarter, its focus is on the history of the city, not on Jewish history or the vagaries of Jewish absence and presence across the centuries. The museum has established similarly organized centers for interpretation elsewhere (for example, in the Pedralbes Monastery and at Refugi 307, a bomb shelter used during the Spanish Civil War). The goal of these interpretation centers is to communicate to contemporary visitors what particular spaces meant in the past and how they changed over time.

El Call: Barcelona's Jewish Quarter, a booklet authored by one of the museum's historians, describes the history of the Call from the first notice of Jewish presence in Barcelona in 850 to the increasingly restrictive laws that governed Jewish life, the Black Death, the Barcelona Disputation in 1263, and the assault on the Call in 1391 and its destruction, which is where the history of the Call ends.

The booklet contains a basic description of the different streets that form the Call and the limited archeological knowledge that is available about them. The city's "production" of Jewish heritage in the Call is about the history of Barcelona, about urban archeology and a neighborhood where Jews once lived while sharing the city with others. In a sense, Jewish presence in Barcelona is reduced to the physical space Jews once occupied.

An examination of Casa de l'Espai Call, the Associació Call de Barcelona, and Urban Cultours shows that debates over Jewish presence and absence in Barcelona are about more than placing signs that provide explanations of the remote past or telling one's own story, even if it is a story about contention with the municipal authorities. Rather, touring the Call means witnessing a constant, active, and often contradictory production of the past. Touring the Call, maybe even touching the gaps in old door frames that may or may not have once held a mezuzah, means facing, as James Young writes, "the complex texture of memory—its many inconsistencies, faces, and shapes—that sustains the difficulty of our memory-work, not its easy resolution" (*The Texture of Memory*, xi). Needless to say, Barcelona is far from the only city in which a tour of eleven narrow streets involves controversy.

Girona's Call

The heritagization of Girona's Call has a longer history than that of Barcelona's Jewish quarter. It dates back to the 1970s and was part of a major urban development initiative led by Joaquim Nadal, the mayor at the time. Unlike Barcelona, where different organizations offer competing narratives about its Jewish heritage, Girona's Jewish quarter is managed by a municipal board, the Patronat Municipal Call de Girona, that the city council and the Autonomous Government of Catalonia established in 1992 to take care of the renovation, revitalization, and promotion of the Call.[19] Members of the board include the municipal government, the Catalan government, and the University of Girona. Governmental and nongovernmental institutions, corporations, and individual members are its sponsors and benefactors. The board also oversees the Museum of Jewish History and the Nahmanides Institute for Jewish Studies.

Since 1992, the Patronat has also sponsored exhibits (including "Visas for Freedom," on the role of Spanish Diplomats during the Holocaust in 2009, and an exhibit on the Jews of Morocco in 2011), film series, activities for young children, and, of course, guided tours of the Call, including tours in dialogue format that were performed in Girona's streets, such as *Les set portes del Call* (The seven doors of the Call, 2004), which was later printed in book form and is for sale in the museum's bookstore. This section will focus on the tour script to outline yet another approach to a visit to a city's Jewish quarter (in addition to the three discussed in the preceding section) and to reveal the ways in which such a tour of the Call produces an informative, perhaps entertaining, vision of the past while defusing key historical conflicts and contradictions, partially concealing, at the end, the impact of anti Semitism in Spain.

Situated among commercial, historical, literary, and nationalist narratives, this tour's script tells a story of convivencia that will appeal to most visitors, and it does so by providing a sense of closure, ultimately effacing the conflicts and ambiguities of the past. *Les set portes del Call* maps a comfortable place between marketing and historical knowledge, between urban development of a city and an engagement with a violent past, and, last but not least, between the absence of a Jewish population in Girona and the presence of Jewish sites that are meant to lure visitors from home and abroad.

Officially, Jews have been absent from the city of Girona since 1492, when the Catholic monarchs signed the expulsion edict. The Jewish population in Girona had already been greatly reduced by the end of the fourteenth century after the riots in 1391. Although the city, at times even referred to as "Little Jerusalem," was undoubtedly a thriving community in medieval times and was considered to be the birth-place—or one of the birthplaces—of the Kabbalah, it was also the scene of countless pogroms and other more subtle forms of anti-Jewish violence. After the expulsion, the Jewish quarter was sealed off and remained hidden until the late 1960s, when construction work in the city's old quarter, the Barri Vell, unearthed a passageway, the Callejón de San Lorenzo, which eventually led to the rediscovery of the old synagogue. In an economically sensible move, the local government began the reconstruction of the Call, and today Girona holds a privileged place on both Spanish and international maps of Jewish heritage travel.

Girona and Barcelona are far from being the only Spanish sites where the reconstruction of the judería is a thriving and also an economically profitable enterprise. Flesler and Pérez Melgosa have observed this same phenomenon elsewhere. In an analysis of a report from a travel magazine on the origins and development of the project to restore the Jewish quarter of the city of Tarazona, Flesler and Pérez Melgosa show that accounts of the discovery and development of Jewish quarters rely on two conflicting discourses:

> One is a cultural narrative that emphasizes chance, mystery and external encouragement as originating forces, while the other one, strictly economic, reveals a programmatic study of tourism trends in larger Spanish towns directed to please the perceived interest of a foreign Jewish population. This desired audience is constructed along stereotypical anti-Semitic lines as highly affluent. The cunning interest in the latter narrative so openly expressed weakens the carefully woven story of innocence, goodwill and desires of reconciliation expressed in the former. ("Marketing Convivencia," 71)

Many of the same contradictions can also be found in *Les set portes del Call*. From the opening pages of the text, the complete identification between the judería and the Barri Vell is evident. Economic development and historical recovery work hand in hand: the interdependence of capital and memory is one of the variables that shape contemporary reconstructions of Jewish Spain.

Les set portes del Call aims not just to enrich a leisurely walk in Jewish Girona but also to function as "a journey through the memory of a people" (Moreno, Salip, and Bosch, *Les set portes*, 14). To accomplish this goal, the text is structured as a dialogue around a tour guide's explanations of different aspects of the history of the Call and the account of Jewish customs, rites, and symbols. Often, the guide responds to questions that some of the visitors ask as they wander along the streets of Girona. These visitors, or characters, consist of Catalans and foreign visitors, Gentiles and Jews, who also become cultural interpreters. The main character is an older Jewish man named Rubén who happens on the tour by chance. I use the term "character" somewhat loosely because the text is a scripted tour guide, not a novel or a play. *Les set portes del Call* is symptomatic of the ways in which open-ended stories of convivencia become just one story in which centuries of anti-Semitism are in the end erased.

Rubén arrives in Girona wondering, "Why is it, that sometimes we get the sense that we know a place, even though we have never set foot before?" (*Les set portes*, 7). Strangely compelled by the movement of leaves in a tree, he wanders around the Barri Vell, where he serendipitously encounters a guided tour of Jewish Girona. Although he at first appears to be shrouded in mystery, his story slowly emerges. The other tourists and the guide find out that he was born in Israel, even though he only admits this reluctantly. He arrived in Girona from France but does not seem to have a home. Rubén is depicted as so thoroughly Jewish and well-informed about all things Jewish, including the cemeteries in Jerusalem, Smyrna, and Salonika (23), that it is as though he were facing a prefigured destiny, as though he knows the end of all stories before they are told (or written). Traveling and displacement have marked Rubén's life. When the visitors come across some recently arrived immigrants, Rubén immediately identifies with them: "He discovers in them signs of fatigue and of haste, signs of fear of expulsion, of having left hurriedly behind the place where they had been. He knows these feelings" (94). Rubén becomes a connection between Girona's Jewish past and the city's present. His empathy with the newly arrived immigrants implies that his intricate knowledge of the conflicts of the past would help to alleviate some of the challenges that immigrants to Spain from North Africa and Eastern Europe face today.

This connection between past and present, however, reflects the oversimplified fusion (discussed in the Introduction) of the medieval convivencia and contemporary encounters, crises, and clashes between different populations. Further, racial and cultural stereotypes also characterize Rubén. He not only has a "slightly crooked nose" (7), he also is identified with the Wandering Jew, a figure that dates back to a medieval legend about a cobbler who, after mocking Christ on the way to crucifixion, was told to wander the world until Christ's return. The Wandering Jew has had many appearances throughout history, from the heart of Europe to Latin America.[20] Today, the figure functions as a "model of modern alienation cum psychological introspection in its various formations" (Hasan-Rokem, "Jews as Postcards, or Postcards as Jews," 508), a description that undoubtedly fits Rubén's characterization. Although he is not the "Eternal Jew" (one of the most virulent images that Nazi propaganda used to spread anti-Semitism), Rubén's association with the Wandering Jew should not be taken lightly, precisely because of what happens once Rubén vanishes from the group.[21]

As the tour is about to reach its end, the guide and some of the visitors begin telling local legends involving the Jewish population that once resided in Girona. The guide chooses to tell the legend of the Wandering Jew to his audience. The mythical character would be "a man who has been found down through the centuries in many places and periods. He wanders across the world without finding peace, without ever dying, condemned to a quest that really is a curse for having denied a drink of water to Jesus when he passed in front of his well, carrying the cross, on the way to the Calvary" (Moreno, Salip, and Bosch, *Les set portes*, 100). Rubén's disdain for this story is clear: his eyes darken and his wrinkles get deeper as he listens to this tale (100). Still, he remains an enigma, even for the guide, because he still holds back his own version of this story. The tour ends with a certain hope for harmony and convivencia: a Moroccan violin player from Fez plays a song by Leonard Cohen, and Rubén finally finds a chance to tell all the visitors a different version of the legend of the Wandering Jew. What bothers him, he explains, is not the story's having been told in the context of the tour but its sheer inhumanity. He does see cruelty in a man's denying his neighbor a drink of water or a moment of rest, but he sees even more cruelty in God's punishment: eternal damnation for what is nothing but a mistake any human could make.

Rubén ends his story with a reference to Walter Benjamin and Portbou, and he shares two of the philosopher's maxims with Yosef, a Jewish boy from Argentina. The first is from *Thesis on the Philosophy of History*: "There is no document of civilization which is not at the same time a document of barbarism" (*Les set portes*, 110). The sentence is written on a memorial plaque inside Portbou's cemetery, where, following Jewish tradition, visitors place stones to commemorate the writer, his life, and his passing. The second is incorporated in Karavan's monument: "It is more arduous to honor the memory of the nameless than that of the renowned. Historical construction is devoted to the memory of the nameless" (113). Suddenly convinced, all the other visitors applaud Rubén's words. Finally, he turns to the boy, and he reminds him that the Wandering Jew can be recognized by the traces of his heavy footsteps: seven nails, which form a cross on the ground. Rubén finally walks away, and the other members of the tour are almost certain that his footsteps have left seven little holes in the shape of the cross. Yet before they are able to find the ultimate proof that Rubén is, after all, the Wandering Jew, young Yosef has playfully skipped behind Rubén, stepping on the traces of his steps, erasing them: "The child has unconsciously erased the myth" (114).

Although the heavy-handed symbolism could be criticized as a literary shortcoming, the text, for what it is—a guidebook—is sufficiently intricate, informed, and researched (it even ends with a bibliography for further reading). The young child's playful gesture at the end, however, stands for something else: leisure and playfulness (the curious child, skipping), carefully packaged in a commercial venture beneficial to local economic interests, erase conflicts of the past behind a hope for a harmonious future. What vanishes, ultimately, are not the traces of the Wandering Jew but one of the thousand and one stories of, in David Nirenberg's terms, the "interdependence of violence and tolerance"(*Communities of Violence*, 7) in the Mediterranean memory of Jewish Spain.

In her article "Beyond Virtually Jewish: New Authenticities and Real Imaginary Spaces in Europe," Ruth Ellen Gruber returns to the argument she made in *Virtually Jewish*, in which, she explains, she "coined the term 'virtually Jewish' to describe how non-Jews 'fill' Europe's so-called Jewish space" ("Beyond Virtually Jewish," 488). In this article Gruber discusses the proliferation of Native American and Wild West theme restaurants and parks in Eastern Europe. She suggests, however, that for "both the virtually Jewish and imaginary Wild West . . . what we actually have is the creation of 'new authenticities'—things, places, and experiences that in themselves are real, with all the trappings of reality, but that are quite different from the 'realities' on which they are modeled or that they are attempting to evoke" (490–491). The medieval Call is not just a space that Jews and non-Jews fill with meaning, it is also the site of conscious attempts to fix its meaning. Jewish quarters, not only in Catalonia but elsewhere, have emerged as a newly 'constructed' authenticity, evoking a remote past and thereby creating an entirely new narrative that might have little to do with the actual past. The challenge that remains is to recognize that these "new authenticities" are a product of multiple and contradictory narratives that come together in sites where institutions, companies, and individuals involved with heritage travel collect memories—or what passes for memories.

Portbou: When Walter Benjamin Became Benjamin Walter

It is fitting that Rubén, the character in *Les set portes del call*, pays a visit to Portbou, located in the province of Girona. Rubén not only stands for all displaced Jews across the centuries, he also stands—or at least shows empathy—for all the displaced, all refugees. His visit to Portbou is therefore not only significant because Walter Benjamin was Jewish but also because today the town itself has gathered multiple meanings in relation to escape, displacement, and exile. Benjamin's death has in many ways become a symbol of the defeats of exile; it is the point where Jewish history and Spanish history intersect in the twentieth century.

On September 28, 1940, Walter Benjamin took his own life in the Hotel França in Portbou. With the philosopher's death, this story of a failed border crossing is no longer just Benjamin's, just as Portbou would never again be just Portbou. The town itself acquired palimpsestic features because the philosopher's death rewrote the town's meaning in history and memory: "Chance occurrences, actions, and statements independent of Benjamin resulted in memories of the writer being linked with a town's atmosphere of a frontier situation, rather than a specific place that can be named" (Scheurmann, "Borders, Thresholds, Passages," 239). Touring Portbou therefore becomes a distinctive and evocative experience.

When Benjamin was on the way to the United States in September 1940, Spain was going to be the last obstacle in his transit to the Americas. Theodor Adorno had helped him procure the necessary paperwork, but Benjamin still lacked a French exit visa. Both the Vichy and Francoist governments changed their rules quickly, if not erratically, in 1940. The missing exit visa was what forced the 48-year-old philosopher to cross the Pyrenees on foot with the help of Lisa Fittko, who was his guide; it was the reason Spanish authorities told Benjamin he was to be sent back to Vichy France. The police stationed at the border did allow him, however, to spend the night at the Hotel França, where he died of a morphine overdose. Benjamin's fellow travelers, German photographer Henny Gurland and her young son, were eventually allowed to stay in Spain, even though they also lacked exit visas. Austrian refugees Carina Birman and Sophie Lippman, who also crossed the border illegally and were in Portbou at the same time as Benjamin, did make it to Portugal. In her memoir, *The Narrow Foothold*, Birman describes the details of her escape, including how she and those who traveled with her were able to bribe the Spanish authorities, thereby buying their passage into Spain.[22]

Even though some have speculated otherwise, it is beyond any doubt that Benjamin committed suicide. Lisa Fittko remembers that Benjamin crossed the border prepared for the worst: "he had enough morphine with him to take his own life with a deadly overdose" (*Escape through the Pyrenees*, 114). Conjectures still abound, however, suggesting that he was the target of an assassination—because he was Jewish, because he was a Marxist, or because he was not Marxist enough. In Mauas's 2005 documentary *Who Killed Walter Benjamin?*, for example, a local butcher asserts that a Jewish man who killed himself would never have been buried in holy ground at the Catholic cemetery in Portbou. Although such deductions might lead to interesting conspiracy theories, there are satisfactory explanations for why Benjamin was laid to rest in a Catholic cemetery: Walter Benjamin had become "Benjamin Walter" on his death certificate, and a cerebral aneurysm, not suicide, was listed as the reason for his demise. A long list of questions have been raised:

Did Walter Benjamin become Benjamin Walter because the Catholic priest, Andrés Freixa, purposely wanted to erase his Jewish identity, converting him against his will postmortem? Did the morphine overdose become an aneurysm because Benjamin was murdered? Most researchers now agree that Walter Benjamin became Benjamin Walter because Benjamin was better known as a first name in Spain.[23] Burying a purported Catholic who died of an aneurysm would certainly have caused fewer administrative headaches than burying a man who was Jewish and who had committed suicide. Benjamin's remains were therefore placed in niche 563 at the local graveyard overlooking the Mediterranean. Henny Gurland paid for a five-year rental of the grave. Once these funds ran out, his remains were moved to a mass grave.[24]

Stories of evasion across the Pyrenees during World War II abound, such as Fittko's autobiography, *Escape through the Pyrenees*, and Sheila Isenberg's *A Hero of Our Own*, about Varian Fry, the young American who saved thousands of refugees by helping them to escape Vichy across the Pyrenees; however, Benjamin's failed attempt to make it into Spain might be the most well-known, or at least the most "visited" or "tourable," escape route. As early as 1979, a plaque was placed on the cemetery walls with the following inscription: "A Walter Benjamin. Filósof Alemany, Berlin, 1892–Portbou 1940." Unveiled only four years after the end of the Francoist dictatorship and in the Catalan language, the plaque represents the first moment of a long and still ongoing memorial process. Another plaque, from the 1990s, bears the well-known inscription that Rubén, the character from *Les set portes del Call*, also mentions. The plaque is inside the cemetery, but it does not mark Benjamin's final grave; instead, it is placed over a triangular-shaped boulder, a community memorial stone, where visitors often leave little stones (a traditional Jewish symbol of remembrance and respect).

Although Benjamin's remains do not lie buried there, one could hardly call the gravestone a fake. If the purpose of this memorial is to bear witness to Benjamin's passing and to pay homage to his life and his work, the gravestone becomes genuine, shaping the public memory of Benjamin himself and of Portbou as a whole, as cultural anthropologist Michael Taussig suggests: "If the grave diggers then erected their own memorial in response to visitors asking to see the grave, who is to say this is any less respectful of the dead or any less fitting a way to register the claims of memory and history?" ("Walter Benjamin's Grave," 25).

The gravestone not only marks the philosopher's passing in memory, it also becomes a lieu de mémoire and an important symbol for the city of Portbou and the multiple sites that form the Ruta Walter Benjamin. These sites also include the train station, a reminder of the trains that crisscrossed Europe during World War II, leading both to freedom and to a terrible death. Karavan himself mentions the significance of the train station, discussing the inspiration for the location of his monument "Passages": "The noise of trains at the big frontier railway station brought to mind the sounds of deportation to the camps. Death, frontier, hope" (Karavan, "1 Corridor, 1 Stairs, 1 Seat = Passages," 101). Trains and train tracks share this significance in Antonio Muñoz Molina's *Sepharad* (discussed in Chapter 1).

Some of the final battles of the Spanish Civil War took place in Portbou, the last Catalan town that many of the defeated Spanish Republicans saw before crossing into France and initiating a long, at times endless, exile. Thus, the small border town with its olive trees and stunning views of the Mediterranean becomes the place where the memory of the Spanish Civil War and World War II merge into one complex realm. Had Benjamin survived, chances are that the first town south of the Pyrenees he reached would have become but a footnote in history, or at least in the history of World War II.

Within Spanish history, however, Portbou itself will always be significant, as will the Ruta Líster, the escape route named after Enrique Líster, a high-ranking official in the Spanish Republican army who escaped to France after the 1939 defeat and who would eventually make it to the Soviet Union. Although most sources confirm that Fittko took Ruta Líster when helping Benjamin across the Pyrenees, Manuel Cussó-Ferrer, director and writer of the 1991 film *The Last Frontier*, warns that today it might not be possible to trace Benjamin's last route exactly. The director crossed the Pyrenees on foot five times while preparing for his film. "Today it is difficult to reconstruct the geographical orientation points experienced by refugees in 1940. Several fires, the bad state of some paths, and the vanishing of landmarks and milestones constituted a great obstacle, hindering any attempt at finding the way Benjamin and other refugees might have taken over the

Pyrenees" ("Walter Benjamin's Last Frontier," 155). Considering that the Ruta Líster would have taken longer than a route located farther east, Cussó-Ferrer suggests that "it seems logical that they most probably did not take the actual 'ruta Líster,' but rather a shorter way, which was not so high up, better protected and also safer" (155–156). Even so, the Ruta Líster and the Ruta Walter Benjamin end up sharing the same meaning, turning Portbou into a site where the refugees of the Spanish Republic and of World War II come together. The Ruta Líster, as Mariana Valverde writes,

> still evokes powerful memories among aging Spanish radicals. The collective memory of the Spanish Left sometimes, though not routinely, acknowledges Benjamin and his cohort of refugees in its evocation of Lister and other refugees of that time. By contrast, the central European memories that pay homage to the victims of Nazism—recollections much more numerous and easy to find in bookstores, on the Internet, and in other common archives than Spanish memories of injustice—invariably reproduce the two-gauge problem at the level of historical memory: nothing is said, in Benjamin scholarship and related commentaries, about the reasons that the paths used by refugees fleeing south were already well known and well traveled before 1940. ("Remembering Benjamin from South of the Pyrenees," 446)

Valverde also raises the question of why the French town of Collioure, where poet Antonio Machado and his mother today lie buried, does not have the same significance that Portbou has. Unlike Benjamin, Machado died of natural causes, but, like the German philosopher, the poet's path across the Pyrenees, in his case from south to north, also led to his death. That there is no monument in France marking the passing of Machado reveals a striking imbalance between how World War II and the Spanish Civil War are remembered. "On the Internet there are images of the tombstone that feature similar, fresh-looking Spanish flowers, so there must be some who still make the trip to Collioure. However, the grand monument to Benjamin that now draws cultural-capital tourism to [Portbou] has no equivalent on the French side of the border" (448).

Karavan's monument may very well be the reason memory tourists are more drawn to Portbou than to Collioure. "Passages," commissioned in 1992 by the German and Catalan governments, inaugurated in 1994, and today administered by the Museu Memorial de l'Exili (MUME), undoubtedly plays an important role in Portbou's prominence as a site of "collected memory." The monument, situated across from the graveyard and overlooking the Mediterranean, is forged out of rusted iron. Visitors are invited to climb down a staircase that cuts right through the cliffs and leads directly to a whirlpool. On the final step, the visitor is faced with Benjamin's words—those that Rubén quotes in *Les set portes del Call*—inscribed on a glass wall: "It is more arduous to honor the memory of the nameless than that of the renowned. Historical construction is devoted to the memory of the nameless." The text appears in Catalan, English, Spanish, French, and German. The monument evokes desolation in the dark tunnel, possibly a passage into the underworld, but also hope with the light shining through the glass wall that separates the visitor from the Mediterranean. Karavan's "Passages," like the monuments that Young discusses in *The Texture of Memory*, "becomes a point of reference amid other parts of the landscape, one node among others in a topographical matrix that orients the rememberer and creates meaning in both the land and our recollections" (7). With "Passages," Walter Benjamin's death in Portbou always means more than the simple fact that Benjamin died in Portbou.

Visits to Portbou itself, especially the monument, have sparked many essays, not only those by Scheurmann, Taussig, and Valverde, but also that by John Collins, for whom Karavan's "Passages" is a piece that "promises to haunt forever" ("From Portbou to Palestine and Back," 68) and that evokes the plight of current migrants in the Mediterranean (67). Collins also observes that "the monument is the most famous sight in Portbou and a place of pilgrimage for wayward writers with a melancholic fondness for cultural studies" (72). Taussig expresses his discomfort with the ways in which Portbou might be turning into the site of a secular Benjamin pilgrimage, creating "an incipient cult around the site of Benjamin's grave, as if the drama of his death, and of the holocaust, in general, is allowed to appropriate and overshadow the enigmatic power of his writing and the meaning of his life. Put bluntly, the death comes to mean more than the life" ("Walter Benjamin's Grave," 6). Taussig elaborates on his uneasiness with the Benjamin pilgrimage: "This cult is at once too sad and too sentimental, too overdetermined an event—the border crossing that failed, the beauty of the place, the horror of the epoch. It really amounts to a type of gawking, I thought to myself, in place of informed respect, a cheap thrill with the frisson of tragedy further enlivened by the calm and stupendous beauty of the landscape" (6).

Although Taussig refers specifically to Karavan's monument, the larger questions he raises can be applied to cultural tourism and heritage travel. One might say that "informed respect" is precisely what the different institutions and individuals that produce tours of the Calls and border-crossing sites offer (or aim to offer) to all travelers. The "gawking" and the "cheap thrill" are always a risk. After all, in the same way that a novelist cannot control how her readers will receive her work, the tour guide or the public officers who administer visits to specific sites are not in control of the experience that the travelers and tourists may have.

As with the Jewish quarters discussed earlier, today it is possible to visit the Ruta Walter Benjamin. MUME administers the route and also runs the Espai Memorial Walter Benjamin (Walter Benjamin Memorial Space). One of the objectives of the organization, as stated on their website, entails "recalling the figure of Walter Benjamin, fostering critical knowledge of his work from a historical perspective, and linking his intellectual legacy with contemporary culture and thought through the adoption of a cross-over and polyhedral view that takes into account all humanistic disciplines."[25] This objective, as well as others, would place the towns of La Jonquera and Portbou "on the memorial map."

Considering this objective, it is hardly surprising that an article on touring Portbou appeared in *Qué Fem*, a leisure-oriented weekend supplement of the Barcelona daily *La Vanguardia*. The article does include information about the circumstances of Benjamin's death, about what to visit in Portbou itself, as well as detailed information about where to stay and where to eat. This might be "memory tourism" at its best, in the true sense of the term: visiting Portbou as a whole, not just the monument, the burial site, or even the train station, becomes an experience of history and memory, as the final comment of the article suggests, referring to Karavan's monument as "an experience that will at least not leave you indifferent."[26] The understated tone may imply a certain incompatibility between memory and tourism; being "not indifferent" suggests a possible engagement with the past, but an engagement that should neither be too difficult to handle nor prevent the visitor from enjoying his or her weekend adventure.

Carina Birman's memoir, *The Narrow Foothold*, also capitalizes on a visit to Portbou. Although the text itself is only sixteen pages, the supplemental materials imply that this is not just a book about Birman's escape but also a virtual visit to Portbou. In a brief note at the beginning of the book, John Retty, the publisher, explains that he accompanied Kathy Duggan (the granddaughter of Sophie Lippman, who traveled with Birman) and the photographer Christopher North "to see for myself the difficulties the refugees faced in crossing the border" (*The Narrow Foothold*, vii). Retty remembers Portbou in the following terms: "My first impression of [Portbou] was its smell of freedom, its friendly inhabitants" (vii). Portbou undoubtedly has historical meaning, but this meaning coexists with projections and desires of the visitors and what they are trying to find, whether the visitor is someone like Hannah Arendt, who visited Portbou in 1940 to look for the grave of her dear friend, which she was never able to locate, or the contemporary memory tourist, who, after reading the piece in *La Vanguardia*, hungers for "an experience that will at least not leave you indifferent."

MUME's goal of placing the Ruta Walter Benjamin "on the memorial map," although not exactly equivalent to "heritagization," nevertheless shares certain aspects of the process. While the institution itself emphasizes research, it also provides actual tours, making it possible to follow the steps of Walter Benjamin and others who either fled from Franco's forces after 1939 or from the Fascist menace coming from the other side of the Pyrenees shortly afterward. MUME, in addition to housing a museum that documents the experience of Republican exile in La Jonquera, also administers a number of other exile routes and the locations that surround them, as well as the Espai Memorial Walter Benjamin website, where much of the available information and bibliography on Benjamin's death can be found.[27] In addition to this virtual presence, a path across the Pyrenees with historical markers is also one of the tours that the museum sponsors. The museum publishes a brochure that contains a summary of the history of Portbou as a site of exile and border crossing for Spanish refugees fleeing fascism during World War II, a very brief sketch of Walter Benjamin's exile, a map of the seven-kilometer route from Banyuls to Portbou over Mount Querroig at the border, information about Karavan's memorial, and a diagram of the sites that can be visited in Portbou, including the train station, the Fonda França where Benjamin took his life, the civic center, the Walter Benjamin memorial, and a sign in the main street (Rambla) in the heart of Portbou that summarizes the circumstances surrounding Benjamin's death.[28]

The Meaning of the Ruins

That Portbou has meaning is beyond a doubt, but the question that arises is who has the right and the responsibility to define and redefine the meaning of this small border town. Portbou has meaning for Germany as well: the Arbeitskreis Selbständiger Kulturinstitute (ASKI), under curator and art historian Konrad Scheurmann's leadership, commissioned Karavan's "Passages" on behalf of the German government in 1990; the monument itself and the responses it has inspired reflect Germany's engagement with the Nazi past.

Portbou holds meanings for individuals, for all those who have visited after reading the piece in *La Vanguardia* and have been moved by Karavan's monument, for those who just happened on the place, traveling around the Catalan coast, and for such individuals as Kathy Duggan, who found the typescript of Carina Birman's memoir (as noted earlier, Duggan's grandmother, Sophie Lippman, crossed the border with Birman in 1940). *The Narrow Foothold* includes photos of Duggan outside the Fonda França where Benjamin died and at the end of the escape route at the foot of the Pyrenees.

Portbou is meaningful within the history of Catalonia as well, specifically as the site of the last battles of the Civil War and as a way station for the Republican exodus. In a brief speech delivered at the opening of Karavan's monument in 1994, Jordi Pujol, then president of the Catalan Generalitat, establishes specific links between Benjamin's story and Catalonia's hospitality toward immigrants and refugees: "He fled from his own country, but above all he fled from intolerance and lack of understanding. At that time he did not find here a Catalonia ready to receive exiles, as we have always aimed to be throughout our history. . . . This memorial is a tribute to freedom and coexistence" ("This Memorial Is a Tribute to Freedom," 144). Pujol presents Catalonia as a nation that under different circumstances would have been hospitable to Benjamin and other refugees. Portbou and Karavan's monument become symbols for the kind of progressive and tolerant nation Pujol envisions. That Benjamin was, after all, a Jewish refugee in flight has significance in relation to more recent developments in Catalonia. Edgar Illas has analyzed the ways in which the foundation of the State of Israel and the revival of Hebrew became powerful symbols for Catalan nationalism in the 1980s and 1990s. Pujol, who presided over the Generalitat from 1980 to 2003, revived a preexisting Catalan philo-Semitism, turning a vision of Israel's success into a particular political program.[29]

Portbou has meaning for Israel and Palestine as well. Before creating "Passages," Karavan was known for his memorial to victims of the Holocaust at the Weizmann Institute at Rehovot in Israel and for the Israeli Pavilion at the 1976 Venice Biennale, dedicated to peace between Israelis and Palestinians. Karavan planted two olive trees in front of the pavilion and wrote "Our Borders Should Be Olive Trees" as an inscription. He has explained the significance of the olive tree at the Portbou monument: "Among the stones and rocks, in the dry dusty soil, scorched by the sun and dried out by the wind, a little old olive tree that fights for its life" (Karavan, "1 Corridor, 1 Stairs, 1 Seat = Passages," 104). Collins picks up on the olive tree symbolism and the role it plays in Palestinian culture: "Karavan's monument highlights the transgressive, even revolutionary nature of Benjamin's work, but it also suggests the belated completion of a journey from the confined, genocidal world of fascism—the world whose horrors so deeply colored the work of a whole generation of Jewish intellectuals who did manage to make the journey to America—to the open sea and the promise of the Jewish state" ("From Portbou to Palestine and Back," 72). For Collins and also for Taussig, Karavan's monument evokes the current crisis in the Middle East. Collins wonders, "How does Palestine look when viewed from Portbou?" (72), while Taussig speculates about whether Benjamin could have been the first suicide bomber ("Walter Benjamin's Grave," 7). Collins's text is more subtle, as he focuses specifically on the ways in which Karavan's monument faces the Mediterranean (Pessarrodona's "bloody sea"), thereby also facing Israel and Palestine. He then continues to reflect: "Were he still alive, however, the iconoclastic thinker buried at Portbou would un-doubtedly ask us to take this picture and, in his famous phrase, brush it "against the grain" ("From Portbou to Palestine and Back," 72).

The issue raised in both essays is whether an examination of Ben-jamin's work and his death in Portbou provides an answer or at least an approach to understanding the current situation in Israel and Pal-estine. In earlier chapters I have argued that evoking the remote past (medieval convivencia, the rise of crypto-Judaism, and the expulsion in the fifteenth century) has helped to articulate coherent and even re-demptive narratives of the present situation. The ways in which traces of Jewish life appear in public spaces in Catalonia—spaces which also belong to itineraries of heritage travel and memory tourism—suggest a similar phenomenon, as seen in Collins's and Taussig's essays. But the faint "Palestina Libre" scrawled on the plaque on Carrer de Marlet in Barcelona's Call also suggests that various interpretations (from the historically informed to the rogue and impulsive) of the relation between past and present will always coexist whenever the heritage traveler and the memory tourist encounter, literally or virtually, the palimpsestic remainders of Sepharad.

Conclusion
Asking the Mediterranean, Waiting for an Answer

The preceding chapters have addressed the contradictions and con-flicts contained within the expression "Jewish Spain" by "asking the Mediterranean," as Marta Pessarrodona suggests in "Weissensee," her poem about the Berlin cemetery that refers specifically to Walter Ben-jamin. The last chapter should have confirmed that the circumstances surrounding the philosopher's death and his memorialization (embod-ied in and symbolized by Karavan's monument) are an intrinsic part of "Jewish Spain," as are the other memory sites that I have discussed. "Asking the Mediterranean" leads to a profound ambivalence con-cerning all things Jewish in Spain; what Jews were (and are imagined, expected, and feared to be) changes according to specific historical circumstances in the nineteenth century, throughout the twentieth century, and in the present day.

Shifting perceptions of Jews, Jewish culture, and Jewish heritage in Spain are shaped by philo-Sephardism and anti-Semitism, discourses that also change over time. Their current incarnations in Spain do, however, reveal continuities with the past. Although anti-Semitism in contemporary Spain operates most forcefully in conjunction with neg-ative views of Israel and the United States, the intolerances of the past also haunt contemporary forms of prejudice and bigotry. Alejandro Baer and Paula López argue that, in relation to anti-Semitism in the Spanish media, a specific "Spanish pattern" emerges:

183

> This includes: (i) a tendency to pro-Arab Manichean thinking when discussing the parties to the conflict, (ii) the overlap of anti-Zionist and anti-American rhetoric, especially prevalent in the liberal press but not absent in the conservative media, and (iii) the use of stereo-

types rooted in religious antisemitism in the portrayal of Israelis and the State of Israel especially in opinion columns and editorial cartoons. What does constitute a specifically Spanish characteristic is the adoption of these discourses across a broad swathe of the political spectrum. ("The Blind Spots of Secularization," 4)

Indeed, Spain currently has "one of the highest levels of antisemitism in Europe" (1), as past and present crises continue to exacerbate forms of prejudice in Spain and the Mediterranean world.

On March 30, 2011, an article with the headline "The Crisis Sparks Anti-Jewish Hatred in Spain" appeared in *El País*. The article cites a Ministry of Foreign Affairs survey from fall 2010 that found that 58.5 percent of the population believe that the Jews are very powerful because they control the economy and the mass media, and a third of the population (34.6 percent) have an unfavorable or totally unfavorable opinion of the Jewish community.[1] It should come as no surprise that prejudices in Spain against Jews (and Muslims and Gypsies) continue to be rampant, and that the economic crisis has only exacerbated negative predispositions. But the article also shows that more individuals identifying themselves as center-left (37.7 percent) have negative feelings toward Jews than the radical right (34 percent), which leads Jacobo Israel Garzón, the president of Spain's Federation of Jewish Communities (FCJE), to state that if the statistics are correct, "Spain would be a unique case in Europe, and the country would have a real problem."[2]

The history of philo-Sephardism and anti-Semitism in twentieth-century Spain shows that these tendencies do not emerge in a vacuum; rather, they are the consequence of conflicting depictions and instrumental uses of Jews and, specifically, of the notion of "Spanish Jews" throughout the century. Although the current conflict in the Middle East might influence attitudes about Jews, this alone does not explain the persistence of anti-Semitism in Spain. This book has aimed to convey the complex stories that lie behind this situation, stories that of course continue to evolve.

In fall 2012, the Spanish government announced that the naturalization process for the descendants of the Sephardim would be eased. Until then, Sephardic Jews already received preferential treatment;

now the government eliminated a two-year residency requirement and proof of financial resources, as well as the stipulation that the applicants renounce their current citizenship. The naturalization process varies depending on the applicant's national origin. Attaining Spanish citizenship through the regular channel requires ten years of legal residence. The period is shortened by half for political refugees and is only one year for noncitizens who have specific ties with the nation, for instance, those born in Spain or married to a Spanish national. For citizens of Latin American countries, the period is shortened to two years, and also for natives of Andorra, Portugal, and Equatorial Guinea. Until 2012, being of Sephardic origin also fell into the two-year category (Díaz-Mas, *The Sephardim*, 195).

The government policies are clearly connected to the colonial era (Sephardic origin implies Iberian origin) as well as to early twentieth-century forms of philo-Sephardism, among them Ángel Pulido's initiatives and his *Spaniards without a Homeland* (1905), Primo de Rivera's royal decree (1924), Ernesto Giménez Caballero's film *Jews of the Spanish Homeland* (1929), and also the shifts in the use of the terms "Spanish Sephardim," "Sephardim," and "protégés" that appeared in the documents that the Spanish government circulated in the late 1940s to give proof of Spain's (and Franco's) benevolence toward Jews.

Philo-Sephardic discourse is also quite evident in the language used to present the new rules. When the changes in the naturalization process were announced, the old theme of nostalgia for Sepharad also reappeared. Indeed, a November 2, 2012, article in *El País* reporting on the new naturalization process included the subheading "The Spaniards Who 'Yearn for Sepharad.'" José Manuel García Margallo, the Spanish foreign minister, explains in the article that the change in legislation aims to "*recover* the *memory* of a Spain that has been *silenced* for many years" and to complete the journey "toward home and freedom" of those Spaniards living in diaspora "who long for Sepharad" (my emphasis).[3] In the same article, Justice Minister Alberto Ruiz Gallardón also mentions the "affection for Spain" of the Sephardim, and the comments of Isaac Querub, president of the Jewish Federations, reveals a conventional and redemptive narrative pattern: "Just as March 31, 1492, the date of the signing of the edict expelling the Jews from Castile and Aragon, was, according to Querub, a day of twilight and darkness, the legal disposition "of the return" announced today will make this day "go down in history as a day of clear blue and bright shining skies for Spain." The contrast between darkness and light indeed suggests the kind of closure and coherence that all the stories and narratives discussed in this book depict as continually desired and persistently elusive. Thus, at second glance the new naturalization process might not provide redemption or closure after all, as a thorny issue lies at its very core: how does one prove Sephardic identity? Once again, a narrative that appears to be tightly woven reveals its remainders.[4]

The *El País* article briefly notes that proof of identity (eventually leading to citizenship) could be provided in the form of "surnames, language, ancestry, or ties to Spanish culture and customs." But any of these factors conjures up complicated relationships with and narratives about identity. Although a surname, for example, might suggest Sephardic origin, it should not be taken for granted as such. As mentioned earlier, Francisco Franco's surname was often considered "proof" of his Jewish origins, a presumption then used to explain the dictator's personal investment in protecting Jews during World War II.

The meaning of "language" is also unclear in this context. The term in the article is, ambiguously, "idioma"; neither Spanish, Judeo-Spanish, Ladino, nor Haketia is specified as a language that might support a claim to Sephardic origin. Ladino might be an obvious choice, but connecting Ladino with Spanish citizenship is particularly tricky because Ladino is not simply associated with Spain; it is a diasporic language that was once, as Aron Rodrigue notes, the language of the transnational Levant and "is for all intents and purposes dead, a casualty of the Holocaust and of the long-term, secular processes of political, social, and cultural change that destroyed the transnational Levant in which it had developed and flourished" ("The Ottoman Diaspora," 884). Thus, it remains unclear which language would provide the necessary connection with Spain.

The requirement for proof of "ancestry" or "ties to Spanish culture and customs" is also equally ambiguous, possibly purposefully so. The marginal and disenchanted voice of Antonio Muñoz Molina's Señor Salama eerily undermines these connections; he mulls over what Spain means for him, considering his circumstances: "Spain is so remote that it is nearly nonexistent, an inaccessible, unknown, thankless country they called Sepharad, longing for it with a melancholy without basis or excuse" (*Sepharad*, 111). The other Spanish intellectuals who interact with Salama in Tangier find him "tedious" despite his "flowery talk" (117–118), showing poignantly that the expected "ties to Spanish culture and customs" will carry the weight of a 500-year history that can neither be ignored nor taken for granted.

One of the most controversial aspects of the recent change is that individuals applying for citizenship would also need to provide evidence of their Judaism. Considering that for centuries individuals had to prove that they were *not* Jewish to remain and survive in Spain makes it difficult not to see the requirement as ironic. When *New York Times* correspondent Doreen Carvajal, author of *The Forgetting River: A Modern Tale of Survival, Identity, and the Inquisition*, first found out about the new stipulation, she saw it as a happy ending to a redemptive narrative: "They held this news conference with top ministers to offer automatic citizenship to descendants of all Sephardic Jews who left during inquisition. Point blank done. It was a romantic notion on my part. I told my husband, I think I'm going to try and get the passport because it closes a circle. It was very poetic."[5]

At first glance Carvajal's comments might appear to echo Querub's statement; however, she explains that Spain's Jewish Federations informed her that she would not qualify for citizenship, at least not immediately, because her ancestors were conversos. The circle does not close, after all, and Carvajal is ultimately left wondering whether this new initiative is about economically beneficial ties with Turkey or Venezuela, which would echo past forms of philo-Sephardism, now that Spain is again submerged, as it was in the early twentieth century, in an economic crisis.[6]

In an op-ed piece published in the *New York Times* on December 8, 2012, Carvajal recognizes that what makes the immigration reform particularly thorny for her is that for descendants of conversos, or *bnei anusim*, like her own family, only religious training and conversion to Judaism under the auspices of Spain's Jewish Federations would facilitate her path to Spanish citizenship.[7] Carvajal expresses her discomfort with the "religious requirements" that now seem to form part of the expedited naturalization process and also suggests that they might echo forceful conversions of the past.[8]

The other very thorny issue is that, although Sephardim have been invited to return to Sepharad, a law that would facilitate the naturalization process of the descendants of the Moriscos (Muslims who converted to Christianity and were expelled in 1609) has not been considered at the same time. Because the naturalization process for the descendants of the Sephardim appears to be more about political and economic opportunity than about cultural and religious pluralism, the new rules appear to be a slightly revised and updated version of philo-Sephardic discourse, which, as argued in earlier chapters, was always more about Spain's challenges and opportunities in specific historical moments than it was about the Sephardim. As we have seen, philo-Sephardic discourse in the early twentieth century and during World War II and its aftermath makes for good stories of homecoming and redemption in which the nostalgic return to Sepharad is a ubiquitous motif.

García Margallo's choosing to discuss the new stipulation in terms of a recovery of Spain's "silenced" memory also fuses the history of the Sephardic diaspora with Spain's debate over its far more recent past, specifically the Civil War and its aftermath. The expression "recovery of historical memory" has a very specific meaning in the debate about Spain's contentious past, which eventually led to the Law of Historical Memory in 2007.[9] As mentioned in Chapter 1, Labanyi argues that the expression should be understood "based on the specificity of the term 'historical memory,' which has come to be used concretely in relation to those forms of memory work that take place in transitional justice contexts" ("The Politics of Memory in Contemporary Spain," 122). The debate about transitional justice in Spain certainly relates multidirectionally to debates about the past in other parts of the world, but lumping this debate together with the expulsion of the Jews in the fifteenth century and the Sephardic diaspora takes both histories out of context. Although a member of Spain's conservative Popular Party spoke of the expedited naturalization process for the Sephardim in terms of the recovery of silenced memory, this should not be taken simply at face value, especially considering that the law was approved during the years of Prime Minister José Luis Rodríguez Zapataro's left-leaning government and that members of the Popular Party opposed the creation of the law.[10] García Margallo's choice of words represents an attempt to conflate two very different histories of violence, therefore changing the political conversation about both "historical memory" of the Spanish Civil War and Spain's relationship with Jews, specifically with the the Sephardim. The recurrence of the myth about Franco's and the Francoist government's alleged benevolence toward Jews in revisionist critiques in right-leaning media further corroborates this interpretation.[11]

The 1492 expulsion, the Spanish Civil War and its repressive aftermath, and the Holocaust are not comparable, much less interchangeable, events. The preceding chapters have shown many instances in which the three events appear to be joined in a "persecutory landscape" (Nirenberg, *Communities of Violence*, 5). This process is problematic (because events, individuals, and institutions are taken out of context) but also necessary (because it allows authors to articulate coherent narratives about the past). In the same chapters I have also made a case for viewing memory as multidirectional, as Rothberg defines the term, "as subject to ongoing negotiation, cross-referencing, and borrowing; as productive and not privative" (*Multidirectional Memory*, 3). Recognizing that memory is multidirectional represents a radical departure from simply equating events of the past with the present.

A quick look at the ways in which Holocaust memory operates in Spain should provide further evidence. Although the Holocaust did not take place in Spain, Spanish history intersects with Holocaust history in a number of ways, for reasons that are geopolitical (the struggle over control of the Mediterranean, refugees' legal and clandestine border crossings, the internment and assassination of Republican exiles, or Rotspanier, in Nazi concentration camps), opportunistic (Franco's shifting alliances with Hitler and Mussolini), and cultural (Spain's historical relationship with the Sephardim). Spain's "memory wars" also have a dynamic relationship with Holocaust memory. Baer has shown that Holocaust memory has invigorated the debate on Spain's contentious past; he argues that, in the Spanish case, "it is, ironically, Jewish memories in their globalized version—those created by the cultural industry and by institutional initiatives—which have paved the way for the public emergence of social memories of Republican deportation" ("The Voids of Sepharad," 107). Discourses about Holocaust memory may resonate with discourses about the memory of the Spanish Civil War and the Francoist dictatorship, but this does not make the actual remembered (and forgotten) events comparable, much less interchangeable.

In Spain, as elsewhere, struggles over the ways in which the past is made present also take place in the cultural arena, and, as Baer notes, cultural production about the Holocaust, specifically cinema, has in many ways shaped public awareness of the Holocaust (99). Antonio Gómez López-Quiñones and Susanne Zepp, editors of the anthology *The Holocaust in Spanish Memory*, confirm Baer's point. The availability of Holocaust memoirs and testimonies (by Primo Levi, Jean Améry, Elie Wiesel, and others) and films (in addition to Spielberg's *Schindler's List* and Benigni's *La vita è bella*, Gómez López-Quiñones and Zepp also mention Polanski's *The Pianist*) has sparked national interest in the Holocaust as well (*The Holocaust in Spanish Memory*, 10). The effects that Hollywood productions have on Holocaust memory and Holocaust awareness need to be understood in a global context. Even so, the success of John Boyne's young adult novel *The Boy in Striped Pajamas* (with more than five million copies of the novel sold worldwide) and of the 2008 film based on the novel serves as a particularly striking example of the ways in which Holocaust awareness in Spain operates in relation to the persistent inscription and reinscription of philo-Sephardism and anti-Semitism. The Spanish translation of the novel appeared in 2007 and remained a bestseller through 2009. This is not the place to go into detail about the novel's historical inaccuracies and inconsistencies; however, it is important to point out that the book was marketed to an adult, not a young adult, audience in Spain.[12] The huge commercial success in Spain of a fiction set in Auschwitz coexists with a new global pattern of anti-Semitism that, according to Baer, "is neither of religious nor of racial nature, although it draws substantially on previous forms of antisemitism, and it can be visibly related to the news from the Middle East" ("The Voids of Sepharad," 95). In Chapter 5, I addressed the range of interpretations of the relation between past and present that will always coexist in the ruins of Sepharad. Specifically, the words "Palestina Libre" on a plaque originally placed on a building to commemorate its Jewish history shows that the perceptions of "Jewish Spain" turn nostalgic visions of the past in the Iberian Peninsula and controversial views of the present in the Middle East into strange bedfellows. The success of *The Boy in the*

Striped Pajamas (both the novel and the film) adds another dimension, leading me to suggest that an explanation for the ambivalence that surrounds "Jewish Spain" might be that Jews in Spain are acceptable as long as their presence is far away in time (before 1492) or far away in place, locked in a silver screen that bears no relation to Spain's realities. It may be that the eastern shore of the Mediterranean is not far enough away, given the extent to which the current conflict in the Middle East informs and shapes current views of Jews much as contemporary Israeli politics is conflated with Jewish history in its entirety. These contradictions become apparent not only in the nostalgic evocation of the Jews of Sepharad and the days of convivencia but also in the fascination that the reading public still has for novels set in the Holocaust, particularly those with child protagonists. Although the role of the child victim is yet another question this book cannot undertake, if we "ask the Mediterranean," the answers are bound to be ambiguous, disturbing, contradictory, and, ultimately, open-ended.

Notes

Notes to Introduction

1. The Catalan term *call* comes from the Latin *callis* (street).

2. Samuel ha-Sardi was one of the most erudite inhabitants of the city; he attended the school of Nathan ben Meir in his youth. In 1225 he wrote the *Sefer ha-Terumot*, a treatise on civil laws and the Talmud.

3. For a more in-depth analysis of this phenomenon, see Baer and López, "The Blind Spots of Secularization," and Baer, "The Voids of Sepharad."

4. Such studies as Federico Ysart's *España y los judíos en la segunda guerra mundial* (Spain and the Jews in World War II, 1973) and Chaim Lipschitz's *Franco, Spain, the Jews, and the Holocaust* (1984) provide a positive evaluation of the events in Spain, ultimately concluding that all possibilities of saving lives, without causing a major commotion in the homeland, were exhausted. Haim Avni's *Spain, the Jews, and Franco* (1982), Bernd Rother's *Franco y el Holocausto* (2005), and Isabelle Rohr's *The Spanish Right and the Jews* (2007) have challenged these conclusions. Ysart and Lipschitz's narratives, which center on Franco as a savior, coexist with the memories of individuals who acted in outright defiance of this same dictator's—or anyone else's—orders. A brief yet significant example would be Marek Halter's biographical sketch of Giorgio Perlasca in *Stories of Deliverance*. Giorgio Perlasca was an Italian who fought for the Nationalists in the Civil War. Finding himself in trouble in Budapest in 1944, he was granted Spanish citizenship. Once Ángel Sanz Briz, the Spanish diplomat, left Budapest, Perlasca continued the work Sanz Briz had already initiated, protecting more than 5,000 Jews in the city. See Halter, *Stories of Deliverance*. Perlasca and Sanz Briz will be the subject of Chapter 3.

5. Unless otherwise noted, all translations are mine.

6. Lisa Fittko, whose story of survival appears in Trudi Alexy's *The Mezuzah in the Madonna's Foot* (a text discussed in Chapter 2) assisted the poet's tragically failed attempt to find freedom in Spain. The details of Benjamin's death and the importance of Karavan's monument will be explored in Chapter 5.

7. In *Dark Continents* Ranjana Khanna notes that, for Nicholas Abraham and Maria Torok, the task of psychoanalysis is to identify the phantom and bring it back into unhindered signification through assimilation (24).

8. Khanna reminds us of the importance of engaging with the remainder: "In fact, to do away with the remainder would be an impossible and unethical assimilation of otherness, a denial of loss and of an engagement with the damage brought about by that loss" (*Dark Continents*, 24).

9. I agree that the *noeuds de mémoire* (or "knots of memory") that Rothberg proposes in "Between Memory and Memory" are a more productive alternative to Nora's concept, making it possible to "stimulate further conceptualization of collective or cultural memory beyond the framework of the imagined community of the nation state" (7). But for the purposes of this book, which precisely engages with the limits of the (Spanish) imagined community of the nation state and with the ways in which an analysis of the Spanish relationship with Jews and Jewish culture makes these limits evident, the concept of *lieux de mémoire* is suitable.

10. As Danielle Rozenberg points out, Castro's interrogation of Spain's "essence" invigorated Islamic and Jewish studies (*La España contemporánea y la cuestión judía*, 342); considering Castro's work is therefore important not because it sheds light on "the structure of Spanish history," as the English translation of the title of his most important work indicates, but because it has allowed scholars to radically rethink what "Spain"—that is, the modern nation—means. Castro's view of the Jews within Spanish history should not be taken for granted, however; it has been the subject of serious critiques in the work of Yitzhak Baer (1966), Benzion Netanyahu (1997), and Albert A. Sicroff (1960). See Subirats, "Nota preliminar" in *Américo Castro y la revisión de la memoria*, 18.

11. Eduardo Subirats points out that the notion that Spain had a "multiethnic and pluri-religious reality" before 1492 has only been put forth by intellectuals in exile ("La peninsula multicultural" in Subirats, ed., *Américo Castro y la revisión de la memoria*, 39).

12. Patricia Grieve's *The Eve of Spain: Myths of Origins in the History of Christian, Muslim and Jewish Conflict* (2009) traces the gendered implications of one of Spain's foundational myths from the Middle Ages to the modern era; Barbara Fuchs's *Exotic Nation: Maurophilia, and the Construction of Early Modern Spain* (2008) explores the role that Moorish heritage plays in the cultural construction of Spain; and David Wacks's *Framing Iberia: Maqāmāt and Frametale Narratives in Medieval Spain* (2007) discusses medieval Iberia in relation to the "frametale": "a type of prose narrative fiction in which a series of unrelated tales or episodes is narrated by characters in an overarching story that provides a context and a pretense for the narration of the tales" (Wacks, *Framing Iberia*, 5).

13. Other important texts are Rozenberg's *La España contemporánea y la cuestión judía*, a comprehensive, sociological study of the intersections of Jewish and Spanish life in the contemporary period, and Ojeda's *Identidades ambivalentes*, an anthropological study of Sephardim in Spain. Both books also challenge the myth of Franco's benevolence toward Jews and conclude that it was fabricated, disseminated, and maintained for political reasons. "Revisiting Jewish Spain in the Modern Era," which initially appeared in 2011 as a special issue of the *Journal of*

Spanish Cultural Studies, edited by Daniela Flesler, Tabea Linhard, and Adrián Pérez Melgosa, was reissued as a book by the same title in 2013; the collection of essays provides a number of innovative case studies centering on a complicated Jewish absence and presence from the nineteenth century to the present. All three works reveal that studying "Jewish Spain" in the contemporary period allows us to zoom in on the main problems that affected and continue to affect Spanish social, political, and cultural life.

In addition, as Andrew Bush shows in his essay "Amador de los Rios and the Beginnings of Modern Jewish Studies in Spain," two pioneering studies of Jewish culture and heritage in Spain were published in the nineteenth century: Adolfo de Castro's *Historia de los judíos de España* (1847) and José Amador de los Ríos's *Estudios históricos, políticos y literarios sobre los judíos de España* (1848).

14. Rozenberg also argues that, since the mid-nineteenth century, Jewish heritage study was used in an opportunistic manner and always with specific political aims (*La España contemporánea y la cuestión judía*, 15).

15. Justin Crumbaugh's *Destination Dictatorship: The Spectacle of Spain's Tourist Boom and the Reinvention of Difference* (2009) discusses the cultural implications of the relations between the Franco regime and the development of tourism. Eugenia Afinoguénova and Jaume Martí-Olivella's anthology on the same subject, *Spain Is (Still) Different: Tourism and Discourse in Spanish Identity* (2007), is also noteworthy, especially because the book includes Flesler and Melgosa's "Marketing Convivencia: Contemporary Appropriations of Spain's Jewish Past."

16. A number of these texts are mentioned in Flesler, Linhard, and Pérez Melgosa's introduction to *Revisiting Jewish Spain*, including novels by foreign authors, such as Noah Gordon's *The Last Jew* (2000), translated into Spanish as *El último judío* in 1999, and Lion Feuchtwanger's *Die Jüdin von Toledo* (1955), translated into Spanish as *La judía de Toledo* in 2000; historical fiction by Spanish authors, such as Lucía Graves's *La casa de la memoria* (1999), Chufo Lloréns's *La saga de los malditos* (2003), Ildefonso Falcones's *La catedral del mar* (2006), Martí Gironell's *El pont dels jueus* (2007), and Agustín Bernaldo Palatchi's *La alianza del converso* (2010); and literary fiction, such as Carme Riera's *Dins el darrer blau* (1994), which won the *Premio Nacional de Literatura* in 1995, and its sequel, *Cap al cel obert* (2000), Antonio Muñoz Molina's *Sepharad* (2001), and Juana Salabert's *Velódromo de invierno* (2001). I will discuss the last two in detail in Chapter 2.

17. For an analysis of texts that also consider the Sephardic diaspora, see Adolfo Campoy-Cubillo's discussion of the works of Esther Bendahan and Mois Benarroch in *Memories of the Maghreb* (2012). The discussion is particularly productive in relation to the writing of other authors of the Sephardic diaspora, such as Albert Cohen, Elias Canetti, and Jacques Derrida.

18. I am referring specifically to Ernesto Giménez Caballero's film *Jews of the Spanish Homeland* (1929). For a discussion of this film, see Friedman's "Reconquering 'Sepharad.'"

19. Rozenberg connects Spanish philo-Sephardism with the search for a new

sphere of influence in the Mediterranean that would make up for the lost empire (*La España contemporánea y la cuestión judía*, 16).

20. In a telling reference to Saenz de Heredia's film *Raza* (1942), which was based on a novel by Francisco Franco himself, Franco's young alter ego wanders the streets of Toledo with his mother; he takes the opportunity to explain to her that coming to Spain "purified" the Sephardic Jews and that they eventually resisted and protested Christ's death before asking Saint James to come and preach the gospel on the Iberian peninsula (Rohr, *The Spanish Right and the Jews*, 117–118; Rother, "España y los judíos," 153; Rozenberg, *La España contemporánea y la cuestión judía*, 256; see also Avni, *Spain, the Jews, and Franco*, 71).

21. Rozenberg also mentions Franco's alleged crypto-Judaism and then challenges this myth by showing that, although Franco is a common Sephardic surname, not all Francos are Sephardim (*La España contemporánea y la cuestión judía*, 254–255).

22. This document, entitled "Spain and the Sephardi Jews," was initially published in 1949 by the Spanish Diplomatic Information Bureau. Avni explains that the goal of the pamphlet was to rebut Israel's vote against Spain in the United Nations General Assembly in 1949. The text is reproduced in Avni, *Spain, the Jews, and Franco*, 179; Baer, "The Voids of Sepharad," 97; and Rozenberg, *La España contemporánea y la cuestión judía*, 250.

23. In his study of Jewish populations in North Africa, Michael Laskier differentiates between Jews who spoke Spanish and Judeo-Spanish and the Judeo-Arab group. The first, descendants of those who were expelled in 1492, settled for the most part in northern Morocco. According to Laskier, "the Sephardim were the most receptive to European ideas and their manners and customs differed from those of the rest of the Jewish population" (*North African Jewry in the Twentieth Century*, 15). The second group, whose ancestors settled in North Africa between 586 B.C.E. and A.D. 70, represents the largest Maghrebi Jewish population. They were speakers of Judeo-Arabic and the local Arabic. In this category Laskier includes descendants of the Sephardim, who did not settle in northern Morocco. "They mingled with the Judeo-Arabs and, over time, had forgotten their Spanish language, assimilating the Judeo-Arabic vernacular" (16). In the late nineteenth and early twentieth centuries, Spanish philo-Sephardism identified the first group with a long-lost pan-Hispanic cultural heritage. In addition, a new but rather small group of Jewish refugees from Eastern Europe began arriving in Morocco in the 1930s. Although I might occasionally refer to the other groups, my analysis centers primarily on the Spanish- and Judeo-Spanish-speaking Moroccan Jews and their identification with Spain.

24. For an in-depth analysis of the ways in which the philo-Sephardic movement "strove to utilize the Jews to advance Spain's colonial expansion in Morocco" in the late nineteenth and early twentieth centuries, see Rohr, "Spaniards of the Jewish Type," 61.

25. Mercenaries fighting for the Nationalists during the Civil War and twenty-first-century Moroccan immigrants have both been associated with the haunting

figure of the Moorish invader from the eighth century (see Flesler, *The Return of the Moor*, 10, and Martin-Márquez, *Disorientations*, 4). Although this figure reveals the prejudices and racism that shape Spain's relationship with Morocco, it also evolves, adjusting to specific historical junctures: the figure of the Moor that appears in texts from medieval or early modern Spain has a very different political meaning from the Moroccan soldier depicted in Civil War cultural productions or the twentieth- and twenty-first-century North African immigrant. Hence, it is important to understand the shifts in the meaning of the "Moorish other" and the "Jewish other" in a discussion that focuses specifically on the Protectorate during the 1930s and 1940s and the representation of others in "historical memory."

26. An exception would be the Algerian city of Oran, occupied by Spain from 1505 to 1708. The Spanish forces returned to Oran in 1732 and finally departed in 1792.

27. The Queen's testament states: "I ask my daughter the Princess and her husband the Prince that, as Catholic Princes, they keep always in mind to honour God and keep alive the Holy Faith, being obedient to the Holy Mother, the Church, and keep the conquest of Africa as the only way to reach the faith of the infidels" (Albet-Mas, "Three Gods, Two Shores, One Space," 590).

28. The "Setmana Tràgica" refers to a series of violent confrontations between the army and protesters, mainly anarchists, communists, and Republicans. The confrontations were triggered when Prime Minister Antonio Maura called up reserve troops to protect Spanish-controlled mines in the Rif region. The large human and material costs of the "Rif War" and Spain's most devastating defeat in Annual in 1921 had severe consequences for the Spanish government. General Primo de Rivera's coup in 1923 ended King Alfonso XII's reign. The military situation in Morocco led to the creation of a new, more organized Spanish colonial army, the Legión Extranjera, led by generals Francisco Franco and Millán Astray.

29. The Spanish Protectorate was only set in place after the French Protectorate was a reality, following the French invasion in 1911.

Notes to Chapter One

1. Even though linguists who study the Judeo-Spanish language differ on a number of points, there seems to be a general agreement that the language Sephardic Jews spoke before 1492 bore some of the traits that would later mark the developments of Judeo-Spanish as a distinct language. It was in exile, shortly before and after 1492, that Judeo-Spanish consolidated itself as the language of the Jewish communities.

2. 1992 was, of course, more than the year during which the Barcelona Olympics coincided with the world's fair in Seville. In addition to the celebrations of and protests against the 500th anniversary of the conquest of the New World, the 500 years that had passed since the expulsion of the Jews also became the subject of numerous commemorations and debates.

3. In his shattering critique of *Sepharad*, Hackl argues that, among many other shortcomings, the novel portrays Sephardim as victims and therefore as "good."

He adds that this is a general tendency in Spanish literature and cites *Velódromo de invierno* as an example ("El caso Sefarad," 20, 29).

4. My use of "frametale" is based on the definition that David Wacks provides in *Framing Iberia: Maqāmāt and Frametale Narratives in Medieval Spain*. Wacks defines the "frametale" as "a type of prose narrative fiction in which a series of unrelated tales or episodes is narrated by characters in an overarching story that provides a context and a pretense for the narration of the tales" (*Framing Iberia*, 5). The original Spanish subtitle of *Sepharad*, "Novela de novelas," was not carried over in Margaret Sayers Peden's 2003 translation.

5. The diplomat is Ángel Sanz Briz, whose actions (and the multiple meanings attached to those actions) will be addressed in Chapter 3.

6. Jo Labanyi suggests that "memory has become an industry generating public interest for economic reasons" and that the publication of Isaac Rosas's *¡Otra maldita novela de la guerra civil!* (Another damn civil war novel!) reveals that the media debate on memory might have reached a limit that expands far beyond the literary realm ("The Politics of Memory in Contemporary Spain," 119).

7. Strictly speaking, Ilse Landermann would belong to what Susan Rubin Suleiman has called the "1.5 generation"; that is, "child survivors of the Holocaust, too young to have had an adult understanding of what was happening to them, and sometimes too young to have any memory of it at all, but old enough to have been there during the Nazi persecution of Jews" (*Crises of Memory and the Second World War*, 179).

8. Lagranja's activities reflect, as Isabelle Rohr has shown, the contradictory rhetoric of the Francoist government toward Jews during World War II. Rohr historicizes the perception of the Sephardim as more Spanish than Jewish: a prolonged stay in the Iberian Peninsula "purified" Sephardim, making them (as opposed to Ashkenazim) redeemable. Rohr explains the differentiation between the Sephardim and Ashkenazim in relation to Spanish colonialism in North Africa: "The revival of philosephardism needs to be understood within the context of Spain's Mediterranean policy, more concretely with the ebb and flow of the Franco-Spanish relationship in Morocco. In the attempt to rationalize these contradictions the regime revived the distinction between the Ashkenazi and the Sephardic Jews, by pinning all ills on the former and arguing that the latter had been 'cleansed' during their stay in Spain" (*The Spanish Right and the Jews, 1898–1945*, 98).

9. Even though the Landermanns are not Sephardic Jews, Miranda promises to help Annelies because a strong friendship with Arvid Landermann, Annelies's husband, binds him to this family's fate.

10. *Velódromo de invierno* is hardly the first Spanish novel in which Hans Christian Andersen's fairytales play a crucial role. Particularly, Ana María Matute's *Primera memoria* (translated into English as *School of the Sun*) is a novel in which the main character, according to María Elena Soliño, grasps "the merciless qualities of Andersen's text" (*Women and Children First*, 180). The original fairytale, unlike the Disney version, does not end with a marriage and a "happily ever after."

It ends instead with the young mermaid's sacrifice because she is unable to kill the woman who is to marry the prince she loves. Even though Andersen's fairytale ends with a strongly religious and prescriptive message—the mermaid becomes a heavenly spirit, closer to her yearned-for eternal life every time children behave well—what seems to capture both Matute and Salabert is the mermaid's loneliness when she knows she can neither return to her kin beneath the waves nor remain "happily ever after" with her beloved prince.

11. In the novel *La noche ciega*, set during the Civil War, Salabert constructs a similar topography. The city of Finis appears again in this work, and a brief reference to Arvid Landermann reveals the connections between the two texts.

12. The German expression "wurden vergast" (were gassed) refers to the deaths of Sebastián's family in the gas chambers. German is the language of extermination; Spanish, the language of memory and the living.

13. In Salonika, which had the largest Sephardic population in Greece, 80 percent of the community was deported during World War II. Most of them died in concentration camps. See Díaz-Más, *Sephardim*, 180.

14. Terms in italic are in the original Judeo-Spanish.

15. The conversos were Jews who had converted to Christianity. Anti-Jewish riots in 1391, the establishment of the Holy Inquisition, and the 1492 expulsion led to massive conversions. It has been speculated that the "New Christians," for fear of being associated with crypto-Jewish and therefore heretic practices, were among the culprits in the anti-Semitic violence in the fifteenth century. The character of Costura in Carme Riera's *Dins al darer blau* (In the last blue) is an example: Costura is a Christian convert who betrays the community of *chuetas* (Majorcan Jews) when they attempt to leave the island and the threat of the Inquisition behind. In Ana María Matute's *The School of the Sun*, the Taronjí brothers play a similar role: the two men, also descendants of the chuetas, are guilty of the death of José Taronjí, a family member who represented a threat to the most conservative sectors on the island. The murder, a repercussion of the Civil War in Spain, is an example of the recurrent motif of "caínismo," the hatred of as well as violence toward members of one's own family or community, that has been widely recognized in the literature of the Spanish Civil War.

16. After the loss of Puerto Rico, Cuba, and the Philippines, Spain no longer had significant colonial possessions. The rediscovery of Sephardic Jews who had maintained the Judeo-Spanish language provided an opportunity to establish neo-colonial ties with Greece, its Mediterranean neighbor to the east.

17. According to María Rosa Menocal, the stories from the *Arabian Nights* lead to and from al-Andalus and are connected to her notion of a culture of tolerance. She writes:

> Petrus Alfonsi brought frame tale tradition to Latin Europe, followed by other collectors and translators from Andalusia. If the frames of these works characteristically present some sort of tyranny—direct or indirect echoes of Scheherazade's plight—the tales within them embody the hope that stories can bring, since by

their very nature they resist clear-cut interpretations and are likely to reveal the different ways in which truths and realities can be perceived. In its insistence that the point of stories, of literature, is to pose difficult questions rather than to propose easy answers or facile morals, this tradition is a central part of the Andalusian legacy to subsequent European culture. (*The Ornament of the World*, 274)
It is no coincidence that one of the stories in *Sepharad* is titled "Scheherazade."

18. Alfredo Campoy-Cubillo points out some of the novel's shortcomings and suggests that Esther Bendahan's novels "reiterate the historical specificity of the Sephardic experience that is missing from *Sefarad*" (*Memories of the Maghreb*, 84). Despite the flaws that Campoy-Cubillo discusses, Muñoz Molina's novel remains a necessary text in a discussion of the nostalgia for Sepharad in relation to World War II and the Holocaust.

19. In a reply to Hackl's critique, the author confesses that fragments of different lives—including the author's—make up this character. A historical Jacobo Salama lived, in fact, in Tangier in the period during which Muñoz Molina's tale takes place. For more information on Eastern European Jewish refugees in Tangier, see Rohr, *The Spanish Right and the Jews, 1898–1945*, 105.

20. In the last tale of the collection, the "key" trope will appear again, when the main character describes what remains of the Jewish quarter in his hometown.

Notes to Chapter Two

1. Jorge Reverte, "La lista de Franco para el Holocausto," *El País*, June 20, 2010.

2. At first, the complete title of Alexy's book was *The Mezuzah in the Madonna's Foot: Oral Histories Exploring Five Hundred Years in the Paradoxical Relationship of Spain and the Jews*. When the paperback edition appeared a year later, in 1994, two new subtitles were added: *Marranos and Other Secret Jews* and *A Woman Discovers Her Spiritual Heritage*. In her second book, *The Marrano Legacy: A Contemporary Crypto-Jewish Priest Reveals Secrets of His Double Life*, the author explains why the subtitles of her first work changed with the paperback edition. After she was interviewed on the radio following the publication of the hardcover edition, a large number of callers—instead of asking about Alexy's book on exile in Spain during World War II—expressed interest in the history of crypto-Jews and inquired where they could find more information about "the book about Crypto-Jews." This then prompted the publishers of the 1994 paperback edition to add the two subtitles: "Marranos and Other Secret Jews" and "A Woman Discovers Her Spiritual Heritage" (*The Marrano Legacy*, 4).

3. These include the testimonies of exiles Nina Mitroni, Hilde and Peter Blau, Leon Nussbaum, Mendel and Ruchel Slucki; rescuers Lisa Fittko, who assisted Walter Benjamin in his failed attempt to cross to Spain, Renée Reichmann, the prominent Hungarian émigrée in Tangier, and a number of individuals who collaborated with the American Jewish Joint Distribution Committee; important personalities who belonged to the Jewish community in Spain, among them Carlos

Benarroch, Samuel Toledano, and Mario Muchnik; and Catholic activists who promoted religious pluralism in Spain.

4. Nirenberg also notes that the 1391 mass conversions

raised, for the first time, systemic doubt about who was a Christian and who was a Jew. At their simplest, these were questions about who had actually converted. Particularly when conversion took place in an atmosphere of mob violence, it could be difficult to ascertain who had in fact been baptized, though the clas-sification was obviously a crucial one, given the Inquisition's interest (at least in the Crown of Aragon) in relapsed converts. But the problem of identification ex-tended far beyond doubts about whether an individual had been baptized or not, for ambiguity could arise in any number of settings. (14)

5. See Gavriel Rosenfeld, "A Flawed Prophecy? *Zakhor*, the Memory Boom, and the Holocaust."

6. Isaac Salama, Antonio Muñoz Molina's fictional Holocaust survivor in *Se-pharad*, struggles with shame throughout his life. The testimonies in *Memorias judías* also reveal the same tension between guilt and shame.

7. See Rothberg, *Multidirectional Memory*, 9. In *Beyond Anne Frank*, Wolf also uses the phrase to discuss the different ways in which hidden children and their parents endured the devastating events of the Shoah: "Hidden children, however, were not seen as survivors and hesitated to apply this label to themselves. Accord-ing to several interviewees, they have been told by camp survivors that they were not really survivors, because 'they had it easy during the war.' This suggests not only a hierarchy of suffering, but also that hidden children have no right to claim survivor status" (Wolf, *Beyond Anne Frank*, 17–19). The problem with this frame-work is that other stories of survival are silenced or devalued. Doris Bergen also uses the phrase in *War and Genocide: A Concise History of the Holocaust* (x).

8. In *Secrecy and Deceit: The Religion of the Crypto-Jews*, David Gitlitz recog-nizes a series of common threads that run through crypto-Judaism "despite the fact that Iberian crypto-Judaism varied considerably from time to time and from place to place" (81). These common threads include that fact that crypto-Jewish prac-tice derives from Judaism but also might contain elements from Christianity, that crypto-Judaism was always persecuted, which explains the secrecy and subterfuge that are part of the practice, and that crypto-Jews always led a double existence: a private and hidden Jewish life and a public and overt Catholic life.

9. For an analysis of the ways in which documents that were produced during the trials of the Inquisition can be studied, see Gitlitz, *Secrecy and Deceit*, chapters 2 and 3.

10. Alexy uses the same language in her second book, *The Marrano Legacy*: "For me, finding out I was a Jew . . . and then denying it and hiding it under a Catholic cover, felt like the ultimate sin of betrayal" (84).

11. Alexy explains her feelings in the following terms: "We were baptized twice. It didn't seem to bother my parents or Fredo [her brother], but I felt like a coward and a criminal. Whatever else being a Jew was all about, I knew they were special,

persecuted for being who they were, just like the heroes and saints I had read about. By lying, by denying I was one of them, I knew I had forever forfeited the right call myself a Jew" (*Mezuzah*, 40).

12. In the foreword to *The Marrano Legacy*, Stanley Hordes, cofounder of the Society of Crypto-Jewish Studies, calls Alexy a "twentieth-century conversa" (ix).

Notes to Chapter Three

1. I use the term "rescue narratives" broadly to refer to instances in which Jews were either protected or saved from deportation to a concentration camp.

2. Yad Vashem provides the following description of the Righteous among the Nations project on the institution's website:

> One of Yad Vashem's principal duties is to convey the gratitude of the State of Israel and the Jewish people to non-Jews who risked their lives to save Jews during the Holocaust. This mission was defined by the law establishing Yad Vashem, and in 1963 the Remembrance Authority embarked upon a worldwide project to grant the title of Righteous Among the Nations to the few who helped Jews in the darkest time in their history. To this end, Yad Vashem set up a public Commission, headed by a Supreme Court Justice, which examines each case and is responsible for granting the title. Those recognized receive a medal and a certificate of honor and their names are commemorated on the Mount of Remembrance in Jerusalem. (www.yadvashem.org/yv/en/righteous/program.asp)

3. See Avni's chapter "Fact and Fiction" in *Spain, the Jews, and Franco*; Rother, *Franco y el Holocausto*, 410; Gerber, *The Jews of Spain*, 263; Rozenberg, *La España contemporánea y la cuestión judía*, 21.

4. In addition to Sanz Briz, Carmen Ruiz de Santaella and Eduardo Propper de Callejón are honored at Yad Vashem in Israel. Other Spanish diplomats who protected Jews in occupied Europe include Sebastián Romero de Radigales, Bernardo Rolland de Miota, and Julio Palencia.

5. Sanz Briz had a long and successful career in diplomatic service and died in 1980, serving as Spain's ambassador to the Holy See. In 1998 Spain issued a postage stamp in his honor as part of a series on human rights.

6. Edith Wischnitzer remembers Perlasca as "an Italian guy who had seen a Jewish kid killed in Italy . . . he became very angry with the Germans, he volunteered to come to Hungary to work, this way he came to the Spanish embassy. He was a second Wallenberg." Edith Wischnitzer, interview 27155, USC Shoah Foundation Institute Visual History Archive, 2011.

7. The letter is dated December 4, 1945. "Records Relating to the Investigation of Giorgio Perlasca by the United States Holocaust Memorial Council, 1945–1990," RG-20.004, USHMM (cited hereafter as Perlasca records).

8. Perlasca records, tape 1, 23:17.

9. Perlasca records, tape 3, 3:04.

10. Jaime Vándor, interview 32735, USC Shoah Foundation Institute Visual History Archive, 2011.

11. Gladitz-Pérez Lorenzo produced and directed a documentary on Perlasca in 1993.

12. For the interviews in which Perlasca tells his story, see Perlasca records.

13. For an account of Perlasca's confrontation with Eichmann, see Halter, *Stories of Deliverance*, 276–280, and Deaglio, *The Banality of Goodness*, 130–137.

14. Historian Wayne Bowen carried out an interview with Serrano Suñer in 1997. The interview is available at the USHMM library, RG-50.030*0454, and online at collections.ushmm.org/search/catalog/irn506738.

15. See, for example, a brief article entitled "Suner Accuses Judaism as Foe of the New Spain," *New York Times*, June 3, 1939. In the article Serrano Suñer emulates Nazi rhetoric and talks about international Jewry as Spain's ultimate enemy.

16. See Avni, *Spain, the Jews, and Franco*, 181; Rother, *Franco y el Holocausto*, 399; Rozenberg, *La España contemporánea y la cuestión judía*, 250.

17. For an account of the lack of a Spanish response to the deportation of all Jews from Salonika, see Fleming, *Greece: A Jewish History*.

18. It is hardly a coincidence that both documents appear reprinted in David Salinas's *España, los sefarditas y el Tercer Reich 1939–1945: La labor de diplomáticos españoles contra el genocidio*. The book, published by the University of Valladolid and the Spanish Foreign Ministry, does not take into account the research (Avni, Marquina Barrio and Ospina) that challenges the myth that Francoist Spain was protecting the Jews.

19. Gladitz-Pérez Lorenzo argues that the newspaper article is very biased because the press was not free in Spain in 1949. She suggests that Sanz Briz read the article before it was printed and that it might even have been censored by him, thus leading to a version of the events that corresponds to what the Spanish government wanted the general public to believe. Gladitz's report is dated August 1, 1990. Perlasca records, accession number 1991.016.

20. This time the members of the Civil Guard are committing acts of heroism.

21. The earliest negotiations between Perlzweig and Cárdenas took place in 1943 and eventually led to the resolution that was passed in December 1944: "At the end of the WJC meeting came the crowning achievement, for Cárdenas, as well as for Spain, in a resolution expressing thanks to Spain for having protected persecuted Jews especially in Hungary" (Rother, "Myth and Fact: Spain and the Holocaust," 58).

22. George Horovicz, interview 44854, USC Shoah Foundation Institute Visual History Archive, 2011.

23. Molho, "Un hidalgo español al servicio de Dios y de la Humanidad en Budapest."

24. Gilbert writes:

On June 26, information brought by four Jewish escapees from Auschwitz exploded on the Allied and neutral world: their report, smuggled out of the death camp itself, made it clear that all previous deportees to Auschwitz over the previous two years had been murdered there and that the Hungarian deportees were even then being gassed. The Jewish leadership in Budapest appealed to diplomats of neutral countries to do what they could to save the Jews of the capital from deportation. In an immediate response, the Spanish Minister in Budapest, Angel Sanz-Briz, and the Swiss Consul-General, Carl Lutz, joined forces to issue protective documents. Sanz-Briz distributed 1,898 such documents, using Spanish Legation writing paper. (*The Righteous*, 387)

25. Renée Reichmann, the matriarch of a prominent Hungarian family that had emigrated to Tangier, played a crucial role in these efforts.

26. Lequerica began his political career as a firm Nazi supporter. As the Spanish ambassador to Vichy, he ordered the deportation of Spanish writer Max Aub to Algeria and also ordered the arrests of many Republican leaders, such as anarchist leader Federica Montseny and Lluis Companys, the former president of the Generalitat of Catalonia, in 1939. Lequerica became Franco's foreign minister in 1944, when the regime in Spain no longer openly supported the Axis and was slowly shifting toward building alliances with the Allies. During his tenure as the ambassador to Vichy, however, Lequerica never stood in the way of diplomats' efforts to protect Jews who were Spanish citizens or under Spanish protection after 1942. Lequerica's story, like so many others, also contains the contradictions of the period.

27. Joshua Goode explains that differentiating racial thought in Spain from elsewhere in Europe has long been a common practice: "Spaniards, for instance, have gone to great lengths to deny any similarity between Iberian racial thought and its northern European counterparts. A common boast, for example, among members of the Spanish fascist party, the Falange Tradicionalista, even before the Civil War and repeated long after World War II, was that Spanish fascism had always remained free of racial or fascist ideas" (*Impurity of Blood*, 3).

28. In what follows I refer to the depiction of Sanz Briz, Raoul Wallenberg, and Giorgio Perlasca in Carcedo's text, not the actual historical figures.

29. See Goytisolo, "La historiografía española y la herencia de Sefarad."

30. Carcedo emphasizes Sanz Briz's compassion and concern for children, regardless of whether they were Jewish (*Un español frente al Holocausto*, 110, 134, 153, 154, 196).

31. According to Gilbert, "on October 23, Sanz-Briz put Giorgio Perlasca, an Italian subject whom he knew and respected in charge of the Spanish safe houses in the city" (*The Righteous*, 400).

32. Gilbert's version of the events also includes eyewitness accounts, such as young Avraham Ronai's. Ronai recalls how Perlasca protected Jews residing in a safe house whom members of the Arrow Cross were ready to take down to the Danube, where they would be shot. Perlasca intervened, threatening that, because the Jews were Spanish citizens, the consequences for Hungarians in Spain would be severe. "Suddenly out of nowhere appeared Perlasca, and began berating the Arrow Cross commander, threatening to cable and report to Madrid this violation of Spanish rights, an act which would have grave consequences for Spanish-

Hungarian relations and cause damage to the career of the Hungarian officer in charge. The ploy worked, and all those assembled were released and allowed to return to the Spanish-protected house from which they had been taken to what had been intended to be their death" (401). Gilbert takes this information from a speech by Mordecai Paldiel at Yad Vashem on September 25, 1989, when Perlasca was awarded a Medal of the Righteous.

33. The 1964 film, directed by Giuseppe de Santis, has been translated as *Attack and Retreat*.

34. Before his brains dried up (from reading too many chivalry novels), Don Quixote was a gentleman named Alonso Quijano.

Notes to Chapter Four

1. According to Virginia Trueba, the figure of Aixa Kandisha belongs to both Moroccan and Jewish folklore. Part male, part female, she is a goat-footed, nocturnal, evil being, both a witch and a demonic seductress. One of the many legends that circulated in Tangier was that on windy nights she knocked on doors before taking the men away with her (Vázquez, *La vida perra de Juanita Narboni*, 161n).

2. Italy, Portugal, Belgium, and the Netherlands later ratified the agreement.

3. The Protectorate covered one-fifth of the Moroccan territory, roughly 22,000 square kilometers. The Rif mountain range, extreme climates, and Berber resistance made this zone particularly hard to control.

4. José Antonio Primo de Rivera founded the Falange in 1933 in an attempt to emulate Italian fascism. Although Franco relied on the Falange during the war and throughout the postwar period, he would later distance himself from the fascist organization.

5. Juan Prim (1814–1870) was a general and a statesman. After leading the troops in the African War, he commanded the army in Mexico and was a hero of the "Glorious Revolution" that ended Queen Isabel II's rule. He was assassinated only two days after the more progressive-leaning Amadeo of Savoy became the king of Spain.

6. Susan Martin-Márquez carries out a thorough analysis of this brotherhood and how it relates to gender roles and the notion of *hispanidad* in *Disorientations: Spanish Colonialism in Africa and the Performance of Identity*.

7. In *Provincializing Europe*, Chakrabarty challenges the colonial and historical temporality in John Stuart Mill's thought:

> According to Mill, Indians or Africans were *not yet* civilized enough to rule themselves. Some historical time of development and civilization (colonial rule and education, to be precise) had to elapse before they could be considered prepared for such a task. Mill's historicist argument thus converted Indians, Africans, and other "rude" nations to an imaginary waiting room of history. In doing so, it converted history itself into a version of this waiting room. We were all headed for the same destination, Mill averred, but some people were to arrive earlier than others. That was what historicist consciousness was: a recommendation to the colonized

to wait. Acquiring a historical consciousness, acquiring the public spirit that Mill thought absolutely necessary for the art of self-government, was also to learn this art of waiting. This waiting was the realization of the "not yet" of historicism. (Chakrabarty, *Provincializing Europe*, 8)

8. Scholars have documented the gendered dynamics of colonialism and post-colonialism that are "from the outset fundamental to the securing and mainte-nance of the imperial enterprise" (McClintock, *Imperial Leather*, 7). Stoler's *Carnal Knowledge and Imperial Power* and Spivak's discussion of the "third-world gendered subaltern" in *A Critique of Postcolonial Reason* are seminal texts that discuss the intricate relationships between gender and colonialism.

9. "Philo-Sephardism," as Isabelle Rohr explains, "soon became a tool in the hands of a neo-colonial lobby, which argued that the peaceful commercial penetra-tion of Morocco would pave the way to colonial expansion there and help regen-erate the Spanish economy" (*The Spanish Right and the Jews*, 19).

10. The dictator's own writing supports this idea: "My years in Africa live within me with indescribable force. . . . Without Africa, I can scarcely explain my-self to myself, nor can I explain myself properly to my comrades in arms" (quoted in Balfour, *Deadly Embrace*, 202).

11. It is important to note here that the Catholic queen deliberately stated in her testament that the conquest of the Islamic enemy was of utmost importance. However, a Spanish conquest of North Africa did not materialize after her death; instead, an "Atlantic shift" marked the birth of modern colonialism in the New World (Vilarós and Ugarte, "Cuando África empieza en los Pirineos," 199–200).

12. Albet-Mas mentions a comparable anecdote: a comic strip character with the name Ben Ali "served as a propaganda element in this sense, being presented as always anxious to accompany his father 'who was off to fight for Spain, against the Jews'" ("Three Gods, Two Shores, One Space," 594).

13. For an analysis of the poem, see Jacobo Israel Garzón's *Los judíos de Tetuán*, 233–236. The ballad and the prose texts use identical expressions to tell this story of unrequited love.

14. In Lope de Vega's play an angry mob murders Raquel; in Bécquer's legend Sara Leví's own father crucifies his daughter to punish her for having fallen in love with a Christian and for her desire to convert to Christianity.

15. Virginia Hagelstein Marquardt argues that "avant-garde movements in the visual arts were aligned with both the communist left and the fascist right" (*Art and Journals on the Political Front, 1910–1940*, 3); in *Vértice*—a direct organ of the Falange, after all—ideological goals supersede the artistic contents. Jordana Men-delson and Estrella de Diego explain that, in such magazines as *Vértice*, "surrealist drawings were appropriated for use in some of the publication's most symbolically important issues, even before the end of the Civil War" ("Political Practice and the Arts in Spain," 99).

16. Adolfo Campoy-Cubillo also points out that "Spain's fraternal relation with the Maghreb was certainly atypical in the context of European colonialism, but it

was also coherent with the official discourse of Spanish exceptionalism articulated by the Francoist regime" (*Memories of the Maghreb*, 9).

17. Albet-Mas argues that Spanish Orientalism was "specifically African and, more precisely, 'Moroccanist'—Spain's 'Orient' turned out to be in the South rather than to the East. The Spanish Orient was, in fact, Morocco, at least from the second half of the nineteenth century onwards, due to several factors: the geographical vicinity of the North African coast, the cultural heritage and historical legacy of Al-Andalus, and the fact that it was the theatre of the new colonial adventure, designed to strengthen the international position of Spain, as well as to serve certain bourgeois interests within Spanish society" ("Three Gods, Two Shores, One Space," 586).

18. Santiago Matamoros, or James the Moor-Slayer, became the patron saint of Spain and has been represented, starting in the ninth century, "in the form of a medieval knight, in the style of Saint George slaying the dragon, but with this mythical animal now being replaced by a Moor, trampled underfoot by the Apostle's horse" (Albet-Mas, "Three Gods, Two Shores, One Space," 589).

19. The author explains later in the text that Sultana Cohén's family comes from Oran. According to Gottreich and Schroeder, the Algerian city was "an integral part of the early modern Sephardi network" (*Jewish Culture and Society in North Africa*, 15).

20. Valis writes:

Lo cursi is one of the most pervasive cultural phenomena of nineteenth—and early twentieth—century Spain. An untranslatable term, *cursi* comes closest in meaning to *kitsch*, but encompasses much more than trash, cheap sentimentality, or tackiness, traits commonly associated with kitsch. In dictionaries, one who pretends to refinement and elegance without possessing them is cursi. Popular imagination explains it more as "querer y no poder" (wanting and not being able to). Lo cursi is a form of disempowered desire, frustrated in its aspiration to a higher order of things in life. (*The Culture of Cursilería*, 31–32)

21. For the alleged superiority of the Sephardim, see note 20 in the Introduction.

22. Rohr writes that "in the wake of the Russian revolution, 'White' Russian officers spread the Protocols [of the Elders of Zion] throughout the world from Western Europe to Japan. The Spanish translation came from a French version, which had been edited by Father Ernest Jouin, an ecclesiastic who took credit for coining the term 'Judeo-Masonic'" (*The Spanish Right and the Jews*, 36). For more on the Falange and freemasonry, see Ferrer Benimeli, *La masonería en la España del siglo XX*, esp. page 92, for Prim's affiliations with freemasonry. Unlike the short prose piece published in *Vértice*, the early ballad "Romance de Sultana Cohén" expresses outrage at Prim's assassination. Vega writes: "Lo mataron los masones. / Los jesuitas le matan. / Fueron los republicanos. / Las balas eran monárquicas" (The Masons killed him / The Jesuits are killing him / The Republicans were guilty. / The bullets were from the Monarchists) (quoted in Israel Garzón's *Los judíos de Tetuán*, 235). Vega's not automatically identifying Prim with the Free-

mason in the poem (which precedes the Civil War) underscores the ideological agenda of the piece published in *Vértice*.

23. In Vega's text the queen's fury results from Prim's treason; the author "ventriloquizes" Queen Isabella II, who, after pledging her jewels for the Moroccan cause, now claims that the peace in Morocco is the result of the Freemasons' conspiring with the British.

24. *La vida perra de Juanita Narboni* was reprinted in 2000 with a superb introduction by Virginia Trueba. For Vázquez's short stories, collected in *El cuarto de los niños y otros cuentos* (2008), Trueba again provided an introduction. *Fiesta para una mujer sola*, with an introduction by Sonia García Soubriet, was published in 2009.

25. In 1982 director Javier Aguirre released his film version of the novel: *Vida/perra*. Aguirre's film features only one actress, Esperanza Roy, and is set in northern Spain instead of Tangier. Vicente Tortajada suggests that the child who in Goytisolo's novel crushes flies in the pages of Spanish classics in the library of the Liceo Español in Tangier is supposed to be a young Ángel Vázquez (*Azahar y vitriolo*, 13).

26. Virginia Trueba describes Vázquez's relationship with the Holländer family in her introduction to a new edition of Vázquez's short stories, *El cuarto de los niños y otros cuentos*.

27. Goytisolo, "Vorwort," *Das Hundeleben der Juanita Narboni*, 5.

28. "Juanita ist ein Resonanzkörper, in dem sich Wesentliches und Nebensächliches vermischen" (Goytisolo, "Vorwort," 6).

29. The MEDEA program supports film projects in the European Union and the Mediterranean basin.

30. Quoted in Vicente Molina Foix, "Mansión de Drácula en Atocha," *El País*, January 29, 2010.

31. The term "paradise" is used to describe international Tangier in the press packet for Benlyazid's film.

32. "Dedicated to a historical Muslim woman, Fatima Fihra (the tenth-century founder of one of the world's first universities), *A Door to the Sky* envisions an aesthetic that affirms Islamic culture while inscribing it with a feminist consciousness, offering an alternative to both the Western imaginary and an Islamic fundamentalist representation of Muslim women. Whereas contemporary documentaries show all-female gatherings as a space of resistance to patriarchy and fundamentalism, *A Door to the Sky* uses all-female spaces to point to a liberatory project based on unearthing women's history within Islam, a history that includes female spirituality, prophecy, poetry, and intellectual creativity, as well as revolt, material power, and social and political leadership" (Shohat and Stam, *Unthinking Eurocentrism*, 165).

33. Juanita's monologue moves back and forth across more than forty years of her own and Tangier's history. The structure of the film, with two brief exceptions, is linear.

34. She describes herself and her sister as "women with a British passport, with Andalusian blood, and who have had the Tangier experience" (Vázquez, *La vida perra de Juanita Narboni*, 221).

Notes to Chapter 5

1. Daniela Flesler and Adrián Pérez Melgosa have published the sole analyses to date of Jewish heritage tourism in Spanish cities, specifically, on Tarazona and Hervás; their 2008 and 2010 essays are cited repeatedly in this chapter. Ethnomusicologist and performer Judith Cohen has discussed the appropriation of Jewish culture in Galicia. See "We've Always Sung It That Way" in *Charting Memory: Recalling Medieval Spain*. In the last chapter of *La España contemporánea y la cuestión judía*, Rozenberg presents an overview of different forms of recovery of Jewish heritage in contemporary Spain.

2. More information on the Exile Memorial Museum can be found on its website, www.museuexili.cat/.

3. Derrida discusses Freud's "A Note upon the 'Mystic Writing Pad'" in his essay "Freud and the Scene of Writing" and argues that the "mystic writing pad" resembles a palimpsest. Although this writing device (nowadays available as a toy) allows for repeated erasure of writing on its surface, traces of older writing remain partially visible. The palimpsest and the writing pad thus provide ways to understand the production of memory.

4. For more information on the works of art, refer to the Walter Benjamin in Portbou website, walterbenjaminportbou.cat/en/content/el-darrer-passatge, sponsored by the Memorial Democràtic and Ajuntament de Portbou.

5. Crumbaugh states that "the representation of the tourist boom was so ubiquitous that tourism came to act as an allegory of the larger changes of the 1960s, offering provisional cohesion and coherence to the disparate, even contradictory, ideas about economic growth, and reconfiguring the relationship between the Franco regime and the Spanish populace" (*Destination Dictatorship*, 2).

6. Crumbaugh, citing Afinoguenova and Martí-Olivella, points out that the "Spain Is Different" slogan "dates back to 1929, when it was used for the first time on posters of the Patrimonio Nacional de Turismo" (*Destination Dictatorship*, 135n1). Crumbaugh understands the slogan as "the kind of doublespeak that typified late Francoism. Spanish exceptionality (its difference) had by then been reinvented as an ornamental inscription on the larger story of integration and modernization" (6).

7. See Curtis and Pajaczkowska, "'Getting There': Travel, Time and Narrative," 202.

8. See the chapter "'McDisneyization' and 'Post-Tourism'" in Rojek and Urry, *Touring Cultures*.

9. Gruber adopts the term "Jewish space" from Diana Pinto's *Beyond Anti-Semitism: The New Jewish Presence in Europe*.

10. The creation of Caminos de Sefarad is an example of the promotion of cul-

tural tourism and an attempt to present Spain not only as a destination for beach holidays but also as a site of cultural history. The development of cultural tourism, including Jewish heritage tourism, began in the 1990s: "This promotion, linked to the concept of the 'historic city' and to cultural and heritage tourism, partakes of the current efforts of the Spanish Tourism Board, which has been trying to project an image of Spain that would appeal to a more discriminating clientele than that which looks for inexpensive beaches: people interested in art, architecture, and cultural heritage" (Flesler and Pérez Melgosa, "Marketing Convivencia," 67).

11. Flesler and Pérez Melgosa explain: "Ironically, many of the Spanish Jewish quarters that are exhibited today as spaces of convivencia and religious tolerance were created together with the imposition of special clothing for Jews, in order to police the frontier between Jews and Christians to break up and prevent the close relationships that arose from 'living together in cities and dressing alike' (Alfonso X, Siete Partidas 7.24.1)" ("Hervás, Convivencia, and the Heritagization," 64).

12. For an analysis of this debate and its meaning, see Kruger, *The Spectral Jew*.

13. See Chapter 2 for an oral history of the Jewish community of Barcelona.

14. See the Urban Cultours website, "Revisiting Jewish Heritage in Spain and the Memory of Sepharad in Catalonia," www.urbancultours.com/.

15. See the Associació Call de Barcelona website, www.calldebarcelona.org/.

16. See the Caminos de Sefarad/Red de Juderías de España website, www.red juderias.org/.

17. Jesús García, "Barcelona divulgará su patrimonio judío con un centro de interpretación," *El País*, May 13, 2006.

18. The term "Montjuïc" is a derivation of Mons Judaicus, where Jews used to reside and work the land.

19. See the Patronat Call de Girona website, www.girona.cat/.

20. See Hasan-Rokem, "Jews as Postcards, or Postcards as Jews," 508.

21. Girona is not the only city in which the figure of the Errant Jew becomes part of a tour. Toledopaisajes, a private entity in Toledo, also lists "The Errant Jew" among the guided tours that it offers (www.toledopaisajes.com/teatralizadas.php).

22. Birman recalls: "I told him of our attempted gold bribery and implored him to abandon the idea of suicide, or at least to await the result of Sophie's dealing with the local authorities, about which he was very pessimistic" (*The Narrow Foothold*, 5).

23. "'Benjamin' was a common first name in Spain, which—unlike in the Germany of that time—in no way indicated that the bearer might be Jewish by birth, but it was unknown as a family name. It thus seemed reasonable to view the name 'Walter,' unknown in Spain, as a last name" (Scheurmann, "New Documents on Benjamin's Death," 268). The confusion over the name made it very difficult to investigate what exactly happened to Walter Benjamin until the necessary documents were located in 1992.

24. See Cussó-Ferrer's "Walter Benjamin's Last Frontier: Sequences of an Approach" for further details, images, and documents about the circumstances of

Benjamin's burial. When Hannah Arendt visited the small cemetery in Portbou only a few months after her good friend's death, she wrote to Gershom Scholem about the beauty of the place: "It is carved in stone terraces; the coffins are also pushed into such stones. It is by far one of the most fantastic and most beautiful spots I have ever seen in my life." She did write, however, that she failed to find Benjamin's gravesite: "It was not to be found, . . . his name was not written anywhere" (quoted in Taussig, "Walter Benjamin's Grave," 3).

25. "Objectives," Museu Memorial de l'Exili website, www.museuexili.cat/.

26. The actual text in Catalan reads: "una experiencia que os deixará, como a minim, poc indiferents." The quotation appears in the article "El darrer passatge: Les últimes hores de vida a l'exili de W. Benjamin a Portbou" (The last passage: The final hours of W. Benjamin's exile in Portbou), *La Vanguardia*, September 9, 2010.

27. According to the MUME website,

The Exile Memorial Museum Consortium is a public body constituted for the establishment and joint management, in the town of La Jonquera, of the Museum under this name, whose object is the exhibition, research, interpretation, and dissemination of information about historical events related to exiles. Moreover, the Consortium manages the Walter Benjamin Memorial Site, located in Portbou, whose main objectives are the study and promotion of the German philosopher Walter Benjamin, to tell the history of the Catalan Pyrenean border during the Second World War and the fostering of a critical commitment to freedom of thought faced with totalitarian systems. ("The Exile Memorial Museum: Walter Benjamin Memorial Site [Portbou]," www.museuexili.cat)

28. The following text appears on the historical marker:

On September 25, 1940, Walter Benjamin together with the German photographer Henny Gurland, her son Joseph, and a number of other people they had met on the mountain, reached Portbou. On the journey from Banyuls-sur-Mer to the Querroig summit, next to the border, they had been led by Lisa Fittko, the wife of his old acquaintance, German journalist Hans Fittko. The conditions of the trek must have been very tough. On top of the problems typical of a mountain path, Benjamin was in poor health, and there was the terrible circumstance of knowing that the Gestapo could stop them at any time.

29. Illas writes:

In these various identifications of the Catalans with the Jews, Israel was the mirror that could best reflect the situation and certain collective desires of the Catalans. The aesthetic-political linkages between the Catalans and the Jews contained perhaps at least three main goals: (1) to present the Catalans as a persecuted community that has strived to preserve its national personality; (2) to portray them as an industrious people that base their wealth on a (liberal) mixture of individual entrepreneurship and collective efforts; and (3) to stress the fundamental importance of their language, which under Francoism functioned as an almost secret code but which never stopped aspiring to become a state language like Hebrew in Israel. ("On Universalist Particularism," 85)

Notes to Conclusion

1. Juan Bedoya, "La crisis dispara el odio antijudío en España" (The crisis sparks anti-Jewish hatred in Spain), *El País*, March 30, 2011.

2. The Federation of Jewish Communities in Spain represents Jewish organizations in their interactions with national and international instituions. For more information, see www.fcje.org/.

3. "La condición de sefardí dará derecho automáticamente a la nacionalidad española" (Being Sephardi guarantees Spanish citizenship), *El País*, November 22, 2012.

4. On May 20, 2013, Raphael Minder reported in the *New York Times* that the naturalization process for Sephardic Jews applying to become Spanish citizens seemed to have stalled. Minder quotes Jacob Levy, a Ladino speaker who expresses disappointment with the ways in which the Spanish authorities have handled the situation.

5. Quoted in Gerry Hadden, "Spain Offers Citizenship to Descendants of Jews Forced Out during the Inquisition," *PRI's The World*, February 7, 2013.

6. Hadden, "Spain Offers Citizenship."

7. The Hebrew term *anusim* is a legal category in Jewish law that refers to the forcefully converted; the *bnei anusim* or *b'nei anusim* are their descendants.

8. Doreen Carvajal, "A Tepid Welcome Back for Spanish Jews," *New York Times*, December 8, 2012.

9. For a discussion of the debates on "historical memory" and the law between 2004 and 2007, see Labanyi, "The Politics of Memory in Contemporary Spain."

10. In *The War and Its Shadow: Spain's Civil War in Europe's Long Twentieth Century*, Helen Graham discusses the "memory wars" in Spain in relation to the debates about the past in the former Yugoslavia and Latin America.

11. Alejandro Baer made me aware of an editorial that appeared in *La Razón*, a right-leaning Spanish newspaper, on May 5, 2013. In a piece entitled "Memoria Histórica," Luis Suárez not only criticizes the Law of Historical Memory but also reiterates the myth of the Francoist benevolence toward Jews during World War II.

12. For a discussion of the book's inconsistencies, see A. O. Scott's book review "Something Is Happening," published in the *New York Times* (Nov. 11, 2006). Erin McGlothlin offers a convincing critique of the book and the film based on Boyne's novel in her article "Rewriting the Fantasy of the 'Wrong' Victim in Jochen Alexander Freydank's *Spielzeugland*." McGlothlin argues that beyond the historical inaccuracies in both texts, the book and the film reenact the fantasy of the "wrong victim." McGlothlin explains that this fantasy was first identified in postwar German discourse by Theodor Adorno and that it "is one that continues to operate in various guises in contemporary representations of the Holocaust, revealing how such texts persist in casting the Holocaust in absolute binaries of 'right' and 'wrong' as well as a related tendency to naturalize the fate of the Jewish victims as inevitable or even predestined" (2).

Bibliography

Afinoguenova, Eugenia. "El discurso del turismo y la configuración de una identi-
dad para España." In *Cine, imaginario, turismo: Estrategias de seducción*, ed.
Antonia del Rey Reguillo, 33–63. Valencia: Tirant lo Blanch, 2007.

Afinoguénova, Eugenia, and Jaume Martí-Olivella. "A Nation under Tourist Eyes:
Tourism and Identity Discourses. In *Spain Is (Still) Different: Tourism and
Discourse in Spanish Cultural Identity*, ed. Eugenia Afinoguénova and Jaume
Martí-Olivella, xi–xxxviii. Lanham, Md.: Lexington Books, 2008.

———, eds. *Spain Is (Still) Different: Tourism and Discourse in Spanish Identity.*
Lanham, Md.: Lexington Books, 2008.

Aganzo, Carlos, Esperanza Moreno, and Antonio Cortijo. *Rutas por las juderías
de España*. Madrid: El País Aguilar, 2008.

Albet-Mas, Abel. "Three Gods, Two Shores, One Space: Religious Justifications
for Tolerance and Confrontation between Spain and Colonial Morocco during the Franco Era." *Geopolitics* 11:4 (2006): 580–600.

Alexy, Trudi. *The Marrano Legacy: A Contemporary Crypto-Jewish Priest Reveals
Secrets of His Double Life*. Albuquerque: University of New Mexico Press,
2003.

———. *The Mezuzah in the Madonna's Foot: Marranos and Other Secret Jews; A
Woman Discovers Her Spiritual Heritage*. [San Francisco]: Harper San Francisco, 1994.

Armistead, Samuel. "Américo Castro in Morocco: The Origins of a Theory." In
*Américo Castro: The Impact of His Thought: Essays to Mark the Centenary
of His Birth*, ed. Ronald Surtz, Jaime Ferrrán, and Daniel P. Testa, 73–82.
Madison, Wis.: Hispanic Seminary of Medieval Studies, 1988.

Avni, Haim. *Spain, the Jews, and Franco*. Philadelphia: Jewish Publication Society
of America, 1982.

Baer, Alejandro. "The Voids of Sepharad: Memory of the Holocaust in Spain."
Journal of Spanish Cultural Studies 12:1 (2011): 95–120.

Baer, Alejandro, and Paula López. "The Blind Spots of Secularization: A Qualita-
tive Approach to the Study of Antisemitism in Spain." *European Societies*
14:2 (May 2012): 203–221.

213

Baer, Yitzhak. *A History of the Jews in Christian Spain*. Philadelphia: Jewish Publication Society of America, 1961.

Balfour, Sebastian. *Deadly Embrace: Morocco and the Road to the Spanish Civil War*. New York: Oxford University Press, 2002.

Beckwith, Stacy N., ed. *Charting Memory: Recalling Medieval Spain*. New York: Garland, 1999.

Benlyazid, Farida. "El cine dirigido por mujeres." *Quaderns de la Mediterrania* 7 (2006): 221–224.

Bergen, Doris. *War and Genocide: A Concise History of the Holocaust*. Lanham, Md.: Rowman & Littlefield, 2003.

Berthelot, Martine. *Memorias judías: Barcelona, 1914–1954; Historia oral de la Comunidad Israelita de Barcelona*. Barcelona: Riopiedras and Fundación Baruch Spinoza, 2001.

Birman, Carina. *The Narrow Foothold*. London: Hearing Eye, 2006.

Boym, Svetlana. *The Future of Nostalgia*. New York: Basic Books, 2001.

Braham, Randolph L., and Scott Miller. *The Nazis' Last Victims: The Holocaust in Hungary*. Detroit: Wayne State University Press, 1998.

Bush, Andrew. "Amador De Los Ríos and the Beginnings of Modern Jewish Studies in Spain." *Journal of Spanish Cultural Studies* 12:1 (2011): 13–33.

Campoy-Cubillo, Adolfo. *Memories of the Maghreb: Transnational Identities in Spanish Cultural Production*. New York: Palgrave Macmillan, 2012.

Carcedo, Diego. *Un español frente al Holocausto: Así salvó Ángel Sanz Briz a 5.000 judíos*. Madrid: Temas de Hoy, 2000.

Caruth, Cathy. *Trauma: Explorations in Memory*. Baltimore: Johns Hopkins University Press, 1995.

Castro, Américo. "Entre los hebreos marroquíes: La lengua española de Marruecos." *Revista Hispano Africana* 1:5 (1922): 145–146.

———. *The Structure of Spanish History*. Translated by Edmund L. King. Princeton, N.J.: Princeton University Press, 1954.

Cervantes Saavedra, Miguel de. *Don Quixote*. Translated by John Rutherford. New York: Penguin, 2000.

Chakrabarty, Dipesh. *Provincializing Europe: Postcolonial Thought and Historical Difference*. Princeton, N.J.: Princeton University Press, 2008.

Childers, William. *Transnational Cervantes*. Buffalo, N.Y.: University of Toronto Press, 2006.

Cinca i Pinós, Maria. *Las mil y una noches: Según el manuscrito más antiguo conocido*. Barcelona: Destino, 1998.

Cohen, Judith R. "'We've *Always* Sung It That Way': Re/Appropriation of Medieval Spanish Jewish Culture in a Galician Town." In *Charting Memory: Recalling Medieval Spain*, ed. Stacy Beckwith, 1–34. New York: Garland, 1999.

Collins, John. "From Portbou to Palestine and Back." *Social Text* 24:4 (2006): 66–85.

Crumbaugh, Justin. *Destination Dictatorship: The Spectacle of Spain's Tourist Boom and the Reinvention of Difference*. Albany: SUNY Press, 2009.

Curtis, Barry, and Claire Pajaczkowska. "'Getting There': Travel, Time and Narrative." In *Travellers' Tales: Narratives of Home and Displacement*, ed. George Robertson, 197–214. London: Routledge, 1994.

Cussó-Ferrer, Manuel. "Walter Benjamin's Last Frontier: Sequences of an Approach." In *For Walter Benjamin*, ed. Ingrid Scheurmann and Konrad Scheurmann, translated by Timothy Neville, 154–161. Bonn: AsKI, 1993.

Cyrulnik, Boris. *The Whispering of Ghosts: Trauma and Resilience*. New York: Other Press, 2003.

Deaglio, Enrico. *The Banality of Goodness: The Story of Giorgio Perlasca*. Translated by Gregory Conti. Notre Dame, Ind.: University of Notre Dame Press, 1998.

Derrida, Jacques. "Freud and the Scene of Writing." In *French Freud: Structural Studies in Psychoanalysis*, translated by Jeffrey Mehlman, 74–117. Special issue, *Yale French Studies* 48 (1972).

Díaz-Más, Paloma. *Sephardim: The Jews from Spain*. Translated by George K. Zucker. Chicago: University of Chicago Press, 1992.

Douglass, Ana, and Thomas A. Vogler. *Witness and Memory: The Discourse of Trauma*. New York: Routledge, 2003.

Felman, Shoshana, and Dori Laub. *Testimony: Crises of Witnessing in Literature, Psychoanalysis, and History*. New York: Routledge, 1991.

Ferrer Benimeli, J. A. *La masonería en la España del siglo XX*. Toledo: Universidad de Castilla–La Mancha, 1996.

———. *La masonería en la historia de España: Actas del I Symposium de Metodología Aplicada a la Historia de la Masonería Española*, Zaragoza, June 20–22, 1983. Zaragoza: Diputación General de Aragón, Departamento de Cultura y Educación, 1985.

Fittko, Lisa. *Escape through the Pyrenees*. Translated by David Koblick. Evanston, Ill.: Northwestern University Press, 1991.

Fleming, K. E. *Greece: A Jewish History*. Princeton, N.J.: Princeton University Press: 2007.

Flesler, Daniela. *The Return of the Moor: Spanish Responses to Contemporary Moroccan Immigration*. West Lafayette, Ind.: Purdue University Press, 2008.

Flesler, Daniela, Tabea Linhard, and Adrián Pérez Melgosa. "Introduction: Revisiting Jewish Spain in the Modern Era." *Journal of Spanish Cultural Studies* 12:1 (2011): 1–11.

Flesler, Daniela, and Adrián Pérez Melgosa. "Hervás, Convivencia and the Heritagization of Spain's Jewish Past." *Journal of Romance Studies* 10:2 (2010): 53–76.

———. "Marketing Convivencia: Contemporary Appropriations of Spain's Jewish Past." In *Spain Is (Still) Different: Tourism and Discourse in Spanish Cultural Identity*, ed. Eugenia Afinoguénova and Jaume Martí-Olivella, 63–84. Lanham, Md.: Lexington Books, 2008.

Frank, Ben. *A Travel Guide to Jewish Europe*. Gretna, La.: Pelican, 1992.

Friedman, Michal. "Reconquering 'Sepharad': Hispanism and Proto-Fascism in Giménez Caballero's Sephardist Crusade." *Journal of Spanish Cultural Studies* 12:1 (2011): 35–60.

Freud, Sigmund. "Mourning and Melancholia." In *The Standard Edition of the Complete Psychological Works of Sigmund Freud, Vol. 14 (1914–1916): On the History of the Psycho-Analytic Movement, Papers on Metapsychology and Other Works*, ed. James Strachey, 237–258. London: Vintage, 2001.

Frye, Northrop. *Anatomy of Criticism: Four Essays*. Princeton, N.J.: Princeton University Press, 1957.

Fuchs, Barbara. *Exotic Nation: Maurophilia and the Construction of Early Modern Spain*. Philadelphia: University of Pennsylvania Press, 2009.

Gerber, Jane. *The Jews of Spain: A History of the Sephardic Experience*. New York: Free Press, 1992.

Gerli, E. Michael. "The Ambivalent *Converso* Condition: A Review Article of *The Evolution of* Converso *Literature: The Writings of the Converted Jews of Medieval Spain*." *Calíope: Journal of the Society for Renaissance and Baroque Hispanic Poetry* 9:2 (2003): 93–102.

Gilbert, Martin. *The Righteous: The Unsung Heroes of the Holocaust*. New York: Henry Holt, 2003.

Gitlitz, David. *Secrecy and Deceit: The Religion of the Crypto-Jews*. Philadelphia: Jewish Publication Society, 1996.

Gladitz-Pérez Lorenzo, Nina. "Der Fall Giorgio Perlasca." *Dachauer Hefte* 7 (1991): 129–143.

Gold, Hazel. "Illustrated Histories: The National Subject and 'The Jew' in Nineteenth-Century Spanish Art." *Journal of Spanish Cultural Studies* 10:1 (2009): 89–109.

Gómez López-Quiñones, Antonio, and Susanne Zepp, eds. *The Holocaust in Spanish Memory: Historical Perceptions and Cultural Discourse*. Leipzig, Germany: Leipziger Universitätsverlag, 2010.

Goode, Joshua. *Impurity of Blood: Defining Race in Spain, 1870–1930*. Baton Rouge: Louisiana State University Press, 2009.

Gottreich, Emily Benichou, and Daniel J. Schroeter, eds. *Jewish Culture and Society in North Africa*. Bloomington: Indiana University Press, 2011.

Gould Levine, Linda. Introduction to *Reivindicación del conde don Julián*. Madrid: Cátedra, 1995.

Goytisolo, Juan. *Count Julian*. New York: Viking Press, 1974.

———. *Disidencias*. Barcelona: Seix Barral, 1977.

———. "La historiografía española y la herencia de Sefarad." *Letras Libres* 4:43 (2002): 32–35.

———. "Vorwort." *Das Hundeleben der Juanita Narboni*. Vienna: Droschl, 2005.

Graham, Helen. *The War and Its Shadow: Spain's Civil War in Europe's Long Twentieth Century*. Portland, Ore: Sussex Academic Press, 2012.

Grieve, Patricia E. *The Eve of Spain: Myths of Origins in the History of Christian,*

Muslim, and Jewish Conflict. Baltimore: Johns Hopkins University Press, 2009.

Grohmann, Alexis. "Errant Text: Sefarad, by Antonio Muñoz Molina." *Journal of Iberian & Latin American Studies* 12:2–3 (2006): 233–246.

Gruber, Ruth Ellen. "Beyond Virtually Jewish: New Authenticities and Real Imaginary Spaces in Europe." *Jewish Quarterly Review* 99:4 (2009): 487–504.

———. *Virtually Jewish: Reinventing Jewish Culture in Europe.* Berkeley: University of California Press, 2002.

Hackl, Erich. "El caso Sefarad: Industrias y errores del santo de su señora." *Lateral: Revista de Cultura* 6:78 (2001): 20, 29.

Halevi-Wise, Yael, ed. *Sephardism: Spanish Jewish History and the Modern Literary Imagination.* Stanford, Calif.: Stanford University Press, 2012.

Halter, Marek. *Stories of Deliverance: Speaking with Men and Women Who Rescued Jews from the Holocaust.* Chicago: Open Court, 1998.

Hasan-Rokem, Galit. "Jews as Postcards, or Postcards as Jews: Mobility in a Modern Genre." *Jewish Quarterly Review* 99:4 (2009): 505–546.

Herzberger, David K. "Representing the Holocaust: Story and Experience in Antonio Muñoz Molina's *Sefarad*." *Romance Quarterly* 51:2 (2004): 85–96.

Hirsch, Marianne. *Family Frames: Photography, Narrative, and Postmemory.* Cambridge, Mass.: Harvard University Press, 1997.

Hoffman, Eva. *After Such Knowledge: Memory, History, and the Legacy of the Holocaust.* New York: Public Affairs, 2004.

Huyssen, Andreas. *Present Pasts: Urban Palimpsests and the Politics of Memory.* Stanford, Calif.: Stanford University Press, 2006.

Illas, Edgar. "On Universalist Particularism: The Catalans and the Jews." *Journal of Spanish Cultural Studies* 12:1 (2011): 77–94.

Isenberg, Sheila. *A Hero of Our Own: The Story of Varian Fry.* New York: Random House, 2001.

Israel Garzón, Jacobo. *Los judíos de Tetuán.* Madrid: Hebraica Ediciones, 2005.

Kammen, Michael G. *Mystic Chords of Memory: The Transformation of Tradition in American Culture.* New York: Knopf, 1991.

Karavan, Dani. "1 Corridor, 1 Stairs, 1 Seat = Passages." In *Dani Karavan: Hommage an Walter Benjamin: Der Gedenkort "Passagen" in Portbou = Dani Karavan: Homage to Walter Benjamin: "Passages" Place of Remembrance at Portbou,* ed. Ingrid Scheurmann and Konrad Scheurmann, 100–111. Mainz: Verlag Philipp von Zabern, 1995.

Khanna, Ranjana. *Dark Continents: Psychoanalysis and Colonialism.* Durham, N.C.: Duke University Press, 2003.

Kinoshita, Sharon. "Medieval Mediterranean Literature." *PMLA* 124:2 (2009): 600–608.

Kirshenblatt-Gimblett, Barbara. *Destination Culture: Tourism, Museums, and Heritage.* Berkeley: University of California Press, 1998.

Krell, Robert. *Child Holocaust Survivors: Memories and Reflections.* [Victoria, B.C.]: Trafford Publishing, 2007.

Kruger, Steven F. *The Spectral Jew: Conversion and Embodiment in Medieval Europe.* Minneapolis: University of Minnesota Press, 2006.

Labanyi, Jo. "Memory and Modernity in Democratic Spain: The Difficulty of Coming to Terms with the Spanish Civil War." *Poetics Today* 28:1 (2007): 89–116.

———. "The Politics of Memory in Contemporary Spain." *Journal of Spanish Cultural Studies* 9:2 (2008): 119–125.

LaCapra, Dominick. *Writing History, Writing Trauma.* Baltimore: Johns Hopkins University Press, 2001.

Laskier, Michael. *North African Jewry in the Twentieth Century: The Jews of Morocco, Tunisia, and Algeria.* New York: New York University Press, 1994.

Leys, Ruth. *From Guilt to Shame: Auschwitz and After.* Princeton, N.J.: Princeton University Press, 2007.

Linde, Charlotte. *Life Stories: The Creation of Coherence.* New York: Oxford University Press, 1993.

Lipschitz, Chaim. *Franco, Spain, the Jews, and the Holocaust.* New York: Ktav Publishing House, 1984.

Lisbona, José. *Retorno a Sefarad: La política de España hacia sus judíos en el siglo XX.* Barcelona: Riopiedras, 1993.

Lukács, György. *The Theory of the Novel: A Historico-Philosophical Essay on the Forms of Great Epic Literature.* London: Merlin Press, 1971.

Marquardt, Virginia Hagelstein, ed. *Art and Journals on the Political Front, 1910–1940.* Gainesville: University Press of Florida, 1997.

Márquez Villanueva, Francisco. *De la España judeoconversa: Doce estudios.* Barcelona: Bellaterra, 2006.

Marquina Barrio, Antonio, and Gloria Inés Ospina. *España y los judíos en el siglo XX: La acción exterior.* Madrid: Espasa Calpe, 1987.

Martin-Márquez, Susan. *Disorientations: Spanish Colonialism in Africa and the Performance of Identity.* New Haven, Conn.: Yale University Press, 2008.

Matute, Ana M. *School of the Sun.* Translated by Elaine Kerrigan. New York: Pantheon Books, 1963.

Matvejević, Predrag. *Mediterranean: A Cultural Landscape.* Berkeley: University of California Press, 1999.

McClintock, Anne. *Imperial Leather: Race, Gender, and Sexuality in the Colonial Contest.* New York: Routledge, 1995.

McGlothlin, Erin. "Rewriting The Fantasy of the 'Wrong' Victim in Jochen Alexander Freydank's *Spielzeugland.*" *New German Critique* 123 (forthcoming, 2014).

Mendelson, Jordana, and Estrella de Diego. "Political Practice and the Arts in Spain, 1927–1936." In *Art and Journals on the Political Front, 1910–1940*, ed. Virginia Hagelstein Marquardt, 183–214. Gainesville: University Press of Florida, 1997.

Menny, Ana. "Entre reconocimiento y rechazo: Los judíos en la obra de Américo Castro." *Iberoamericana* 38 (2010): 146–150.

Menocal, María Rosa. *The Ornament of the World: How Muslims, Jews, and Christians Created a Culture of Tolerance in Medieval Spain.* Boston: Little, Brown, 2002.

Meyerson, Mark. "Letters on 'Inflecting the *Converso* Voice.'" *La corónica* 25:2 (1997): 179–182.

Molho, Isaac. "Un hidalgo español al servicio de Dios y de la Humanidad en Budapest." *Tesoro de los judíos sefardíes* (Jerusalem) 7 (1964): 32–40.

Moreno, Joan, Rosamaria Salip, and Josep Maria Bosch. *Les set portes del Call.* Girona: CCG Edicions, 2004.

Muñoz Molina, Antonio. *Sepharad.* Translated by Margaret Sayers Peden. Orlando, Fla.: Harcourt, 2003.

Netanyahu, Benzion. *Toward the Inquisition: Essays on Jewish and Converso History in Late Medieval Spain.* Ithaca, N.Y.: Cornell University Press, 1997.

Nirenberg, David. *Communities of Violence: Persecution of Minorities in the Middle Ages.* Princeton, N.J.: Princeton University Press, 1996.

———. "Enmity and Assimilation: Jews, Christians, and Converts in Medieval Spain." *Common Knowledge* 9:1 (2003): 137–155.

———. "Figures of Thought and Figures of Flesh: 'Jews' and 'Judaism' in Late-Medieval Spanish Poetry and Politics." *Speculum* 81:2 (2006): 398–426.

———. "Mass Conversion and Genealogical Mentalities: Jews and Christians in Fifteenth-Century Spain." *Past and Present* 174:1 (2002): 3–41.

———. "What Can Medieval Spain Teach Us about Muslim-Jewish Relations?" *CCAR Journal: A Reform Jewish Quarterly* 59:4 (2002): 17–36.

Nora, Pierre. "Between Memory and History: Les Lieux de Mémoire." Translated by Marc Roudebush. *Representations* 26 (Spring 1989): 7–24.

Ojeda, Mata M. *Identidades ambivalentes: Sefardíes en la España contemporánea.* Collado Villalba, Madrid: Sefarad Editores, 2012.

Paldiel, Mordecai. *The Righteous among the Nations: The Unsung Heroes of the Holocaust.* New York: HarperCollins, 2007.

Pennell, C. R. *Morocco: From Empire to Independence.* Oxford, UK: Oneworld, 2003.

Perra, Emiliano. "Legitimizing Fascism through the Holocaust? The Reception of the Miniseries *Perlasca: Un eroe italiano* in Italy." *Memory Studies* 3:2 (2010): 95–109.

Pessarrodona, Marta. *Berlin suite: Edición bilingüe.* Barcelona: Edicions del Mall, 1985.

———. "En defensa de Israel." In *En defensa de Israel,* ed. Marcos Aguinis, 221–231. Zaragoza: Libros Certeza, 2004.

Pinto, Diana. *Beyond Anti-Semitism: The New Jewish Presence in Europe.* New York: American Jewish Committee, 1994.

Portelli, Alessandro. *The Death of Luigi Trastulli, and Other Stories: Form and Meaning in Oral History.* Albany: SUNY Press, 1990.

Preston, Paul. *The Spanish Holocaust: Inquisition and Extermination in Twentieth-Century Spain*. London: HarperCollins, 2008.

Pujol, Jordi. "This Memorial Is a Tribute to Freedom." In *Dani Karavan: Hommage an Walter Benjamin: Der Gedenkort "Passagen" in Portbou = Homage to Walter Benjamin: "Passages" Place of Remembrance at Portbou*, ed. Ingrid Scheurmann and Konrad Scheurmann, 144–145, translated by Silke Graefinghoff and Ingrid Scheurman. Mainz: Verlag Philipp von Zabern, 1995.

Ricoeur, Paul. *Memory, History, Forgetting*. Chicago: University of Chicago Press, 2004.

Robertson, George, ed. *Travellers' Tales: Narratives of Home and Displacement*. London: Routledge, 1994.

Rodogno, Davide. "Italiani brava gente? Fascist Italy's Policy toward the Jews in the Balkans, April 1941–July 1943." *European History Quarterly* 35:2 (2005): 213–240.

Rodrigue, Aron. "The Ottoman Diaspora: The Rise and Fall of Ladino Literary Culture." In *Cultures of the Jews: A New History*, ed. David Biale, 863–885. New York: Schocken, 2002.

Rohr, Isabelle. "'Spaniards of the Jewish Type': Philosephardism in the Service of Imperialism in Early Twentieth-Century Spanish Morocco." *Journal of Spanish Cultural Studies* 12:1 (2011): 61–75.

———. *The Spanish Right and the Jews, 1898–1945: Antisemitism and Opportunism*. Brighton, UK: Sussex Academic Press, 2007.

Rojek, Chris, and John Urry. *Touring Cultures: Transformations of Travel and Theory*. New York: Routledge, 1997.

Romeu Ferré, Pilar, and Miguel Iaffa. *The Former Major Synagogue of Barcelona*. Barcelona: Associació Call de Barcelona, c. 2007.

Rosenfeld, Gavriel David. "A Flawed Prophecy? *Zakhor*, the Memory Boom, and the Holocaust." *Jewish Quarterly Review* 97:4 (2007): 508–520.

Roskies, David. *Against the Apocalypse: Responses to Catastrophe in Modern Jewish Culture*. Cambridge, Mass.: Harvard University Press, 1984.

Rothberg, Michael. "Between Memory and Memory: From *Lieux de mémoire* to *Noeuds de mémoire*." *Yale French Studies* 118–119 (2010): 3–12.

———. *Multidirectional Memory: Remembering the Holocaust in the Age of Decolonization*. Stanford, Calif.: Stanford University Press, 2009.

———. *Traumatic Realism: The Demands of Holocaust Representation*. Minneapolis: University of Minnesota Press, 2000.

Rother, Bernd. "España y los judíos: De los albores del siglo XX a la guerra civil." In *Los judíos en la España contemporánea*, ed. Uriel Macías Kapón, Yolanda Moreno Kapón, and Ricardo Izquierdo Benido, 153–172. Cuenca, Spain: Ediciones de la Universidad Castilla–La Mancha, 2000.

———. *Franco y el Holocausto*. Madrid: Marcial Pons Historia, 2005.

———. "Myth and Fact—Spain and the Holocaust." In *The Holocaust in Spanish Memory: Historical Perceptions and Cultural Discourse*, ed. Antonio Gómez

López-Quiñones and Susanne Zepp, 51–53. Leipzig, Germany: Leipziger Universitätsverlag, 2010.

Rozenberg, Danielle. *La España contemporánea y la cuestión judía: Retejiendo los hilos de la memoria y de la historia.* Madrid: Casa Sefarad-Israel, 2010.

Salabert, Juana. *La noche ciega.* Barcelona: Seix Barral, 2004.

———. *Velódromo de invierno.* Barcelona: Seix Barral, 2001.

Salinas, David. *España, los sefarditas y el Tercer Reich, 1939–1945: La labor de diplomáticos españoles contra el genocidio nazi.* Valladolid: Secretariado de Publicaciones e Intercambio Científico Universidad de Valladolid; Madrid: Ministerio de Asuntos Exteriores, 1997.

Scheurmann, Ingrid. "New Documents on Benjamin's Death." In *For Walter Benjamin,* ed. Ingrid Scheurmann and Konrad Scheurmann, trans. Timothy Neville, 265–277. Bonn: AsKI, 1993.

Scheurmann, Ingrid, and Konrad Scheurmann, eds. *Dani Karavan: Hommage an Walter Benjamin: Der Gedenkort "Passagen" in Portbou = Dani Karavan: Homage to Walter Benjamin: "Passages" Place of Remembrance at Portbou.* Translated by Franz Fechner and Konrad Scheurmann. Mainz: Verlag Philipp von Zabern, 1995.

———. *For Walter Benjamin: Documentation, Essays, and a Sketch.* Translated by Timothy Nevill. Bonn: AsKI, 1993.

Scheurmann, Konrad. "Borders, Thresholds, Passages: On Dani Karavan's Concept for a Memorial to Walter Benjamin" In *For Walter Benjamin,* ed. Ingrid Scheurmann and Konrad Scheurmann, trans. Timothy Neville, 237–254. Bonn: AsKI, 1993.

Shohat, Ella, and Robert Stam. *Multiculturalism, Postcoloniality, and Transnational Media.* New Brunswick, N.J.: Rutgers University Press, 2003.

———. *Unthinking Eurocentrism: Multiculturalism and the Media.* New York: Routledge, 1994.

Sicroff, Albert A. *Les controverses des status de "pureté de sang" en Espagne du Xve au Xviie siècle.* Paris: Didier, 1960.

Smith, Paul J. *Representing the Other: "Race," Text, and Gender in Spanish and Spanish American Narrative.* Oxford: Clarendon Press, 1992.

Soliño, María E. *Women and Children First: Spanish Women Writers and the Fairy Tale Tradition.* Potomac, Md.: Scripta Humanistica, 2002.

Spivak, Gayatri C. *A Critique of Postcolonial Reason: Toward a History of the Vanishing Present.* Cambridge, Mass.: Harvard University Press, 1999.

Stoler, Ann. *Carnal Knowledge and Imperial Power: Race and the Intimate in Colonial Rule.* Berkeley: University of California Press, 2002.

Subirats, Eduardo, ed. *Américo Castro y la revisión de la memoria: El Islam en España.* Madrid: Ediciones Libertarias, 2003.

———. "La península multicultural." In *Américo Castro y la revisión de la memoria: El Islam en España,* ed. Eduardo Subirats, 39–50. Madrid: Ediciones Libertarias, 2003.

Suleiman, Susan Rubin. *Crises of Memory and the Second World War.* Cambridge, Mass.: Harvard University Press, 2006.

Taussig, Michael. "Walter Benjamin's Grave." In *Walter Benjamin's Grave*, 3–32. Chicago: University of Chicago Press, 2006.

Terdiman, Richard. *Present Past: Modernity and the Memory Crisis.* Ithaca, N.Y.: Cornell University Press, 1993.

Todorov, Tzvetan. *The Fragility of Goodness: Why Bulgaria's Jews Survived the Holocaust; A Collection of Texts with Commentary.* Princeton, N.J.: Princeton University Press, 2001.

Tortajada, Vicente. *Azahar y vitriolo.* Seville: Editorial Renacimiento, 2002.

Trueba, Virginia. Introduction to *La vida perra de Juanita Narboni*, by Angel Vázquez. Madrid: Cátedra, 2000.

Valis, Noël. *The Culture of Cursilería: Bad Taste, Kitsch, and Class in Modern Spain.* Durham, N.C.: Duke University Press, 2002.

Valverde, Mariana. "Remembering Benjamin from South of the Pyrenees: The Two-Gauge Problem." *Public Culture* 21:3 (2009): 440–450.

Vázquez, Ángel. *El cuarto de los niños y otros cuentos.* Valencia: Editorial Pre-Textos, 2008.

———. *La vida perra de Juanita Narboni.* Edited by Virginia Trueba. Madrid: Cátedra, 2000.

Vega, Luis Antonio de. "Itinerario lírico de Sultana Cohén." *Vértice* (August 1938): n.p.

La vida perra de Juanita Narboni. Directed by Farida Benlyazid. Barcelona: Cameo media, 2006. DVD.

Vilarós, Teresa M., and Michael Ugarte. "Cuando África empieza en los Pirineos." *Journal of Spanish Cultural Studies* 7:3 (2006): 199–205.

Wacks, David. *Framing Iberia: Māqāmat and Frametale Narratives in Medieval Spain.* Boston: Brill, 2007.

Wolf, Diane. *Beyond Anne Frank: Hidden Children and Postwar Families in Holland.* Berkeley: University of California Press, 2007.

Yerushalmi, Yosef. *Zakhor: Jewish History and Jewish Memory.* Seattle: University of Washington Press, 1982.

Young, James. *The Texture of Memory: Holocaust Memorials and Meaning.* New Haven, Conn.: Yale University Press, 1993.

Ysart, Federico. *España y los judíos en la segunda guerra mundial.* Barcelona: DOPESA, 1973.

Index

223